"We're All Infected"

Contributions to Zombie Studies

White Zombie: Anatomy of a Horror Film. Gary D. Rhodes. 2001

The Zombie Movie Encyclopedia. Peter Dendle. 2001

*American Zombie Gothic: The Rise and Fall (and Rise)
of the Walking Dead in Popular Culture*. Kyle William Bishop. 2010

*Back from the Dead: Remakes of the Romero
Zombie Films as Markers of Their Times*. Kevin J. Wetmore, Jr. 2011

*Generation Zombie: Essays on the Living Dead
in Modern Culture*. Edited by Stephanie Boluk and Wylie Lenz. 2011

*Race, Oppression and the Zombie: Essays on Cross-Cultural Appropriations
of the Caribbean Tradition*. Edited by Christopher M. Moreman
and Cory James Rushton. 2011

Zombies Are Us: Essays on the Humanity of the Walking Dead.
Edited by Christopher M. Moreman and Cory James Rushton. 2011

The Zombie Movie Encyclopedia, Volume 2: 2000–2010. Peter Dendle. 2012

Great Zombies in History. Edited by Joe Sergi. 2013 (graphic novel)

Unraveling Resident Evil*: Essays on the Complex Universe
of the Games and Films*. Edited by Nadine Farghaly. 2014

"We're All Infected": Essays on AMC's The Walking Dead
and the Fate of the Human. Edited by Dawn Keetley. 2014

Zombies and Sexuality: Essays on Desire and the Walking Dead.
Edited by Shaka McGlotten and Steve Jones. 2014

"We're All Infected"

Essays on AMC's
The Walking Dead *and*
the Fate of the Human

Edited by
DAWN KEETLEY

CONTRIBUTIONS TO ZOMBIE STUDIES

McFarland & Company, Inc., Publishers
Jefferson, North Carolina

LIBRARY OF CONGRESS CATALOGUING-IN-PUBLICATION DATA

"We're all infected" : essays on AMC's The walking dead and
the fate of the human / edited by Dawn Keetley.
        p.   cm. — (Contributions to Zombie Studies)
Includes bibliographical references and index.

ISBN 978-0-7864-7628-2 (softcover : acid free paper) ∞
ISBN 978-1-4766-1452-6 (ebook)

1. Walking dead (Television program)   I. Keetley, Dawn,
1965– , editor of publication.

PN1992.77.W25W47 2014
791.45'72—dc23   2013050953

BRITISH LIBRARY CATALOGUING DATA ARE AVAILABLE

On the cover: A zombie from the first season of *The Walking Dead*
television series, 2010 (AMC/Photofest)

Printed in the United States of America

McFarland & Company, Inc., Publishers
  Box 611, Jefferson, North Carolina 28640
    www.mcfarlandpub.com

To Nick,
who is starting to appreciate zombies,
and Helen,
who doesn't … yet

Table of Contents

vii

Preface

This collection brings together an introduction and thirteen original scholarly essays on AMC's television series, *The Walking Dead* (with some discussion of Kirkman's comic series). Collectively, the essays argue for *The Walking Dead* as a ground-breaking zombie narrative, most importantly because it is the first such narrative in which the survivors are already infected. No zombie bite is needed to spread the contagion; it is immanent in human bodies—deposited there by some event (or natural mutation) that has yet to be explained in either comic or TV series. If the early twenty-first century ushered in the viral zombie (notably in *28 Days Later* [2002]), it has also, in *The Walking Dead*, introduced the viral human, biologically imbricated with the zombies that now, and into the future, form the conditions of its existence.

Since "we" are, in *The Walking Dead*, unambiguously also the zombie, the social and political allegories mapped out by the essays in the first section, "Society's End," are all inevitably allegories in which human and zombie are not pitted against each other but symbiotically bound together. And human and zombie are bound together, above all, through their mutual violence. The characters of *The Walking Dead* are obsessed with guns, and their obsession metonymically represents what one essay calls the "terror/security paradigm"— Americans' broader anxiety about constant threat and a corollary urgent security. This anxiety, above all others, shapes *The Walking Dead*, as it has shaped the post–9/11 United States. The violence considered by the essays in the first section takes multiple forms: it is the violence of terrorism and natural catastrophe; it is self-justifying violence, violence perpetuated for self-defense and for survival; it is racist violence—immediate and brutal, as well as long-term and exploitative; it is the violence of mass crime and lawlessness, as well as of law enforcement; and it is the violence of mourning. While *The Walking Dead's* immense popularity is no doubt in part due to its routine representations of violence, the essays in this collection all argue that the series challenges the violence in which it also indulges.

If the immanent presence of the virus serves as the foundation of *The Walking Dead's* stories of imbricated human and zombie violence, it also functions as the bedrock of the series' contemplation of an equally important, more existential question: what does it mean to be human? The essays in the second section of this collection, "Posthumanity," all suggest that *The Walking Dead* offers a thoroughly posthuman zombie narrative, and each essay fundamentally decenters—contesting, critiquing, or expanding—reigning notions of the "human." Several of the essays argue for the centrality in the series of the body, of its drives, instincts, neurons and muscles. We share a "blind corporeality" with the zombie—and this fact dethrones a particular notion of the human as aligned with some intangible mind or soul and as more-or-less autonomous. Other essays address how the "human" is closely bound up with (indeed defined by) language and time, both of which, in our current moment, seem to be disappearing, as we suffer widespread illiteracy and a mass forgetting of the past; thus we seem, like the zombies themselves, to be slipping into a non-human aphasia and a monstrous timelessness. While the zombies of *The Walking Dead*, then, represent an exterior threat, to which the survivors respond with unremitting violence, they also represent an interior "threat," some non-human yet finally entrenched part of ourselves.

This collection of essays is part of an emerging critical conversation about *The Walking Dead*, and our collective work is indebted to the two prior anthologies—*Triumph of "The Walking Dead,"* edited by James Lowder (Benbella Books, 2011) and *"The Walking Dead" and Philosophy*, edited by Wayne Yuen (Open Court, 2012). The essays in this collection were all written during the course of the third season of *The Walking Dead*, and I think I can speak for all the contributors when I say we all hope the conversation continues as the series continues—and that the series might indeed, as Robert Kirkman hopes, never end.

I would like to thank Laura Kremmel for her invaluable editorial work on this project—and for our conversations about *The Walking Dead* (and gothic/horror more generally). Rita Kurtz also added her incisive editorial assistance, and the book would definitely not be what it is if not for both of them. Lehigh University generously provided a research grant that helped me with editorial costs. Finally, I'd like to thank Kurt who has, I suspect, for my benefit, pretended a greater interest in zombies than he really feels but who has nonetheless offered countless provocative comments about *The Walking Dead* that continue to inspire me. He has also read what I've written and made my writing, as well as my thinking, much clearer than it would have been otherwise. I hope you keep watching, talking, and reading with me.

Introduction

"We're All Infected"

DAWN KEETLEY

The history of the zombie's lurch onto the American screen is oft-rehearsed, so here I will just sketch the principal movements of the zombie narrative with the goal of marking the distinctiveness of *The Walking Dead*.[1] The zombie originated in Haiti, where soulless bodies were reputedly brought back from the dead by a priest, or *bokor*, and sent to labor in the fields.[2] After W. B. Seabrook penned his exotic account of Haitian voodoo in his 1929 *The Magic Island*, film-makers wasted no time bringing the zombie to mainstream audiences—most notably in *White Zombie* (1932) and *I Walked with a Zombie* (1943). Both films exploited the idea of a body without a soul, subject to absolute control by another. Eliding the racialized imperial relationship between the U.S. and Haiti from 1915 to 1934 as well as the longer history of Afro-Caribbean slavery in which Haitian zombie rituals were rooted, the enslaved "zombie" in both films was a hyper-sexualized white woman, forced to do the bidding of white "priests." Despite their curious erasure of racial slavery, these first white zombies nonetheless embodied anxieties about loss of autonomy and about one person's dominion over another.

By all accounts the most momentous event in the history of the cinematic zombie was George A. Romero's groundbreaking *Night of the Living Dead* (1968).[3] Romero's revolutionary film abandoned the singular body bereft of soul typical of both Haitian ritual and early cinema and introduced, instead, a mass contagion of living death. Explained vaguely as the result of radiation from a Venus probe, the epidemic in *Night* led not only to fatally infectious bodies rising from their graves but also to their single-minded urge to eat human flesh. The threat Romero's zombies pose is less soul-death than real, violent death—the spread of what a TV announcer in the film calls an "epidemic of mass murder." If early zombies embodied the threat of slavery, Romero's zombies are death incarnate. Born in the graveyard and in the morgue, they harness anxieties not only about our own inevitable mortality but also about the escalating violence of the world (Vietnam, racial violence in the South, high-profile assassinations). In *Night*, fear of *becoming* a zombie (from early cinema) was knit to a basic fear *of* the zombie—metaphor of our increasingly violent world.

The next paradigm shift occurred in 2002 with Danny Boyle's *28 Days Later* and the birth of the fast, viral zombie.[4] In Romero's films, any corpse not shot, stabbed, or beaten in the head would rise to devour the living (the consequence of that vaguely imputed radiation). While Romero's zombies move at a shambling but inexorable pace that matches the pace of (natural) death, the zombies of *28 Days Later* are pure contagion, spreading like a virus— the speed of the infection allegorized by the terrifying and unpredictable speed of "the infected." Drawing obviously on early twenty-first-century fears of a global pandemic (and influenced by SARS, H1N1, mad cow disease, anthrax, West Nile virus, and the avian flu, among others), the viral zombie also evokes the terrorist, an inescapable part of our landscape since 9/11. The new zombies, as Nick Muntean and Matthew Thomas Payne point out, are "enraged corpses"[5] who live among us: they emerge out of faceless crowds and suburban homes; they rage down city streets, across bridges, through subways and parks. The war on the viral zombie is like the war on the terrorist—a war against "some constantly shifting Other which can be anyone at any time."[6] An iconic moment occurs in *28 Weeks Later* (2007) when the U.S. soldiers lose control of the newly-reclaimed "safe zone" in post-infection London. The virus has just re-emerged and as the crowd panics and streams out of the containment area, the soldiers are first ordered to shoot only the infected. Within seconds, though, it becomes clear that they can't tell the difference between the infected and the merely panicked, and so they are commanded to shoot everyone. Viral zombies bleed into human and the difference between them (between "them" and "us") is represented as an impossible distinction.

The viral zombie film also allegorizes the hyper-speed of contemporary networked postmodernity. As Fred Botting puts it, the contemporary subject is a "shocked subject": "numbed, automatic, zombie-like, it is a victim of sense and sensation and also a hypermodern organism stimulated, hyperactivated and reactive, an effect of an incessant 'bombardment' of images and signs."[7] Neither life nor death move in slow, steady rhythms anymore. The "infected" of *28 Days Later*, *28 Weeks Later,* and *Dawn of the Dead* (2004) simply don't have time to die. Death, moreover, does not come from the graveyard as in the opening of Romero's *Night of the Living Dead*. The brilliant first scenes of *28*

Days Later make it clear that death now streams from those shocking images disseminated by the media.[8] The "rage virus" that decimates London is explicitly created by television images of global mayhem: lab monkeys are strapped down and forced to watch these continuously streaming images and then are given an inhibitor. Their own natural aggression and, more importantly, immersion in violent TV imagery mix to form the postmodern viral zombies of the new millennium.

Although not a distinct paradigm shift, a particular thread in zombie narrative is worthy of note: the humanizing of the zombie.[9] While zombies often incarnate the absolute "Other"—not least because they typically lack any interiority and are driven only to kill—some zombies have been cast as able to restrain the urge to devour us; they thus stand in for more human and recognizable others—the oppressed and the marginalized. In Romero's *Land of the Dead* (2005), for example, the living dead display vestigial traces of memory, going about routine business that clearly defined their lives before death. Tired of the slaughter inflicted by marauding humans, the zombies finally revolt and, led by the African-American "Big Daddy," destroy the exploitative wealthy elite ensconced in the glistening high-rise walls of Fiddler's Green. The distinct "humanity" of the zombie horde is clearly in service to its function as allegory of the underclass; indeed, the film is at pains to align the zombies with the poor, oppressed, and racially marginalized among the human survivors, who are equally barred from Fiddler's Green. The humanity of the zombie, in Romero's rather explicit parable, *is* the humanity of the socially, racially, and economically abject.[10]

The Walking Dead signals still another paradigm shift. Robert Kirkman's ongoing comic series, begun in 2003, and AMC's TV series, which first aired on October 31, 2010, constitute the first ongoing, serialized zombie narrative—born of Kirkman's expressed desire for a "zombie movie that never ends."[11] While *The Walking Dead* radically evolves on the horizontal plane through ongoing serialization, it similarly proliferates on the vertical plane—its stories mutating through numerous media to enrich the central story arcs of the comics and the TV series. There are video games, a "social game" for Facebook, a board game, two novels,[12] and "webisodes" on AMC's website, short videos that follow minor characters from the main storyline. *The Walking Dead* is a fully-realized, continuous post-apocalyptic universe, in which the narrative does not end with the death of its protagonists (witness the death of Lori Grimes in season three) and in which there is no easy end for the survivors, whether it is by death or miraculous restoration of the familiar social order. The threat posed by the "walkers" is ongoing and relentless—as are the hopes of finding some kind of safe space, the dashing of those hopes, and the dramatization of humanity's propensity for venality, debasement, and self-destruction.

As much as fans of both the comic and TV series might rejoice in the prospect that *The Walking Dead* will go on without end, such potential infinitude makes utopian moments particularly hard to come by, if not impossible (which accounts in part for the series' rather bleak nihilism).[13] Fredric Jameson has famously argued that while the principal work of mass culture is to manipulate the audience's anxieties, it also inevitably contains within it utopian elements, moments of hope, or what he calls the "fantasy bribe."[14] In zombie films, the utopian moment, the promise of hope, typically comes right at the end: Fran and Peter flying away from the zombie masses at the mall in *Dawn of the Dead* (1978); John, Sarah, and McDermott on a tropical island at the end of *Day of the Dead* (1985); Jim, Selena, and Hannah at the farmhouse, getting the attention of an airplane, realizing civilization has not been entirely destroyed at the end of *28 Days Later*. Even the bleakest of endings—the survivors' arrival on the island at the end of *Dawn of the Dead* (2004) only to find it infested with zombies, as well as the shots of the infected raging toward the Eiffel Tower at the end of *28 Weeks Later*—are mercifully foreclosed by the abrupt cut to black. The "fantasy bribe" in such films is an end of suffering and terror, not as scanty a bribe as it might seem given the literally heart-pounding frenetic pace of the viral zombies of both films. As a serial narrative, however, *The Walking Dead* will not end and so cannot create easy utopian moments. Any metaphoric (or real) island the survivors find will be encroached upon; any community they create will be besieged from without and within— and the viewer will be there to watch. When Rick says to Carl, in the season two episode, "Better Angels," as he hands him a gun, "People are gonna die ... there's no way you could ever be ready for it," his words are a warning to the viewer too. They are words that echo, returning as a flashback in the season three scene in which Carl has to shoot his mother ("Killer Within"). They will inexorably return again and again, raising for viewers the painful questions: Who will *we* have to see die? Who will *we* have to lose? Can we continue watching if Glenn dies, or Maggie, or Daryl, or *Rick*? Can we not watch? We know only that there will be no cut to black. No fantasy bribe here.

Precisely because *The Walking Dead* is an ongoing serial narrative, it is distinctive in its orientation to the *human survivors* and to their struggle to re-constitute something that looks like a viable social order in the post-apocalyptic world. Kirkman himself indicates this orientation in the brief synopsis repeated on the back of each graphic novel: "In a world ruled by the dead, we are forced to finally start living."[15] Kyle Bishop goes so far as to claim that the distinctiveness of *The Walking Dead* is that it "isn't about zombies at all; it's about human character."[16] While Bishop's point is well-taken, *The Walking Dead* is inevitably also about zombies. *Especially* because *The Walking Dead* is a long-term serial narrative, the fate of the survivors is inextricably interwoven with the zombies. Kirkman, after all, writes that we are forced to start living *"[i]n a world ruled by the dead."* The more the survivors seek to create sanctuaries where walls shut out the walkers, the more the walkers amass outside those walls. Every time the humans venture beyond the always-vulnerable walls, zombies threaten. Sound, movement, the very smell of humans draws zombies to them. There is no human future without zombies, and it is exactly this symbiotic co-existence, apparently without end, of the human and the non-human that makes *The Walking Dead* so compelling. The future the humans face is never without threat; the societies they construct must always involve security first; death, which has always been imminent, is now more imminent than ever.[17] The zombie has forced a radical and inescapable transformation in human progress. Zombies are the remorseless environment in which humans, from now on, will evolve. They are our future—and we are theirs.

If *28 Days Later* ushered in the viral zombie, *The Walking Dead* introduces the viral human, biologically imbricated with the zombies that form the conditions of its existence. In *Safety Behind Bars*, volume three of the graphic novel series, Rick discovers that bodies re-animate even if they haven't been bitten: "We're all infected," he declares.[18] In the TV series, Rick similarly proclaims, "We're all infected" in the final episode of season two ("Beside the Dying Fire"), finally divulging a secret to the rest of his group that scientist Edwin Jenner revealed to him at the end of the first season ("TS-19"). The fact that humans already carry the zombie virus leads inevitably to Rick's pronouncements, in the comic series, that they—the humans—*are* the walking dead. As he says at the end of volume four, *The Heart's Desire*: "You see them out there. You **know** that when we die—we **become** them. You think we hide behind walls to protect us from **the walking dead!** Don't you **get it? We are the walking dead!**"[19] That the humans are carriers of the zombie virus means that the absolute opposition between human and zombie, along with the series of binaries that structure that opposition—human/non-human, normal/monster, living/dead, mind/body, rational/irrational, conscious/unconscious—are impossible to maintain. Humans and zombies are not opposed but are now evolving together. The zombie is not just the threat humans face, the environment within which humans evolve; the zombie now forms a constituent part of the evolving human. In some ways, the zombie narrative has come full circle, back to the symptomatic anxieties of the films of the 30s and 40s inspired by Haitian folklore. In voodoo religion and early film, the fear was not of being consumed by the zombie horde but of becoming a zombie. In *The Walking Dead*, while the zombie horde still pursues, the deeper fear is precisely of becoming (or even of already *being*) a zombie; only there's no predatory priest or evil master trying to enslave one's soul: there's only the indifferent processes of life and death.

"All they do is kill": Society's End

Since "we" are, in *The Walking Dead*, unambiguously also the zombie, the social and political allegories latent in the series are inevitably allegories in which human and zombie are not pitted against each other but rather are symbiotically bound together. Ever since *Night of the Living Dead*, the zombie has been a figure that, in its proximity to us, is able to mobilize social and political critique—and a great deal has been written about Romero's films, in particular, as commentaries on their contemporary culture. Indeed, film critic Robin Wood has claimed that Romero's *Dead* movies offer "the most uncompromising critique of contemporary America ... that is possible within the terms and conditions of a 'popular entertainment' medium."[20] Scholarship has incisively analyzed *Night of the Living Dead* as a parable about, variously, U.S. race relations in the civil rights era, Vietnam, nuclear paranoia, feminism, and the youth movement[21]; *Dawn of the Dead* as a commentary on entrenched American consumerism[22]; *Land of the Dead* as a scathing and not particularly veiled critique of the post–9/11 Bush era (Romero himself identified its evil antagonist as Donald Rumsfeld)[23]; and *Diary of the Dead* (2007) as an allegory of the dehumanizing effects of our now near-total immersion in media technologies.[24] Some critics observe the persistence of the zombie's meaning through its various incarnations, notably as the sign of the subject under capitalism whether as worker or consumer.[25] Other critics map the zombie's changes, especially in the post–9/11 landscape, and describe its increasing identification with epidemic, trauma, terror, and pervasive networked information systems.[26] Muntean and Payne have aptly noted that the zombie's "blank and dead visage" provides a screen onto which perpetually shifting meanings can be cast. The zombie horde is "a monstrous tabula rasa," a fact that accounts for its enduring ability to materialize our shifting fears and anxieties and to mobilize historically-contingent social critique.[27]

As the essays in the first section of this collection make clear, the obsessive object of scrutiny in *The Walking Dead* is the human propensity for violence, a propensity mirrored in the zombies, who are defined by their drive to devour, and then reflected back on the humans, who are themselves infected with the "zombie virus." Writing about the comics, Gerry Canavan has astutely argued that the series is fundamentally about violence—that it is a "war myth." Zombie narratives, Canavan claims, "depict total, unrestrained violence against absolute Others whose very existence is seen as anathema to our own," and they are "ultimately about the motivation for and unleashing of total violence."[28] Given the violence against the walkers that is a staple of both the comics and the TV series, it's hard to disagree with Canavan's argument that *The Walking Dead* is a fantasy of "total violence." Indeed, Rick's rallying words to the group of survivors early in season one seems to set the series in exactly the direction Canavan describes. Disarming the unruly and racist Merle Dixon, Rick tells him: "Things are different now. There are no niggers anymore. No dumb-as-shit inbred white trash fools either. Only dark meat and white meat. There's us and the dead" ("Guts"). Rick subsumes all differences into "us" (the living) and "them" (the dead), and there will be no mercy for "them." Moreover, Rick's banishing of all racial difference (shaping his post-apocalyptic world as "post-racial") allows it to creep back in unrecognized—and killing the zombie can thus easily become, as Canavan points out, merely the "thinnest sublimation" of the violence against the racialized colonial object.[29]

As important as Canavan's essay is, though, his argument is predicated on an absolute separation of survivor and zombie; he claims, for instance, that the zombie is "anti-life which is always inimically and hopelessly Other," that the zombie, always subject to the gaze, "cannot look."[30] The essays in this volume all unsettle Canavan's founding premise—the absolute "Otherness" of the zombie. This distinction becomes simply an untenable one in *The Walking Dead* (however much Rick may espouse it at the beginning). And while it is true that many fans may indeed embrace the series for its apparent licensing of unrestrained savagery, for its "unleashing of total violence" (literally against zombies, unconsciously against real marginalized others), the essays in this collection all argue that, at every turn, the series questions the license it also, on some level, undoubtedly offers.

It is not surprising, of course, that violence preoccupies *The Walking Dead* in our post–9/11 world—in the world of continuous war against terrorism, wars in Iraq and Afghanistan, and high-profile shooting sprees appearing on the news with frightening regularity. As the first two essays in this collection, in particular, describe, safety and security are obsessive preoccupations in both the post–9/11 U.S. and in *The Walking Dead*—and the threats on both counts come not only from the zombies outside the walls (the "others") but from the humans within the walls ("us"). As I write this introduction, news reports indicate that the American diplomatic mission in Benghazi, Libya, was, fatally, not secure enough when four Americans, including the ambassador, were killed by Islamist militia in September 2012. On December

14, 2012, a twenty-year-old long-time resident of Newtown, Connecticut, opened fire at Sandy Hook Elementary School, leaving twenty small children and seven adults dead. An anguished media debate ensued about whether American schools are safe enough. A National Rifle Association spokesperson, Wayne LaPierre, called for armed guards in all schools as a response to Newtown, a call that outraged many, those who cannot reconcile elementary school classrooms and armed guards. "The only thing that stops a bad guy with a gun is a good guy with a gun," said LaPierre, voicing what could be the tag-line of *The Walking Dead*.[31] Whether it be our embassies abroad, then, or our elementary schools at home, we are a nation preoccupied with security.

The Walking Dead's infamous villain, the Governor, certainly espouses the virtue of guns and, more broadly, of a "secure society," a community defended by guns and fortified fences. In a conversation with Milton, Andrea, and Michonne early in season three, the Governor talks of his dream of rebuilding "community." "With lots of guns and ammo," says Milton, drily. "It doesn't hurt," replies the Governor, blithely ignoring the scientist's sarcasm. Andrea adds, "And really big walls," referring to the Governor's obvious pride in his town's walls, continuously patrolled by armed militia. At the end of the same episode, as the Governor speaks to "his people" about the deaths of several soldiers (he claims walkers killed them but, actually, he did), he reminds them: "They didn't have our walls, or our fences" ("Walk with Me").

The Governor's obsession with guns and walls, though, is everyone's obsession on *The Walking Dead*. No one who has watched the show can fail to be aware of either the importance of fences (and securing them against the walkers and other, dangerous, humans) or the omnipresence of guns—the use of guns, training people in how to use guns, debates over who should have guns, giving guns to children, retrieving guns, lamenting the scarcity of guns. Encapsulating the ubiquity of guns in this new world, in "Walk with Me," Merle says he would "piss in [his] pants" if someone walked up to him *without* a gun trained on him. That's the "son of a bitch you'd really wanna be scared of," he adds.

This preoccupation with guns metonymically represents our broader abiding anxiety about constant threat and a corollary urgent security. The guns within the series refract the world beyond the show, as Americans have been constantly on the alert to the erosion of their right to protect themselves (and equally convinced that they *need* to protect themselves) since Barack Obama was elected in 2008. This fear coincides neatly with pervasive, manufactured, often only partially tongue-in-cheek talk about the zombie apocalypse (sign of some absolute threat to security) and the concomitant need for guns. Guns designed for zombies (them), however, are often turned on humans (us) as is tragically illustrated over and over not only in *The Walking Dead* (where Carl, for instance, has to use the gun Rick gave him on both Shane and his own mother) but also in the fact that one of the guns touted by an article in *Guns and Ammo* as one of the "8 Best Guns for the Zombie Apocalypse," the AR-15 rifle, was used to kill first-graders in the Newtown school shooting.[32] One of "us" killing not zombies but "us."[33]

All the essays in the first section of this collection address the problem of violence, what Steven Pokornowski calls the "terror/security paradigm," a paradigm that shapes *The Walking Dead*, just as it has shaped the post–9/11 United States. The essays ask: how do the survivors fight the walkers, protect themselves from the walkers, without becoming *like* them—without losing essential characteristics of freedom, civilization, even humanity itself? One of the tragedies of the series is that the survivors so often seem to become the zombies as they fight them; they lose their lives in fighting for their lives. Such is the truth the ill-fated Dale tries to instill in the group, telling them that if they execute a human being merely because of the *fear* that he might be dangerous, then they are already dead ("Judge, Jury, Executioner"). In a moment of supreme irony in season two, Shane proclaims of the walkers: "They're not people. All they do is kill" ("Pretty Much Dead Already"). Shane says this as he is about to release the walkers from Hershel's barn—where Hershel put them precisely because he could not, would not, kill them, still hoping for a cure for this particular last "plague" in a long line of plagues humans have suffered and survived. Shane says this as he is about to force the survivors to slaughter them all—as he is on the verge of launching his plot to kill Randall and then Rick and not long after he killed Otis. Perhaps Shane's comment could more aptly have been, "They *are* people. All they do is kill."

Despite its being about a futuristic post-apocalyptic world, *The Walking Dead* is steeped in the past. The series thus suggests that, in the end, our propensity for violence may be not only historically-contingent—about, say, a particularly post–9/11 obsession with terrorism and the secure state—but also an enduring human condition manifest throughout history. As the Governor puts it, talking about the importance of re-establishing civilization: "It's about getting back to *who we were*—who *we really are*" ("Walk with Me"; emphasis mine). The tenses here, and their slippage, is crucial—"who we really *are*" is about getting back to "who we *were*"—as if the (stable) essence of humanity lies in human history.

The Governor echoes another zombie narrative here, one that is similarly interested in reclaiming "who *we were*." At a critical moment in Max Brooks' *World War Z* (2006), the survivors confront the question of whether or not to go to war with the zombies, to take back the planet rather than merely existing in the corners that were left to them. One character contemplates the implications of this choice: "We had to reclaim our planet. We had to prove to ourselves that we could do it, and leave that proof as this war's greatest monument. *The long, hard road back to humanity*, or the regressive ennui of Earth's once-proud primates. That was the choice, and it had to be made now."[34] As in the Governor's formulation, these lines suggest the road to the future goes back to the past: "the long, hard road *back* to humanity." It is a road to be violently taken, one that culminates in humans reclaiming their position as "the planet's dominant life-form." Survival in *World War Z*, as well as for the Governor and other characters in *The Walking Dead*, is not actually (only) about survival but about *dominance*, with which the human seems virtually synonymous: the "road back to *humanity*" is also the road back to becoming "the planet's *dominant* life-form."[35]

For the Governor, as for the survivors in *World War Z*, the human past is something to be desired, recapitulated. "We will rise again," the Governor continues—words that, when spoken by a southerner somewhere in Georgia, accrue very particular and less-than-utopian meaning ("Walk with Me"). Re-creating the old civilization, the old South, inevitably involves re-creating violent, exclusionary social structures (as the Governor indeed does, enslaving "walkers" as well as killing anyone who defies him). The dystopian implications of the Governor's words are only intensified in light of the recent zombie apocalypse. We will indeed "rise again"—to repeat old mistakes, to cannibalize and destroy each other once more, and not always in the obvious ways of taking a chunk from someone's neck or burying an axe in his head. Sarah Juliet Lauro and Karen Embry have argued that the zombie, in its violent cannibalism, perfectly embodies our current moment: we "feed off the products of the rest of the planet."[36] This parasitic feeding off of others is not, though, of "the current moment"; it is also of the past, which *The Walking Dead* never allows us to forget.[37] "Remember the Alamo!" says Daryl, pushing a just-murdered man out of a shack to distract the walkers so the group can escape ("When the Dead Come Knocking")—a recapitulation, of sorts, of Shane's shooting Otis in the leg and leaving him as live bait to distract the zombies, so *he* could escape ("Save the Last One"). "Our" life for "theirs"—whether they are dead, undead, or still living. Our lives, it seems, are always bought at the cost of others.

The Walking Dead continually assembles images from the past, always reminding us that our violent "cannibalistic" tendencies are by no means of recent origin—that *The Walking Dead*'s present (our imagined future) is actually also our past. The second destruction of Atlanta during the zombie apocalypse calls to mind the first destruction during the Civil War, and, indeed, the title of the penultimate episode of the second season, "Better Angels," is drawn from Abraham Lincoln's first inaugural address, delivered on the eve of the Civil War. In this episode, Shane's plot to kill Rick comes to fruition, forcing Rick to kill Shane. Brother killing brother—the central thematic of season two, driven by Rick and Shane's escalating conflict—is exactly what Lincoln still hoped to avert in March 1861: "We are not enemies, but friends. We must not be enemies," Lincoln exhorts, calling on his fellow Americans to find "the better angels of our nature" and preserve the Union, prevent war. Those "better angels" seem nowhere in evidence, however, either on the battlefields of mid-nineteenth-century America or in *The Walking Dead*. Instead of better angels, we find only corpses, whether scattered or staggering across the fields of the South. Lincoln presciently warns, moreover, against the tendency to scapegoat another for the failure of our better angels in words that resonate with the central thematic of *The Walking Dead*: "You can have no conflict without being yourselves the aggressors."[38] When walkers overrun Hershel's farm at the end of season two, it is quite clear the survivors brought it on themselves (by a gunshot, no less). The fact that Hershel's pastoral farm, moreover, is set in a landscape itself evocative of the nineteenth century and that the walkers evoke troops streaming over the hill signals that the apocalypse of *The Walking Dead* is a repeated apocalypse—past folded into present, Civil War into zombie war. After the war comes Reconstruction: "We will rise again," says the Governor. The past repeats itself: the dead rise from their graves, repeating the carnage of history.[39]

While zombie narratives are always about violence, the essays in this collection argue that *The Walking Dead* is unique in representing how humans mirror the walkers, offering repeated iterations of human dissolving into zombie *because of* their shared propensity for violence. Shane's comment about walkers ("All they do is kill"), which is also about the survivors, makes this mirroring clear. The zombie virus, then, is seemingly inherent human aggression, repeated in past, present, and future.

"The you part": Posthumanity

If the immanent presence of the zombie virus serves as the foundation of *The Walking Dead*'s allegories of human violence, then it also serves as the bedrock of the series' contemplation of an equally important, albeit more existential question: what does it mean to be human? The essays in the second section of this collection all suggest that *The Walking Dead* offers a thoroughly posthuman zombie narrative—and I mean this term, first, in its most basic sense: the series is posthuman because it fundamentally decenters the human.[40] If Max Brooks' profoundly humanist *World War Z* positions the human as "the planet's dominant life-form" and celebrates humanity's reclamation of what it once was (the "long, hard road back to humanity"), then *The Walking Dead* questions both the accuracy and the desirability of humanity's dominance.[41] After all, to the extent that the human is fundamentally violent, the decentering of both humanity's dominance and even the human itself need not necessarily be dystopian. Each essay in the second section, then, considers how *The Walking Dead* contests, critiques, or expands reigning notions of the "human."

A crucial precursor to *The Walking Dead* is Richard Matheson's *I Am Legend* (1954), a novella that itself interrogates both human supremacy and the human.[42] The lone protagonist, Robert Neville, is not only brutally violent but is also disturbingly blind to his own inhumanity. He is, it turns out, a monster unaware of his own monstrosity. Apparently the last hope of humanity, Neville is in fact the last of an extinct breed; another species has evolved through the bacterium that killed most humans. Will this species be less violent? Matheson leaves that question unanswered, although Ruth, one of the new breed, does allow Neville to take suicide pills rather than seeing him publicly butchered—a butchery *he* has not demurred from enacting on both living and dead.[43] As humanity evolves in tandem with a new life-form—the vampire bacterium in *I Am Legend*, the zombie virus in *The Walking Dead*—there is always hope for positive change.

In its thoroughgoing decentering of what we know as the "human," *The Walking Dead* is different, I suggest, from the generally humanist orientation of many zombie narratives—and, by this, I mean those narratives that position the human as the ideal from which we fell and to which we must return (as *World War Z* exemplifies). Despite its critique of some particular humans (mostly thinly-disguised stand-ins for members of George Bush's administration), Romero's *Land of the Dead*, for instance, is profoundly humanist. Watching the unusually human zombies of Uniontown at the beginning of the film, the protagonist, Riley Dembo, says that they "used to be us" and "are learning to be us again"—setting "us," the human, as the standard. And at the end, Riley refrains from shooting at them because they are simply "Looking for a place to go. Same as us." "Same as us" is the refrain of *Land* with its persistent efforts to show that the zombies actually aren't that different from "us," an aspirational example.

28 Days Later also demonizes some few humans while preserving the human in general as the ideal. Lauro and Embry have noted how the zombie whom the rather despicable troops of Major Henry West have kept chained up in their courtyard is set free by Jim, proceeding to savage the soldiers and enabling the escape of Jim, Selena, and Hannah. Zombie sacrifice enables human freedom from rape, exploitation, and death—and leads to what Lauro and Embry note is a "humanist rather than a posthuman future": Jim, Selena, and Hannah learn that "everything—humanity, government, and most likely capitalism—has survived the attack"—a happy ending.[44] As the zombies are humanized, in both *Land of the Dead* and *28 Days Later*, the films mark the "good" as synonymous with the human. The zombies are then expelled, either through violence (in *28 Days Later*) or through a form of liberal multicultural tolerance that sends them off to find their own place (*Land of the Dead*). The banishing of the zombies in both films means the concomitant foreclosure of the risk that they might ever be incorporated into the human. *The Walking Dead*, however, is notable for refusing this expulsion: with its zombie virus immanent in human bodies (the viral human) and with its prolonged narrative about zombies and humans evolving symbiotically, *The Walking Dead* necessarily decenters both the humanist plot and the human.

Of course the decentering of the human as "ideal," or even distinctly separate from the zombie, risks disturbing the pleasure fans might seek in vicariously participating in "total violence" against the zombie.[45] Not surprisingly, then, there seems to be some fan resistance to suggestions that the zombies are not utterly abject others intent only on killing us. In the season three episode, "When the Dead Come Knocking," the Governor's scientist, Milton, brings to fruition his experiment to test whether the walkers retain any trace of their (human) consciousness. One blog post ranted about this plot turn:

> At this point, I do not need to know any more about Zombie Science. You die. You turn. You need to feed on brains. The end. So seeing Milton's big experiment with the dying Coleman was another eye rolling debacle. That being said, Andrea's reaction to the experiment actually made her the most likeable that she had been in forever. She was completely dismissive of the notion that zombies retain any of their former selves, and she was quick to dispatch of Zombie Coleman when he lunged for Milton. Can we be done with Zombie Science now, please?[46]

The writer here demonstrates the tension between avidly and unthinkingly "dispatching" zombies and the notion that they may have some kind of consciousness or may be, in some sense, residually who they were. Perhaps dispelling, then, some of the pleasures inherent in zombie destruction, the essays in the second part of this collection explore, in some way, "zombie science"; they explore how *The Walking Dead* interrogates, even dislodges, the human by refusing the total erasure or abjection of the zombie that justifies "total violence."[47]

The Walking Dead is posthuman not only in its decentering of the human, though, but also in its (related) preoccupation with the body, a preoccupation that dethrones a particular notion of the human as tantamount to mind (or soul) and as more-or-less autonomous. Cary Wolfe has used the term posthuman to describe those who insist on our embodiment, who resist fantasies of disembodiment (exemplified by dreams of cyborgs or robots). As he writes: "Posthumanism in my sense isn't posthumanism at all—in the sense of being 'after' our embodiment has been transcended—but is only posthuman*ist*, in the sense that it opposes the fantasies of disembodiment and autonomy, inherited from humanism itself." Wolfe argues that posthumanism comes not only *after* but also *before* humanism "in the sense that it names the persistent embodiment and embeddedness of the human being in ... its biological ... world."[48] *The Walking Dead*, then, is posthumanist not least because bodies are always irreducibly present, a fact obviously incarnate in the zombie body itself and in the series' constant and spectacular dismemberings of the zombie body, as well as in its imbrication of human and zombie bodies through the indwelling virus. Graphically manifesting the co-mingling of human and zombie, the survivors in *The Walking Dead* have, more than once, smeared zombie guts on their bodies (as Rick and Glenn do in "Guts" and Michonne does in "Hounded"). The zombie body of *The Walking Dead* is indeed, as Lauro and Embry write, a "dissolution of consciousness"—a challenge to the fantasy of postmodern disembodiment.[49]

The posthuman zombie body, above all, questions the mind/body split, the Cartesian dualism, that has long defined the human. Descartes' "I think, therefore I am" has had a long and certainly not uncontested history, but it has also had profound after-effects in people's entrenched belief that the essence of the human, of who we are, lies mostly in some intangible essence— mind, reason, personality, soul, etc.—that is apart from the body.[50] The after-effects of the Cartesian idea are also evident in the widespread belief in human agency. Agency is persistently defied, after all, by the concrete reality of the body. As Katherine Hayles puts it, in the "posthuman view, conscious agency has never been 'in control,'"[51] and it has never been in control precisely because of the body—the body's automated processes, its ungovernable drives and instincts, its neurons and reflexes, and its slow entropic fall into decay and death. Aside from being in large part automaton, the body is also striated with history: it is "the net result of thousands of years of sedimented evolutionary history, and it is naïve to think that this history does not affect human behaviors at every level of thought and action."[52] Our bodies define us ("we" cannot exist beyond them).

The essays in this section take seriously the proximity of human and zombie and the challenge the zombie poses to notions of the human that are grounded in the Cartesian philosophical tradition. The zombie reminds us that we have a body: it manifests our own often disavowed corporeality (and mortality). A crucial part of the body that we share with zombies is the brain, a part of the body particularly important to personality, to identity. Not surprisingly, *The Walking Dead* is replete, even obsessed, with zombie heads: they are what must be destroyed (multiple times in every episode) or fetishized (as Jenner does with his fMRIs of the brain, and as the Governor does with his fish tanks of floating heads). They are the target of so much dread and perverse attachment precisely because the head, the brain, is the part of the body that most completely defines both zombie *and* human. Deborah Christie has argued that the zombie incarnates "our discomfort with that boundary space that exists in us all, that objectness of our inherent material makeup whereby we transition from human to post–(as in no longer)–human."[53] Disturbingly, as the preoccupation of *The Walking Dead* with heads and brains reminds us, the inner zombie, the "objectness" of the human, exists in the very same space with the source of the conscious self. Edwin Jenner calls that conscious self "the you part," demonstrating to the survivors, using an fMRI, where in the brain the essence of identity inheres. Of course, this is also where the zombie inheres ("TS-19").

As both Hayles and Wolfe make clear, the recognition of our essential embodiment, and the inevitable subject/object split that our embodiment introduces *within us*, constitutes a form of poshumanism that is by no means (only) about futurity. Just as *The Walking Dead's* allegories of violence always fold present and future into the past, the genealogy of thinking about the human as embodied also has roots in the past, in a tradition of thought that actually does acknowledge, has always acknowledged, "the objectness of our inherent material makeup."[54] Philosopher Roberto Esposito has traced back to late eighteenth-century French physiologist Xavier Bichat the notion that humans are traversed by something non-human.[55] For Bichat, every living being has a "double biological layer"—"one vegetative and unconscious" (which he called "organic") and one "cerebral and relational" (which he called "animal"). Riven by these two heterogeneous forces, we are actually determined, Bichat claimed, "in our passions, and even in our will" by what he called the "blind corporeality of [our] vegetative life."[56] Once this "blind corporeality" is acknowledged, the notion of the autonomously human, of "personhood"— the sovereignty that each human being exercises over his or her organic being— becomes fundamentally compromised.

Needless to say, the zombie—both those that amass beyond the survivors and the zombie lodged within—is a perfect representation of our "blind corporeality." Esposito writes of our "non-human aspect" that it is "in the first case ... destined to overcome us and in the second to be mastered by us,"[57] which perfectly encapsulates the drama of *The Walking Dead*—grounded in the survivors' efforts (and failures) to overcome the zombie hordes as well as their efforts (and failures) to overcome their own blind instincts, impulses, and drives. The zombies of *The Walking Dead*, in short, perpetually remind us of the "other than human" within—and our struggle is not only against the external zombies but against what is inevitably inside of us. Both forces, interior and exterior, wreak havoc on every institution humans have ever built—and they always have.

The essays in the first section, "Society's End," highlight primarily the social and political allegories of *The Walking Dead* as each considers what the apocalypse means (in terms of our present and possible future) and the various constituent causes of the looming threat of collapse.

Philip L. Simpson's "The Zombie Apocalypse Is Upon Us! Homeland Insecurity" explores how *The Walking Dead's* emphasis on battening down a secure domestic space allegorizes the post–9/11 United States, in which a series of human and natural catastrophes (9/11, Katrina, the recession, political gridlock) have heightened Americans' anxieties. Simpson explores the leadership that emerges in such a world, specifically the slide from liberal humanism, indeed, from any kind of collective democracy or gender equality, to Hobbesian anarchy and to a patriarchal "strongman" leadership secured with violence. Through its first three seasons, the series has offered fleeting alternatives to the "strongman," but they have all ultimately fallen to the powerful mandate of securing the besieged "home."

Steven Pokornowski's "Burying the Living with the Dead: Security, Survival and the Sanction of Violence" continues the collection's interrogation of the terror/security paradigm that has predominated in the U.S. since 9/11. Reading *The Walking Dead* comic series, Pokornowski argues that the survivors of the zombie plague, determined to secure their own lives above all, deem themselves perennially justified in slaughtering the infectious zombie, the figure of Giorgio Agamben's "*homo sacer*"—one who can be killed with impunity. Like the zombie, the elided racial figure of the series is also bare life, vulnerable to destruction to preserve the life of others. Such slaughter, however, ends by reducing *all* life to bare life, destroying the very life the sanction of violence is meant to preserve.

Like Simpson and Pokornowski, P. Ivan Young, in "Walking Tall or Walking Dead? The American Cowboy in the Zombie Apocalypse," explores the overwhelmingly destructive consequences of violence for those who perpetuate it. Young shifts the context through which the violence of *The Walking Dead* is understood, reading it as a distinctly "western" incarnation of post–9/11 America. Young notes the series' repeated invocations of western tropes as well as its specific parallels to George Stevens' *Shane* (1953). While the western is, however, a genre traditionally sustained by opposed moral absolutes—the mythic cowboy and his villainous nemesis—the zombies of *The Walking Dead* signally fail to be the perfect villains. Instead, they serve as a "symbolic white space," mirroring the western heroes (Rick Grimes and Shane Walsh) in the act of killing. In *The Walking Dead's* post-apocalyptic western landscape of open space, farms, barns and saloons, first Shane and then Rick are unmasked as nothing more or less than ruthless murderers.

Angus Nurse's "Asserting Law and Order Over the Mindless" reads *The Walking Dead* through the lens of criminology—reading at the same time very much against the grain of the previous three essays. With its zombies representing mass lawlessness, *The Walking Dead* explores various potential responses to pervasive crime, including a reactive non-confrontational crime control approach (embodied in Rick Grimes). Nurse argues, however, that in the end, *The Walking Dead* offers a critique of contemporary liberal law and order policy—in particular, of the failure of the reactive policing model. The series suggests that a more aggressive law enforcement response is required in the face of rising crime.

Laura Kremmel's "Rest in Pieces: Violence in Mourning the (Un)Dead," like Nurse's essay, claims that *The Walking Dead* dramatizes a *necessary* violence in response to the conditions of the post-apocalyptic world. The pervasiveness of death, as well as the threat that the undead body poses to the living, thoroughly problematizes conventional mourning practices for the survivors of the apocalypse. Kremmel argues that as the dead turn on their distraught and grieving communities, and as the survivors struggle with varieties of "ambiguous loss," violence against the dead (even "hate mourning") becomes necessary to protect not only the living but also in order to facilitate closure. Violent mourning rituals offer certainty of death, preservation of the loved one's memory, and separation from the dead through heightened abjection.

Christine Heckman's "Roadside 'Vigil' for the Dead: Cannibalism, Fossil Fuels and the American Dream" locates *The Walking Dead's* particular cannibalistic violence within America's history of slavery and the dispossession of Native Americans. Heckman connects this history to a similarly exploitative dependence of the United States on "undead" fossil fuels, marked in the TV series by the preoccupation with repeated shots of stalled and abandoned cars and with a pervasive anxiety about scarcity of gas. Heckman argues that these interdependent, parasitic relationships constitute an impossible white, middle-class American dream. The United States' voracious consumption of people and resources, in *The Walking Dead's* allegory, seems destined to usher in its demise, its apocalyptic self-consumption.

Paul Boshears, in "Mass Shock Therapy for Atlanta's Psych(ot)ic Suburban Legacy," also argues for the destructiveness of a particular kind of white, middle-class American dream. While Heckman writes about the importance to that dream of mobility more generally, Boshears argues for the centrality, in *The Walking Dead*, of white flight to the suburbs, a phenomenon illuminated by the series' location in Atlanta. Tracking the numerous traumas constitutive of Atlanta's history—from the Trail of Tears to the death of most of the city's powerful elite in a 1970 plane crash in Paris, as well as the dissociation induced by white flight to the suburbs, Boshears argues that *The Walking Dead* both evokes these traumas in its setting and in its aesthetic of violent shocks and also serves as a form of mass therapy for its viewers.

In "Apocalyptic Utopia: The Zombie and the (r)Evolution of Subjectivity," the first essay in the second section, Chris Boehm forges a transition from the essays that consider the series' social and political allegories to those in "Posthumanity." Boehm argues that zombies are embodiments of pure death-drive, and thus they not only destroy a social order predicated on exclusion but also open the space for something new. Because everyone in *The Walking Dead* is already infected with the zombie virus, moreover, the revelation that "we" are "them" allows the survivors to see from their own "inner zombie," their own space of pure drive. The series' vision of the new human, infected with the "virus of drive," the "renewing potential of negativity," holds out the hope not just for evolutionary movement beyond social structures predicated on exclusion but for positive social change; it is an ethical mode of being that allows for a re-conception of the social order.

In "Nothing But the Meat: Posthuman Bodies and the Dying Undead," Xavier Aldana Reyes offers another version of the new, evolving subjectivity of *The Walking Dead*. The series presents, Aldana Reyes argues, an alternative to a fleshless posthumanism that imagines a mind free of corporeal encumbrances. Reading the walkers of *The Walking Dead* as the "dying undead," sentient creatures who are distinctly not (yet) dead, Aldana Reyes claims that they embody the fundamental materiality of human consciousness—that they mark the biological as thoroughly constitutive of the human.

My "Human Choice and Zombie Consciousness" also reads the zombie as determining corporeal interior. The zombies of *The Walking Dead* allegorize, specifically, "zombie consciousness"—the neurons, reflexes, and muscles that constitute a realm of automatic functions, directing what we do beyond our conscious control. While the series tries, in its existentialist protagonist, Rick Grimes, to counter the anxiety that humans are far from conscious, reasoning free agents, Shane Walsh exemplifies forms of zombie consciousness: survival instinct, muscle memory, and mimetic desire.

In "'Talking Bodies' in a Zombie Apocalypse: From the Discursive to the Shitty Sublime," Gary Farnell makes a quite different argument from the two preceding essays, arguing against the notion that humans are inevitably, primarily, their organic part. Farnell maintains that the zombie body is in fact the "shitty sublime" that the human survivors must try to overcome, specifically through language. Representing a particular contemporary crisis of illiteracy, as our speech is increasingly "emptied of content and sapped of substance," zombie aphasia marks a kind of deadness. Language, Farnell claims, is what makes meaning and makes us human. As "talking bodies," tethered to the organic, the zombies of *The Walking Dead* are both threat and reassurance that *we* are not dead inside, that we can make ourselves in and through language.

Gwyneth Peaty's "Zombie Time: Temporality and Living Death" also argues that the zombies of *The Walking Dead* represent a fundamental threat to the human as we know it. They embody a vanishing past, an endless devouring present, and an unimaginable future. They are "monstrous timelessness," a rapacious, relentless consumption that endangers both past and future. In the face of a living death that devours time and mortality, the survivors struggle to reinstate both. Through memory, photographs, and ritual they try to retain the past and the present. The human, Peaty argues, demands time—demands, paradoxically, mortality. Time has disappeared, however, in the post-apocalyptic, posthuman world; it has slipped into "zombie time," and the survivors must struggle to reassert time in order to keep the "human" alive.

The collection ends with Dave Beisecker's afterword, "Bye-Gone Days: Reflections on Romero, Kirkman and What We Become," which positions *The Walking Dead* in a context that highlights the zombie narrative as a story of revolution, of wholesale, continual change. Within this story of revolution, the zombies do not function as metaphor—they don't "mean" anything, and they certainly are not our irreducible "other." As Beisecker puts it, the zombies are "the situation" and not "the metaphor." Zombie narratives are about how we humans survive the revolution, how we adapt to change, and whether, and with how much grace, we recognize that the zombies are not only not that much different from us but also they might well be what we become. And what we all become, Beisecker points out, is old and infirm, an inescapable meaning of the often bewildered-looking zombie at a time when the baby-boom generation is entering old age *en masse*.

The Walking Dead, "the zombie narrative without end," is indeed distinctive for its emphasis on futurity: it is the perfect medium for imagining, in Beisecker's words, "what we become." Zombies embody what Elizabeth Grosz has called an "open-ended but relentless force to futurity" that "undoes all stability and identity."[58] Zombies mark doubly what we might become, both in themselves and in what their relentless presence does to the human survivors. If life is always emerging, always becoming, then the forces of natural selection that exert their transformative pressure on humanity inevitably include, after the imagined apocalypse, zombies. What does human life become in this new environment? That story is still unfolding.

NOTES

1. The place to start for a comprehensive overview of zombie narratives, beginning with Haitian folklore and ending, fleetingly, with *The Walking Dead*, is Bishop's *American Zombie Gothic*. The important collection of essays, *Better Off Dead*, edited by Christie and Lauro, is organized into three sections that map the major paradigms shifts I lay out here: "the classic mindless corpse, the relentless instinct-driven newly dead, and the millennial voracious and fast-moving predator." Christie and Lauro, Introduction, 2. Within that collection, essays by Boon, "The Zombie as Other," and Dendle, "Zombie Movies and the 'Millennial Generation,'" offer particularly useful overviews. Muntean and Payne's "Attack of the Livid Dead" gives a good summary of the characteristics of both the pre–9/11 zombie and the post–9/11 zombie.

2. For discussions of the Haitian origins of the zombie, see Bishop, *American Zombie Gothic*, 37–93; Kordas, "New South, New Immigrants"; Inglis, "Putting the Undead to Work"; and McAlister, "Slaves, Cannibals, and Infected Hyper-Whites."

3. Matheson's 1954 novella *I Am Legend* must be mentioned here as a powerful influence on both Romero and the zombie narrative in general. According to Hervey, Romero's script for *Night of the Living Dead* was, from the first, "inspired by *I Am Legend*." Hervey, *Night of the Living Dead*, 10.

4. I'm omitting the zombie comedy from this brief history, though it has been a continuous presence since the 1980s—realized most perfectly, perhaps, in Edgar Wright's *Shaun of the Dead* (2004).

5. Muntean and Payne, "Attack of the Livid Dead," 246–247. See also Wetmore's discussion of the "angry dead," which he argues have dominated horror cinema since 9/11. Wetmore, *Post–9/11 Horror*, 154–155.

6. Muntean and Payne, "Attack of the Livid Dead," 255.

7. Botting, "Zombie London," 158.

8. Steven Shaviro presciently argued, of Romero's early films, that zombies uncannily resembled images: "Romero's zombies could almost be said to be quintessential media images," he writes, "since they are vacuous, mimetic replications of the human beings they once were." "Perception itself," he continues, "becomes infected, and is transformed into a kind of magical, contagious contact." Shaviro, *The Cinematic Body*, 84, 95. See also Birch-Bayley, "Terror in Horror Genres," which reads the "millennial zombie" of post–9/11 film in terms of the global media.

9. Bishop, *American Zombie Gothic*, 158–196, discusses films that "humanize" the zombie.

10. Two other films, *Homecoming* (2005) and *Fido* (2006), are also notable in this regard, figuring zombies as the war veteran and the worker.

11. Qtd. in Bishop, *American Zombie Gothic*, 206. Bishop argues in his book, published in 2010, that one of the developments he sees ahead for the zombie is "the serialization of large-scope storylines, primarily through video games, graphic novels, and season-long television productions." He repeats later, "the most insightful and revolutionary development

in store for the zombie lies in its potential for serialization." Bishop, *American Zombie Gothic*, 198, 206. Such potential has clearly been realized in all incarnations of *The Walking Dead* (comics, TV, video games, novels, webisodes etc.).

12. Both novels are written by Robert Kirkman and Jay Bonansinga—*The Walking Dead: Rise of the Governor* (2011) and *The Walking Dead: The Road to Woodbury* (2012).

13. Maberry calls the comic series "one of the bleakest, most downbeat and nihilistic stories ever told, even in a genre known for those qualities." Maberry, "Take Me to Your Leader," 22.

14. Jameson, "Reification and Utopia in Mass Culture," 144.

15. Kirkman, Adlard, and Rathburn, *Something to Fear*, back cover.

16. Bishop, *American Zombie Gothic*, 206; see also Bishop, "The Pathos of *The Walking Dead*."

17. Liaguno notes that the extreme and relentless violence (largely precipitated by the zombies) functions precisely to highlight the human drama: "The violence *is* important because it frames the narrative in such unyieldingly bleak and punishing circumstances, which only makes the human interaction, action, and reaction to the unfolding events all the more pronounced, ultimately heightening the audience's response to and expectations of the show's characters." Liaguno, "Happy (En)Trails," 125.

18. Kirkman, Adlard, and Rathburn, *Safety Behind Bars*.

19. Kirkman, Adlard, and Rathburn, *The Heart's Desire*.

20. Wood, *Hollywood from Vietnam to Reagan*, 287.

21. See Hervey, *Night of the Living Dead*, especially 95–98, 107–118; Lightning, "Interracial Tensions in *Night of the Living Dead*"; Higashi, "*Night of the Living Dead*: A Horror Film about the Horrors of the Vietnam Era"; Grant, "Taking Back the *Night of the Living Dead*"; Bruce, "Guess Who's Going to Be Dinner"; and Lowenstein, "Living Dead."

22. See Harper, "Zombies, Malls, and the Consumerism Debate"; Loudermilk, "Eating 'Dawn' in the Dark"; and Bishop, "The Idle Proletariat" and *American Zombie Gothic*, 129–157.

23. See Tait, "(Zombie) Revolution at the Gates"; Lowenstein, "Living Dead," especially 108–116; and Lewis, "Ztopia."

24. See Lowenstein, "Living Dead," especially 116–123; Laist, "Soft Murders"; Keetley, "Zombie Evolution"; and Birch-Bayley, "Terror in Horror Genres."

25. See Shaviro, "Capitalist Monsters."

26. See Muntean and Payne, "Attack of the Livid Dead"; Wetmore, *Post–9/11 Horror*, especially 153–155, 159–164; and Birch-Bayley, "Terror in Horror Genres."

27. Muntean and Payne, "Attack of the Livid Dead," 240, 242.

28. Canavan, "'We *Are* the Walking Dead,'" 433, 439, 442.

29. Ibid., 433.

30. Ibid., 433, 437.

31. Mariano Castillo, "NRA Clear on Gun Debate Stance: Arm Schools," CNN.com, December 21, 2012, http://www.cnn.com/2012/12/21/us/connecticut-school-shooting/index.html?hpt=hp_t2.

32. Patrick Sweeney, "8 Best Guns for the Zombie Apocalypse," *Guns and Ammo*, November 15, 2011, http://www.gunsandammo.com/2011/11/15/the-8-best-guns-for-zombie-killing/; Steve Almasy, "Newtown Shooter's Guns: What We Know," CNN.com, December 18, 2012, http://www.cnn.com/2012/12/18/us/connecticut-lanza-guns/index.html.

33. Dendle briefly discusses recent zombie films in relation to school shootings (notably Columbine). Dendle, "Zombie Movies and the 'Millennial Generation,'" 185–186.

34. Brooks, *World War Z*, 267, emphasis mine.

35. Ibid., 267.

36. Lauro and Embry, "A Zombie Manifesto," 93.

37. Muntean and Payne make the crucial point, in talking about post–9/11 zombies in *28 Days Later* and the *Dawn of the Dead* re-make, that, in their representation of rage and violence, zombies are not a phenomenon of the present but the past—"the exhumed specters of the unprecedented horrors of the past one hundred years"—of a century marked throughout by global brutal violence. In the end, they argue, 9/11 was not a break from history, an anomaly, but " a paroxysm *of* history." Muntean and Payne, "Attack of the Livid Dead," 248.

38. Lincoln, "First Inaugural Address," paragraphs 34 and 35.

39. In season three, with Woodbury, the Governor's walled city, we seem to go back even further—to Rome. "Rome wasn't built in a day," says one of Woodbury's citizens. It is, however, being (re)built, along with fortified walls and gladiator fights.

40. My discussion of posthumanism and embodiment is informed by Webb and Byrnand's wonderful essay, "Some Kind of Virus: The Zombie as Body and as Trope."

41. Brooks, *World War Z*, 267.

42. Not surprisingly, Robert Kirkman has said that *I Am Legend* is one of his favorite books. "'The Walking Dead' Creator Robert Kirkman: Why the Zombie Trend Just Won't Die," Bookish.com, October 14, 2011, http://blog.bookish.com/why-the-zombie-trend-just-wont-die.

43. Matheson, *I Am Legend*, 170.

44. Lauro and Embry, "A Zombie Manifesto," 107.

45. Canavan, "'We *Are* the Walking Dead,'" 442.

46. "The Walking Dead—S03E07—'When the Dead Come Knocking' Review," Mediaglitch.net, November 26, 2012, http://www.mediaglitch.net/reviews/2012/11/the-walking-dead-s03e07-when-the-dead-come-knocking-review/.

47. For essays that explore the complicated notion of humans, and zombies, in *The Walking Dead*, see Riley, "Zombie People," and the essays in the first section of Yuen's "*The Walking Dead" and Philosophy*, all of which address the philosophical debates about zombies: Hawkes, "Are You Just Braaaiiinnnsss or Something More?"; Littman, "Can *You* Survive a Walker Bite?"; Greene, "What Your Zombie Knows"; Delfino and Taylor, "Walking Contradictions"; and McKendry and Da Silva, "I'm Going to Tell Them about Wayne."

48. Wolfe, *What Is Posthumanism?*, xv.

49. Lauro and Embry, "A Zombie Manifesto," 101.

50. As Hayles argues, the "posthuman does not really mean the end of humanity. It signals instead the end of a certain conception of the human, a conception that may have applied, at best, to that fraction of humanity who had the wealth, power, and leisure to conceptualize themselves as autonomous beings exercising their will through individual agency and choice. What is lethal is not the posthuman as such but the grafting of the posthuman onto a liberal humanist view of the self." Hayles, *How We Became Posthuman*, 286–287.

51. Hayles, *How We Became Posthuman*, 288.

52. Ibid., 284.

53. Christie, "A Dead New World," 71.

54. Ibid.

55. Elizabeth Grosz, too, has also recently been engaged in this project. She explores "what is before, beyond, and after the human: the inhuman, uncontainable condition of the human, the origin of and trajectory immanent within the human." She identifies the "inhuman" as the "animal, plant, and material forces that surround and overtake the human." Grosz, *Becoming Undone*, 11.

56. Esposito, *Third Person*, 6.
57. Ibid., 12.
58. Grosz, *Becoming Undone*, 3. Grosz is talking about the effects of the Darwinian revolution, which, one could certainly argue, are being continued in the symbiotic evolution of zombie and human in *The Walking Dead*.

PART I
SOCIETY'S END

The Zombie Apocalypse Is Upon Us!

Homeland Insecurity

PHILIP L. SIMPSON

A significant factor in the contemporary popularity of the zombie apocalypse genre in narrative fiction, such as the basic cable channel AMC's series *The Walking Dead*, is its focus on "the day after" the apocalypse—"day after" here referring to the possibility of human survival and reconstitution of the social order after the undead have overrun civilization.[1] In many visions of the zombie apocalypse, such as the last two episodes of George A. Romero's original trilogy, the narrative takes place in the gap between the fall of civilization and the potential final triumph of the undead, in which humanity is extinguished for all time.[2] *The Walking Dead* occupies that same narrative space, although it is too early in the run of the show (or for that matter, the graphic novels upon which it is based) to say if humanity is doomed. The post-apocalyptic attempt to rebuild human society, or at least to fortify some kind of domestic space to keep the undead at bay, is what gives the typical zombie narrative much of its momentum, but it is also what invests it with bleakness, in that the desired safe domestic space may exist only within the realm of human hope and desire.[3] While zombie narratives focus on the process of struggling to batten down a domestic space that can never really be secured, that same domestic space, when found, often becomes a prison (literally in the case of *The Walking Dead's* third season)— besieged from the outside by the undead and other rapacious groups of human survivors, bedeviled on the inside by the tensions and prejudices of the destroyed old social order resurrecting zombie-like within the new emerging order.[4]

The zombie apocalypse as signifier is likely a symptom of the elevated social anxiety attending a series of recent catastrophic events in American history, inaugurated by the terror attacks of 9/11 and the live televised collapse of the World Trade Center towers. Charles B. Strozier makes the case that this event, more than anything else in recent American experience, evokes apocalyptic thinking at a level not seen since the worst days of the Cold War, when nuclear annihilation seemed imminent. One of the mass psychological effects of the awareness of living under the shadow of apocalypse, Strozier identifies, is a kind of numbing or emotional shut-down, a symbolic death.[5] Likewise, Jane Caputi states that, if numbness is "one of the hallmarks of consciousness in the Nuclear Age, what is repressed nevertheless inevitably returns, and these wide-ranging feelings consistently appear in various symbolic and metaphorical forms in the popular arts."[6] Caputi designates the ghouls of the original *Night of the Living Dead* (1968) as avatars of this kind of nuclear-age numbness. If one extrapolates from Caputi's work into the present age of eternal war, it stands to reason that zombies as popular culture monsters might have subsided somewhat in the popular imagination from the end of the Cold War throughout the 1990s. And, not surprisingly, they would then shamble back to life in the aftermath of 9/11, with the reawakening of a range of American global anxieties seeking adequate symbolic forms.[7] As it turns out, this is more or less what happened, heralded by movies such as Danny Boyle's *28 Days Later* (2002), Zack Snyder's remake of Romero's *Dawn of the Dead* (2004), Edgar Wright's zombie romantic comedy ("zom-rom-com") *Shaun of the Dead* (2004), and Romero's own return to the genre with *Land of the Dead* (2005) and *Diary of the Dead* (2007).[8]

This essay contends that the popularity of *The Walking Dead* is due in large part to its focus on the human effort, embodied in sympathetic everyman Rick Grimes and his folk, to re-establish a domestic sphere of safety in the post-apocalyptic world. As such, the series can be read as an allegory of post–9/11, post–Katrina, post–economic-collapse America, frozen by political gridlock between liberalism and a renascent conservatism. As one of its central projects, *The Walking Dead* interrogates what it means to be a leader during the downfall of civilization. As the leader of the story's central group of survivors, Rick begins his journey as one kind of hero: compassionate, humane, idealistic, sentimental, loving, and caring. The brutal necessities of his new world, however, quickly illustrate the shortcomings of the very qualities that made him such a sympathetic character. He must not only fight the dead but learn to fight and kill the living, who compete with him and his people for the few available resources.[9] In the age of terror (in this context, the terror of vulnerability highlighted by recent American catastrophes), Rick Grimes is the American everyman, whose hands have become of necessity "grimy" as he fights foreign and domestic enemies.

In the post–9/11 world of never-ending war, not to mention the economic disaster wrought, ironically, by the American home mortgage market, visions of recouped tranquil domesticity exert incredible nostalgic power. This domestic nostalgia frequently manifests in odd ways, such as naming a new bureaucratic monstrosity the Department of Homeland Security, which antithetically invokes the absence of security by its very name and indeed reifies national insecurity in the very act of attempting to recover, restore, and reassure. Domestic security and insecurity are inseparable, a notion that *The Walking Dead* dramatizes in horrific fashion. Rick's quixotic attempt to secure a safe homeland or domestic sphere for his group resonates dearly with the American viewing public traumatized by the nightmare of recent history, but it also reminds them that true security is unattainable in a violent world.

Fictional portrayals of apocalyptic disaster, such as *The Walking Dead*, often privilege an entropic, blatantly Hobbesian perspective.[10] In these representations, more often than not, civil society falls into irreparable ruin and human nature into savagery, succumbing to devastating macrocosmic forces that only the strongest and most brutal of humans can survive. Thematically, then, *The Walking Dead* is structured upon a tension between a progressive ideology (represented by Dale in its purest form and in more pragmatic form by Rick) and a more fear-bound, conservative ideology (represented by Shane). This narrative tension refracts the increasingly polarized American populace, which has embraced the zombie apocalypse as a "fun" way of exorcizing its demons through recuperative allegory. While the ideological pull is to and fro during the second season of *The Walking Dead*, the clear winner at the end of the season is the Hobbesian view. In the first half of the show's third season, Rick, through his newfound pragmatism, has formed his group into a much more organized search-and-destroy squad, one that moves into and takes over a new domestic zone—fittingly a literal prison—with calm, professional dispatch. In the second half of the season, as the showdown between Woodbury and Rick's group escalates, Rick descends into secretive, isolated madness before negotiating his way back to his sense of shared humanity and bringing the Woodbury survivors into the secured prison. The show's thematic pattern thus far, however, suggests that whatever security is to be found in the prison will be short-lived, with the group at high risk of atomizing once more.

The Hobbesian Post-Apocalypse

Rick and a few of the stronger members of his group of survivors in *The Walking Dead* tend to bear out the Hobbesian tendency in post-apocalyptic fiction.[11] The first two seasons constitute a contest among two strongmen leaders—Rick and Shane—for control of a group of weaker survivors. Specifically, Shane's strongman theories of leadership are tested against Rick's initially more humanitarian views. Shane and Rick, on some level, are equally matched. They are trained sheriff's deputies, capable with the weaponry needed to survive in this new reality. They are resourceful, courageous, and determined to live. Both are natural, charismatic leaders. Rick innately possesses more compassion than Shane, however—a trait in keeping with the show's nostalgia for old-fashioned liberal humanism. In the first season, for instance, Rick goes back to Atlanta to rescue Daryl's obnoxiously racist brother, Merle, who was left handcuffed on a roof. He never finds Merle (not until season three, anyway), and this plot thread exists primarily to demonstrate Rick's concern for a suffering human being, regardless of how disagreeable that person is. Rick's sympathy for those in distress even extends to the walkers who would kill him. He expresses sorrow for a gruesomely mutilated female zombie he encounters in the park during the pilot episode, and, later, he reminds the other survivors that a corpse they are cutting up in order to cloak their human scent with zombie guts was once a human being like themselves. While Rick's empathy for the walkers disappears as the group becomes more desensitized through the necessity of perpetual destruction, especially in season three, he clearly harbors deep reservoirs of compassion, even love—a love he seems to have marginally recovered by the end of season three.

By contrast, Shane acts much more in accord with a Hobbesian view of human nature. He believes that Rick's expansive capacity for love is a weakness that blinds him to the danger in which he places the group by looking for those left behind—in particular, the danger Rick's altruism poses to Lori and Carl. Love him or hate him, Shane is a passionate, tempestuous man. The zombie apocalypse in some way fulfills his lawman's desire to be a protector, but it also unleashes his inner caveman.[12] He severely beats Ed Peletier, for example, in reprisal for Ed's physical abuse of his wife, Carol; he shoots Otis in the leg and leaves him to the walkers; and he kills Randall in an attempt to lure Rick into a fatal ambush in the woods. His rage leads him to defy Rick and Hershel by releasing the walkers from Hershel's barn to be shot down. What drives Shane most is his desire for his own survival and the survival of those he increasingly considers to be his possessions: Lori and Carl. After Rick returns to the group in the first season to reclaim his wife and son from Shane and depose him as leader, Shane becomes even more of a tortured, repressed, and angry man than he had been before. His frustrated rage manifests in a drunken near-rape of Lori in the Centers for Disease Control stronghold at the end of the first season and continues to contort his thinking and actions throughout the second season, culminating in his failed murder attempt of Rick at the season's climax.

Shane is not the only one who doubts Rick's leadership ability. Rick doubts his own ability, which is perhaps, in and of itself, a progressive trait. When one of his leadership choices in season two results in Sophia Peletier going missing, Rick questions himself in his "Garden of Gesthemane" moment before the bloodied statue of Christ in the country church. He asks for a sign that he is on the right path—a prayer answered in ambiguous fashion when Carl has his instance of grace when he sees the deer in the woods but is shot seconds later ("What Lies Ahead"). Just as Rick doubts himself and sees no clear sign that what he is doing will lead to any good, the group itself becomes fractured over Rick's competence as a leader. As the season progresses, the impulsive and aggressive Shane emerges from his second-banana position to become someone who offers a pragmatic alternative to Rick's idealism and Hamlet-like equivocation.

The ground is especially fertile in season two for Rick's followers to question his leadership. A sense of anomie in the group is evident from practically the beginning of the second season, with a fever-stricken T-Dog (before fading to near invisibility in the rest of the season and being summarily dispatched early in season three) complaining to Dale that the group is going to leave both of them behind because Dale is old and he is black. "I'm the one black guy," says T-Dog presciently. "You realize how precarious that makes my situation?" ("Bloodletting"). This potential for T-Dog to emerge as a voice of discontent with "The Man," however, never really goes anywhere. T-Dog explicitly distances himself from his own words by blaming them on his fever and asking Dale not to say anything to the others about what he said. Nor does Daryl's first-season anger over what happened to his brother Merle really coalesce into any kind of rebellion against Rick's authority—just the opposite. When Daryl is lost and injured in the woods, he hallucinates his brother, who scolds him for throwing in his lot with Rick: "A joke is what you are. Playin' errand boy to a bunch of pansy-asses, niggers and democrats" ("Chupacabra"). With that memorable line, Merle articulates a (stereotyped) disenfranchised rural white male's assessment of Rick and the diverse group he leads, resurrecting the dead world's harsh political polarization between conservatism and liberalism. From Merle's perspective (and presumably Shane's), Rick is a "liberal" whose softness is endangering the group (read here, national) security.

Shane fatally underestimates Rick's capacity to protect the group, however, suggesting, by extension, that it is equally fatal to mistake America's current crisis of confidence for weakness. After Shane's mid-season rebellion in destroying Hershel's captive walkers, Rick reclaims his authority by shooting the undead Sophia, who had been kept, unbeknownst to the group, in the barn. This moment marks an acceleration in Rick's hardening as a leader; from this point forward, he finds himself in the position of having to kill human survivors. The two men in the bar are the first people he kills. Shane is next. Killing Shane represents Rick's justified vanquishing of the last real internal threat to his leadership—an act of self-defense, yes, but a reclamation of the power that the stronger, more decisive Shane had usurped from Rick (including the sexual possession of Rick's wife) since the beginning of the apocalypse.

Rick's victory, in the narrative's terms, represents the moment that he proves himself worthy enough to be the lawfully-sanctioned agent responsible for the group's continued safety, a move that includes, to some extent, a repudiation of the thoughtfulness and collaborative style that had earlier marked his leadership. In the wake of Shane's death, when some of the survivors and even his wife express dismay over his action, Rick gives them an ultimatum to leave or stay, and then lays down the law: "Get one thing straight. You're staying? This isn't a democracy anymore." He also expresses bitterness at his subjects over the exigencies that his leadership role has pushed him to: "I didn't ask for this. I killed my best friend for you people" ("Beside the Dying Fire"). Rick has made the transition from idealist to pragmatist, coming into line with Shane's mathematical calculation that the search for Sophia (as sanctioned by Rick) spread the group too thin and consumed too many resources. Little by little, the story has whittled away the softer alternatives to the hard-line "Shane way." Rick, the one-time humanitarian, embraces his inner Shane, inaugurating the fiercer "Rick-tatorship" and priming the allegorical pump for some pointed character parallels between Rick's post-apocalyptic despotism and that of the more sinister but equally conflicted Governor of season three.

The series suggests, via other characters, alternatives to a "Rick-tatorship" kind of social structure, but they never particularly go anywhere, largely because the narrative insists on closing them down in favor of a focus on Rick's character arc. The narrative's stance on the viability of Dale's outspoken liberal humanism as an alternative to Rick's burgeoning patriarchal dictatorship is made clear when Dale, walking alone in the field after his rhetorical defeat in the argument for Randall's life, is horribly mauled by a lone walker. Before his death, Dale repeats to the group Daryl's private statement that the group is broken—another way of saying that its loose democratic structure, under a benign leader who makes consensus-based decisions, is changing into something more despotic, more Hobbesian. Dale's agonizing death dramatizes the shift away from humanism to a more authoritarian regime implemented by Rick, who, for a while, had wavered between the poles represented by Dale on one side and Shane on the other. He comes down definitively on Shane's side in the moment when phallic power is symbolically transferred between them, when Shane is penetrated by Rick's knife and dies, and he stays there until the last few minutes of the last episode of season three, when he renounces his Rick-tatorship in favor once more of collaborative decision making.

Implicit in the Rick/Shane dynamic is an examination of masculinized political leadership. The narrative's favoring of the traditionally masculine profession of law enforcement as a proper prerequisite for post-apocalyptic leadership is a revealing choice.[13] The parallels between Carl and Rick are another, emphasizing the generational transfer of patriarchal power.[14] Like his father, Carl, too, has been shot, which the boy points out to his father as he returns to health. Moved by Carl's statement, Rick bestows his deputy's hat upon Carl, a signifier of the passing of the crown from father to son. Unlike his father, however, Carl awakens from his symbolic death with an immediate turn to callousness, even ruthlessness. The same boy who briefly emerged from a coma to talk about a transcendent vision of the deer in the forest—a graceful moment that inspired Rick to give a despairing Lori hope for Carl's future—recovers to muse, while feeding chickens, that everything is food for something else. He next tells the grieving Carol that she is an "idiot" for believing that she will see Sophia again in heaven. His new cold-hearted vision, as encapsulated in these statements, is far removed from the boy who was moved by the sight of the deer. He agrees with his father's shooting of Carl's former friend, Sophia, urges the execution of Randall, and becomes complicit in Rick's murder of Shane by destroying walker–Shane, who, even in zombie form, still bears the visage of a man who became a surrogate father to him in Rick's absence. Even though Carl later expresses remorse for inadvertently leading the walker that killed Dale to the farm, the clear implication is that Carl, as Lori fears, may grow up accepting cruelty and violent death as the norm in the post-apocalyptic world. Not having as much experience with pre-apocalyptic existence, Carl seems destined to have much less trouble adjusting than Rick does. If Lori is the group's "First Lady," as Carol calls her, then Carl is potentially its future "President"—a patriarchal heir-apparent who comes into his own as a hard-line member of the group in season three, dramatically illustrated by his shooting his reanimated mother after she dies during an emergency C-section and then fatally shooting a frightened Woodbury soldier who was about to surrender.

Alternatives to Strongman Rule

In light of this whittling-down of leadership dominance potentials to just two powerful men, the second season of *The Walking Dead* denies the viability of a more communal approach to survival. Even Dale never truly poses a collective or communitarian alternative to strongman rule. He never questions the need for a strong male authority figure; he asks only that Rick, in that role, exercise decency. The *Vatos*, a group of Hispanic men who stayed behind in Atlanta to care for their sick and elderly, has been the only compelling alternative to Rick's individualistic brand of leadership (or the Governor's). As the episodes have been aired, the fate of the *Vatos* remains unknown. In a telling sequence, however, which was deleted from the first episode of season two, "What Lies Ahead," but which is available as an extra on the Blu-Ray DVD, Rick's group flees the CDC and heads back to the *Vatos* for temporary shelter. Instead, they find that an unknown group of plunderers has breached the *Vatos* stronghold and killed everyone execution-style, including the elderly. Assuming one accepts this deleted sequence as part of the narrative, the communal, utopian possibility represented by the *Vatos* is thoroughly discredited as hopelessly naive, just as Dale's progressive philosophy is toward the end of the season. *The Walking Dead*, instead, suggests a Hobbesian leaning, that catastrophe brings out the worst in human nature and that strongmen leaders have no choice but to compete for dominance over a loosely allied group of passive survivors. Even the apparent triumph of democratic leadership and teamwork at the end of season three, as Rick abdicates his leadership role (and presumably his own potential to be a Governor-style tyrant) in favor of group decisions, is a fragile one. It is also worth noting that the badly outnumbered prison defenders, who admittedly routed the Woodbury attackers, are spared from further assault only because the Governor slaughters his own army in frustration at their retreat. So the tyrannical Governor, in essence, spares the prison—for now. It remains to be seen in season four how the prison's new leadership structure will fare in the post-apocalypse world.

Female alternatives to masculine leadership are equally sparse in the show. The gender politics in *The Walking Dead* are, for the most part, strictly and conventionally delineated in the post-apocalyptic world, in which women are consigned to doing laundry, cooking, and bearing babies while men make the life-or-death decisions, take on leadership roles, stand watch, and go out on hunter-gatherer scavenger missions.[15] In this sense, the most traditional gender roles of the pre-apocalyptic world are re-inscribed into the post-apocalyptic.[16] The show so far has consistently raised the possibility of female empowerment only to decisively shut it down.

One of the most traditional women in the storyline is Carol, who more often than not in the first two seasons is depicted as doing laundry and cooking for her male protectors, Rick and Hershel. Her role as launderer even saves the group at the CDC, when the grenade she took from Rick's clothes when washing them shatters the bulletproof glass, allowing them to escape the decontamination blast. As a devout Christian woman who has endured years of verbal and physical abuse from her husband, she has adopted a strategy of meek submission to Ed but, in turn, developed a fierce protectiveness over her daughter, Sophia, upon whom she believes Ed has sexual designs. When their camp is overrun by walkers and Ed is killed, Carol is liberated to become an independent mother. She takes out her suppressed aggression toward her husband by repeatedly stabbing his corpse, acknowledging that at times she had prayed for Ed's death. She also develops a romantic attraction to another man (Daryl). For these transgressions of her traditionally prescribed female role, the narrative strikes back. She loses her daughter through the agency of another man's well-meaning, but wrong, decision and suffers more verbal abuse from Daryl as he reacts to the shock of Sophia's second death—mirroring, to a lesser extent, what she suffered with her husband.

Other women in the narrative also suffer greatly for transgressing traditional gender roles. Maggie, as a self-assured woman who goes on scavenging missions into town and defies her father's command to stay away from the "Asian boy," Glenn, is one such transgressor. Maggie, however, relinquishes her independence to Glenn by breaking down into sobs and allowing him to drive the car in which they escape to Hershel's farm; she is later humiliated and threatened with rape by the strongman Governor.

Andrea, who rejects Carol's practice of cooking and laundering for men, later emerges from her suicidal loss of faith to become an empowered woman who wants to enter the traditional male sphere of shooting guns, a desire consistently denied to her by the patriarchal Dale and Shane because she is supposedly unstable. She demonstrates another kind of agency when she engages in sex with Shane and, in season three, with the Governor. However, the narrative repeatedly puts her back in her "place." When she accidentally shoots Daryl in her zeal, she seemingly confirms Dale's hypothesis that she is unstable. When zombies overrun the farm and she is separated from the group and becomes a de facto member of the Governor's community (even sharing his bed), she is arguably suffering a symbolic exile into the wilderness for her liaison with Shane and her insistence on shooting guns. Though she tries to negotiate a peace between Woodbury and the prison, thus trying to end her exile, she is punished by being strapped to the Governor's "torture chair" and left for the resurrected Milton to bite her.

Lori Grimes fleetingly exercises her autonomy by deciding to abort her baby rather than have it born into such a world (invoking the specter of the so-called "morning after" pill in a plot twist of dubious medical authenticity), but she immediately turns away from that choice to embrace a pro-life stance.

Her story too ends in tragedy when she demands the emergency C-section that she knows will kill her but save her baby—an even more radically pro-life moment than that of the second season. She appears intermittently throughout the rest of the season as a "ghost," a silenced woman seen only by Rick as a manifestation of his own guilt. Tellingly, she is mute, or at most, uttering unintelligible sounds over a telephone to Rick.

The narrative's last strong female character to date is Michonne, the katana-wielding warrior introduced at the end of season two. Resourceful and strong enough to survive on her own in the zombie-infested wilderness with the aid of her katana and her two "pet walkers," even this powerful woman is rendered repeatedly powerless throughout the season, with her phallic katana often being seized from her by men. Though she always regains her weapon, she is constantly on the defensive as she seeks to integrate herself into Rick's group, a desire largely unreciprocated until the very end of the season. Rick goes so far as to offer her up to the Governor as a prisoner (knowing this will result in Michonne's gruesome death by torture) to save his group before he has a change of heart and recants on the bargain, though not before Merle, acting as Rick's agent, has taken her off to the Governor. While Michonne is able to save herself by talking Merle into letting her go before being handed off to the Governor, she has spent most of the season subordinate to the whims of strong men. The one possibility of a strong female alliance, that between Andrea and Michonne and therefore a "world without men," so to speak, is dealt with largely off-screen and is seemingly forgotten as the season progresses. The storytelling strategy of invoking then renouncing strong female agency allows the show's creators to suggest, at least, subversive or alternative social structures through the camouflage of allegory, but also to undermine nontraditional values for those viewers who may, otherwise, be offended. Any boundary-crossing by women, the slightest move toward claiming male prerogatives, is typically punished by subsequent plot twists.

The sense of hopelessness inherent in the Hobbesian post-apocalyptic zombie text of *The Walking Dead* is well suited to the historical moment's determined re-inscription of the traditional values of male strength and female domesticity as a recuperative strategy in the wake of 9/11.[17] While it is worth noting that every historical era demonstrably perceives its crises to be uniquely worse than anything that has come before, Henry A. Giroux diagnoses this era's apocalyptic despair as having its roots in the rampant authoritarianism of the post–9/11 backlash, during which a "bullying rhetoric of war, a ruthless consolidation of economic forces, and an all-embracing, free-market apparatus and media-driven pedagogy of fear supported and sustained a distinct culture of cruelty and inequality in the United States."[18] Shows like *The Walking Dead*, then, are useful mechanisms for producing cultural meanings that force us to reflect on officially-sanctioned violence.

The 9/11 terrorist attacks and all the disasters that followed marked a watershed moment in the American nation's shock at having to confront the dire possibilities of an apocalyptic future.[19] It has become a critical truism that levels and types of cultural anxiety can often be tracked by the kind of monsters that a given culture produces for entertainment purposes, entertainment indirectly drawing upon headlines to give otherwise fantastic plots some degree of realism or authenticity. The zombie is that monster for post–9/11 America. The United States now feels itself to be under siege in a never-ending war, not on a specifically-identified country or countries but on the concept of "terror" itself, an amorphous enemy that has no specific identity and is ever threatening because it can never be defeated. The nation shies away, furthermore, from the undeniable evidence of its own self-inflicted class inequities, the failures of capitalism, its degenerating infrastructure, and political partisanship and gridlock. The replicating zombie constitutes the perfect metaphor for the dangers of the age, from the biological to the natural, to the nuclear, to the terrorist. The plight of Rick Grimes, an essentially good man forced into hard, perhaps soul-destroying, decisions by these apocalyptic circumstances, finds a sympathetic American audience imagining (perhaps fearing) itself doing much as he does in his evolution from decent family man to dehumanized killer. Of course, the joke is on the audience, for as the graphic novel and the television series make clear, the real "walking dead" of the title are the human characters, who are infected with the same disease as the walkers and are doomed to become them upon dying. What clearer metaphor could there be for the nagging American anxiety than that there is no better future waiting and that we ourselves are monsters or potential monsters? Against that kind of backdrop, Rick's journey to find his family and bring them to a safe harbor in a world gone mad represents an achingly poignant American desire to do the same: to retreat from the never-ending geopolitical perils of the post–9/11 world, to create a post-apocalyptic domestic utopia where one can feel secure once again.

NOTES

1. Deborah Christie discusses the larger implications of the zombie apocalypse as an opportunity for the human characters to evolve to a state that is often called the post-human. She argues that apocalyptic readings of zombie texts tend to focus on the human survivors' effort to restore the status quo in the post-apocalypse, when the texts themselves make the case that "society has evolved beyond humanity, mutating to accommodate a new life-form that both is and is not identifiably human, which proves most clearly that it is our definition and even prioritization of *humanity* that has been flawed from the outset."

Christie, "Dead New World," 68. In other words, zombie texts are case studies in how conceptions of what it means to be human are undergoing profound transformations in the post-human era.

2. Stephanie Boluk and Wylie Lenz specify: "The zombie narrative situates itself in that deferred space between catastrophe and posthistory where the march of time begins to shamble ... but is incapable of reaching its logical conclusion.... To truly go beyond would mean arriving at a point at which there can be no sequel, no return of either the living, the dead, or the living dead. The endless deferral and refusal to cross this threshold serves as the precondition for the serial renewal of apocalyptic desire." Boluk and Lenz, "Introduction: Generation Z, the Age of Apocalypse," 12.

3. As always, there are exceptions to the generally pessimistic tone of zombie apocalypse narratives. Max Brooks' novel *World War Z* (2006), for one, posits the zombie apocalypse as a transformational ten-year period in world history that allows humanity to transcend its ethnic and national differences and to unify to defeat the zombie enemy. For a discussion of the "hopeful" zombie apocalypse in Brooks' novel and other works, see Collins and Bond, "'Off the page,'" 187–204.

4. Michael J. Gilmour speaks to the domestic space aspect of the zombie narrative in this way: "The uninfected take refuge *inside* some kind of fortress ... while the shambling infected are *outside*, gradually breeching whatever defenses those in peril construct.... Without such violation of space—the dead mingling with the living, the infected with the uninfected—there is no story." Gilmour, "The Living Word," 91. Christopher Zealand traces this genre convention back to the original Romero trilogy of zombie films, which "presents a variation on the basic theme of surviving a siege from without and discord from within." Zealand, "National Strategy," 234. Each domestic space so far depicted in *The Walking Dead* has collapsed according to this formula.

5. Strozier, "World Trade Center Disaster," 49.

6. Caputi, "Films of the Nuclear Age," 101.

7. Linda Badley argues that, "as apocalyptic horrors of biological warfare, contagion, and terrorism have become all too real and war once again appears to be perpetual, zombies have returned with a vengeance and in a range of mutated forms. They speak for the cultural moment—expressing paranoia, alienation, and a sense of ever-present threat." Badley, "Zombie Splatter Comedy from *Dawn* to *Shaun*," 49.

8. Kyle William Bishop makes the case that the American zombie film subgenre had for all practical purposes died out by the end of the 1980s and throughout the decade of the 1990s. It died precisely because, during this relatively prosperous domestic period, no pressing sense of national urgency or disaster afflicted the American people. However, all that changed with the televised carnage of 9/11, a disaster that completely shattered the American confidence in its post–Cold War supremacy. Surely, it is no coincidence that shortly after 9/11, the zombie film subgenre was resurrected by Danny Boyle's *28 Days Later* (2002) and its lightning-fast "zombies," which are not actually reanimated corpses but living humans infected with a rage virus that so depersonalizes its victims that they may as well be zombies (read here, rage-filled Muslims). Given the framing context of 9/11 and all the political and economic shocks that have followed, Bishop concludes: "Because the aftereffects of war, terrorism, and natural disasters so closely resemble the scenarios depicted by zombie cinema, such images of death and destruction have all the more power to shock and terrify a population that has become otherwise jaded to more traditional horror films. The most telling barometer of this modern age, therefore, is to be found ... in the unstoppable hoards [sic] of the zombie invasion narrative." Bishop, *American Zombie Gothic*, 11–12.

9. The advertising tagline for the show's third season, "Fight the Dead, Fear the Living," reinforces how central this theme has become.

10. Jonathan Maberry identifies the most common thread in the vast range of apocalyptic tales as "the dim view they take of civilization." According to Maberry, humanity's higher ideals in these narratives fall in direct proportion to the decline in services and resources of civilization. Maberry, "Take Me to Your Leader," 18.

11. For an examination of the philosophies of Thomas Hobbes and John Locke through the prism of *The Walking Dead*, see Jason Walker, "What's Yours Still Isn't Mine."

12. Craig Fischer argues that, symbolically, "Shane's long-deferred desire for Lori might be the unconscious cause of the catastrophe, the male sex drive displaced into the wholesale *Thanatos* of zombie cannibalism." Fischer, "Meaninglessness," 76.

13. Of this aspect of the show, Danee Pye and Peter Padraic O'Sullivan write, "All of the characters operated within a patriarchal society prior to the outbreak, so it's no surprise that they begin to recreate patriarchal norms as they rebuild new societies." Pye and O'Sullivan, "Dead Man's Party," 109. The writers argue that the show sometimes provides clues that gender is learned, not biologically determined. However, these clues are few and far between and almost always negated by subsequent events.

14. David Hopkins explores the Rick/Carl parallels at great length in his essay, "The Hero Wears the Hat."

15. Ashley Barkman puts it this way: "In *The Walking Dead* [sic] post-apocalyptic world, the roles of men and women are clearly demarcated by a feminist's nightmare: men 'hunt' while women 'gather'—traditional gender roles are almost organically claimed." However, Barkman problematically ends up defending the show's depiction of gender by claiming that men are better suited biologically for leadership in survival situations demanding violence. She concludes: "Gender is beyond social construction ... women and men are different in how they solve problems and assert authority." Barkman, "Women in a Zombie Apocalypse," 99, 104.

16. Kay Steiger's disappointment with *The Walking Dead's* gender politics is palpable: "Frustratingly, some of the worst gender dynamics in today's world are replicated in the ones with murderous zombies." Steiger, "No Clean Slate," 105–106.

17. Susan Faludi characterizes the post–9/11 American response as reflexive, laying bare formerly concealed impulses, such as "the denigration of capable women, the magnification of manly men, the heightened call for domesticity, the search for and sanctification of little girls." Faludi, *Terror Dream*, 14. This claim encapsulates the themes and movements of *The Walking Dead* as post-9/11 entertainment, right down to the search for Sophia, whose tragic fate only serves to sanctify her more.

18. Giroux, *Zombie Politics and Culture in the Age of Casino Capitalism*, 57.

19. Kevin J. Wetmore points out that world domination by vampires and ghosts has all been imagined in cinema before, but that after 9/11 "fear is generated by a takeover of the world by the angry dead." Wetmore argues that the zombie is perfectly suited to this cultural moment's fear of terrorism because in the American imagination the Middle Eastern terrorist is so consumed by anti–Western hatred that he is essentially mindless—an automaton programmed to attack Americans. Wetmore, *Post–9/11 Horror*, 166.

Burying the Living with the Dead

Security, Survival and the Sanction of Violence

Steven Pokornowski

> The proposition that existence stands higher than a just existence is false and ignominious, if existence is to mean nothing other than mere life.
>
> —Walter Benjamin, "Critique of Violence"

The Living Dead, Health and Security

The connection between zombies and health is obvious: reanimated by some mysterious force, the dead rise from our nightmares and their graves to spread fear, pain, and pestilence. Since 1968, when George A. Romero redefined the figure of the zombie in *Night of the Living Dead*, we've been trained to fear the flesh-hungry hordes at our door—or, as more recent iterations such as *28 Days Later* (2002) and *The Walking Dead* would have it, at our backs. Zombies and medicine are still more tightly interwoven, however. Not least, the virus and Western interest in the zombie arose out of the same cultural moment and embody overlapping social anxieties. The representational deployment of both zombie and virus in outbreak narratives, moreover, serves to perpetuate an ethically and politically problematic logic of self-defense, spurred by fear. My argument in this essay is twofold. First, I assert that the representation of the zombie as a figure of bare life, and the resulting sanction of violence against it, reduces *all* life to bare life. When left unchecked, this broad sanction of violence begins to destroy precisely those lives that it set out to defend. Second, I propose that a multidisciplinary perspective informed by biopolitical, posthumanist, and critical race theories can offer a way to resist this representational problematic at the levels of both consumption and production—can offer, in fact, a political and ethical critique that takes into account the role of social constructions of humanity and race in maintaining sovereignty.

In what follows, I will examine the historical relation of the zombie and the virus. I will then consider how this biopolitical inflection of the zombie sets in motion a fear of infection, in turn inciting a logic of self-defense and the sanctioning of violence. Focusing primarily on *The Walking Dead* comic series (2004-present), I will analyze this troubling chain reaction and demonstrate how the logic of self-defense provokes what we might call, following Roberto Esposito, an autoimmune reaction, which destroys the very life it sets out to protect. My argument relies on the recent migration of medical terms into the terrain of theory, but while the self-destructive obsession with survival and security that this essay addresses may have become more apparent after 9/11, it is actually much older. I will thus turn to Romero's *Night of the Living Dead* to demonstrate how a perspective informed by the theoretical influence of a racially-aware biopolitics can reveal previously-obscured issues of security and violence hinging on race and class. Recognizing that the logic of survival put forth in zombie narratives is racially-motivated, based on exclusion, and that it reflects real-world issues of race, class, and sovereignty, is a crucial step toward identifying and resisting the violent, self-destructive politics of fear popularized by zombie narratives.

The Zombie-Virus Nexus

The marriage of flesh-eating zombies with medicalized causes is often seen as having its inception with *Night of the Living Dead*; it has been a staple, however, of zombie representations from the beginning. Around the time that W.B. Seabrook introduced American audiences to the zombie in his 1929 study of Haiti, *The Magic Island*, and the Halperin brothers released the 1932 film inspired by that study, *White Zombie*, another figure that defied the limits of life and death was coming into focus: the virus. The invention of the electron microscope in 1931 allowed for the visualization of the formerly elusive virus, which had previously been identified as a filterable agent of infection, smaller than bacteria. By 1938, the virus had come fully into view, as electron micrographs of the tobacco mosaic virus ushered in a new era of visual prowess: the clinical gaze had begun to penetrate deeper than ever.[1]

It is tempting to consider this dual emergence of the virus and the zombie as mere coincidence, but I argue that it was more than that; both figures raised questions about the limits of life. In an article that came out just before the publication of Seabrook's text, A.E. Boycott explained that studies of the virus had reinforced the need to think of life on a continuum, rather than in a binary with the non-living.[2] Boycott places the filterable virus on a continuum of life in the "intermediate group," that is "not so live as a sunflower and not so dead as a brick."[3] Meanwhile, Seabrook was busy recounting how he learned that whites in Haiti "were surrounded by another world invisible, a world of marvels, miracles, and wonders—a world in which the dead rose from their graves and walked."[4] At nearly the same cultural moment, two invisible worlds emerged, each harboring a dangerous object that defied simple notions of life and death.

In the 1920s and 1930s, the virus joined the bacterium as an agent of infection from an invisible world, an enemy threat to the human body.[5] A representational paradigm quickly taken up by educational and popular culture, this trope became standard in mid-century government public health films, Public Service Announcements, and science fiction films and novels, alike.[6] Though the zombie was not originally seen as an enemy, in both Seabrook's portrayal of Haitian culture and the early films inspired by it, zombies were nonetheless unclean, taboo creatures. Seabrook himself originally thought that zombies could be explained by biological causes and were the result of exploitation of the infirm.[7] This Western tendency to pathologize, which Seabrook enjoins, was still more evident in Jacques Tourneur's 1943 film, *I Walked with a Zombie*, in which the main character learns that the zombified ward she will be caring for has a "tropical fever," thus explicitly biologizing the zombie and reinforcing its relation to infectious, microscopic life.

The medicalized zombie at the center of the outbreak narrative came to full fruition in Romero's masterpiece, *Night of the Living Dead*. Romero's infected, shambling zombies were even more inextricably bound up with viruses and medicine than their predecessors. As Deborah Christie points out, Romero's ghouls owed a great debt to the vampires in the 1964 film, *The Last Man on Earth*, the first adaptation of Richard Matheson's 1954 novella, *I Am Legend*.[8] Matheson's plot and its first filmic adaptation center around the catastrophic effects of a mysterious virus that radically affects all human life on earth with the exception of one man with an acquired immunity. The story thus falls loosely under the "outbreak narrative" formula identified by Priscilla Wald, which begins with "an emerging infection, includes discussion of the global networks throughout which it travels, and chronicles the epidemiological work that ends with its containment."[9] By drawing from Matheson and making *Night of the Living Dead* an outbreak narrative, Romero united the microscopic fear of invasion and infection posed by the virus with the macroscopic threat of invasion and infection posed by the zombie. Previously invisible worlds collided, and the visually elusive virus was made manifest in the figure of the zombie. For the first time, in *Night of the Living Dead*, we could see the enemy before us, and we didn't need a *magic* bullet to shoot it dead. But we were also left with a new problem: how do we secure ourselves from this infectious, shambling threat?

Autoimmunity, (In)Humanity and the Sanction of Violence

One of the primary preoccupations of *The Walking Dead* is precisely its exploration of the cost with which security is gained. Early in the comics, *The Walking Dead* very consciously does away with the political and ethical dilemmas that fighting off hordes of the living dead might pose. In their place emerges an unquestioning agenda of extermination, justified as self-defense. Upon closer inspection, however, the events that appear to validate this self-defensive position demonstrate that its acceptance banishes the private and the familial, replacing them, at best, with a self-imposed quarantine, and, at worst, with a self-imposed imprisonment. The living characters of *The Walking Dead* become uncanny doubles of their *homo sacer*-like, undead predators. Put another way, the protagonists' simple classification of the walking dead as monsters animated by less-than-bare life simultaneously reduces their own humanity to bare life, as they champion security and power at the cost of a richer social, political, and communal life. As I shall demonstrate, fictionalized events from *The Walking Dead* mirror the contemporary biopolitical dangers outlined by Giorgio Agamben, Roberto Esposito, Eugene Thacker, and others. The troubling representations of *The Walking Dead* traumatically repeat and reinforce a logic of survival and security that alienates others and lionizes bare life at all costs, implicitly reinforcing the political status quo.

Scholars have already noted the striking similarities between the figure of the zombie and Agamben's now canonical biopolitical theory of *homo sacer* and bare life.[10] Agamben draws the distinction between bare life and political life from Aristotle.[11] He claims that bare life, which is exemplified for him in the titular figure of the archaic Roman *homo sacer*, embodies life that *"may be killed and yet not sacrificed."*[12] Agamben goes on to assert that, in modern politics, the extension of the state of exception to the political rule brings the realm of bare life from the "margins of political order" to the center of politics.[13] In other words, the extension of exceptional or emergency politics to the status quo also extends the pervasiveness of bare life—an embodiment necessary for exceptional, exclusionary politics. Bare life goes from being exceptional to being foundational in its relation to sovereignty. The increased realm of indistinction between political life and that life excluded from politics, moreover, causes an ever-expanding political exclusion to become the centerpiece of political authority and power. The outside moves in, the exclusion is included, bare life becomes political, and all of these binaries become indistinguishable.[14] Consequently, modern Western democracy "does not abolish sacred life but rather shatters it and disseminates it into every individual body, making it into what is at stake in political conflict."[15] Agamben asserts, in other words, that, rather than being encapsulated in individual figures—discrete, sacred people who stand as exceptions to the general rule—bare life becomes disseminated among all citizens. The elevation of the state of exception from sovereign tool to democratic rule causes political life and bare life, which were once distinct, to "become one." This move makes all life bare life and thus able to be killed with impunity but not sacrificed.[16]

The usefulness of this theory in reading zombie literature is striking. Even the earliest zombie films take place in what Agamben refers to as "zones of indistinction," places that escape or elude laws and sanctions—from the colonial castle of *White Zombie* to the mysterious island of *King of the Zombies* (1941).[17] In the case of post–Romero zombie narratives, such as Lucio Fulci's *Zombi 2* (sometimes known in the U.S. as *Zombie*, 1979) or even Danny Boyle's *28 Days Later*, the locus typically shifts from a colonially-inspired zone of indistinction to a national and, by extension, global state of exception. In these fictional worlds, which darkly mirror our own, if we take Agamben's theory seriously, the undead masses, like *homo sacer*, are slaughtered with impunity.

Developing this idea further, Eugene Thacker has explicitly connected the zombie and the microbe, arguing that both exist in the zone of indistinction "[b]etween the life that must be protected and the life that must be protected against, between the healthy and the infected."[18] This oscillation between terms extends to several other domains that are key to biodefense but that similarly complicate understanding the living dead or, for that matter, the microbial, as enemies or sub-lives to be killed without remorse or repercussion. Thacker explains that "[w]hatever bare life is, it matters a great deal, since it now obtains a ubiquity as the protected, the infected, or the nonhuman vector between them. What we have here is not just the biological life or political life, but a *whatever-life*, in which biology and sovereignty, or medicine and politics, continually inflect and fold onto each other."[19] Thacker elucidates how the slippery nature of bare life, or "whatever-life," evades simple categorization as biological, constantly slipping into the political. And as the margin between the life to be protected and the life that can be killed to protect it becomes fluid, the object of sanctioned violence becomes increasingly indistinguishable from the subject protected by it. As Esposito might put it, immune reaction protecting life slides into the autoimmune reaction destroying it.[20] My analysis of Robert Kirkman and Tony Moore's *The Walking Dead* discloses how the immune slips into the autoimmune, how the sanction of violence in self-defense devolves into more generalized violence—and how bio-defense slides into an indefensibile thanatopolitics.

In the eleventh issue of Kirkman and Moore's *The Walking Dead*, the protagonist, Rick Grimes, and his temporary host, Hershel, have a crucial debate about handling the living dead. Hershel explains that rather than killing the walking dead in his area, he and his family have been rounding them up in the barn "until [they] can figure out a way to **help** them." With mutual outrage, Rick and Hershel go on to castigate one another, exposing two opposing logics common in zombie narratives. Rick explains that the only responsible way to secure oneself against zombies is to kill them, a position he supports with three claims. First, he insists on their lack of humanity, saying emphatically that "[t]hose things **aren't** human. They're undead **monsters**." Second, he claims that killing zombies is merciful; it puts "them out of their misery."[21] Finally, and most importantly, he explains that killing zombies is an act of self-defense.[22] Hershel's rebuttal is that, since they know nothing about the walking dead, neither why corpses are reanimating, nor what is wrong with them, he doesn't "want to have **blood** on [his] hands if ... these people **are** alive."[23] The narrative soon portrays his reasoning as tainted by personal interest, however, as well as evincing sentimentality and weakness: he is prominently featured crying as he explains that he "just couldn't kill" his reanimated son. Despite the fact that Hershel makes perhaps the most logical, grounded claim in this argument, later events will reinforce his position as untenable. Near the end of the same issue, the zombies kept in the barn break free and infect several of Hershel's remaining children, until all are slaughtered at point blank range by Rick and his trigger-happy group. Shortly thereafter, Hershel admits—tears once again streaming down his face—that Rick was right.[24]

This episode marks a turning point in the politics of the series. According to Rick and his group, the reason to slaughter the zombies in the barn is to enact a preemptive strike; they argue that it is safer to kill a contained threat than it is to wait for it to break free. This line of thinking mirrors that which Esposito sees as constituting "the most acute point of [the] autoimmunitary turn in contemporary biopolitics," preventive war, which is the "self-confuting figure of a war fought precisely to avoid war."[25] When considered this way, the immune reaction interested in protecting a biopolitics—or a politics of life—begins to cross over into a thanatopolitical, autoimmune reaction, invested in the production of death rather than the maintenance of life. *The Walking Dead* does more than show the shift from a biopolitics to a thanatopolitics; it also demonstrates what is lost in that transition.

After leaving Hershel's farm, Rick and his group stumble onto a prison, which serves as the main setting for a significant number of the comic's issues. Working with a small group of surviving inmates—whom the ex-police officer Rick and his group (ironically and symptomatically) mistake for guards—the survivors manage to make the prison a livable, defensible abode; the cost of their security, however, is a life spent living in a series of cages. The prison setting emphasizes the protagonists' reduction of their own lives to bare life and eerily echoes Agamben's claim in *Homo Sacer* that the camp has become the *nomos* of our time.[26] The diminution of the protagonists' political life is demonstrated throughout their tenure at the prison, where authority is, at best, turbulently established. In fact, the main authority figures of the group of protagonists, Rick and Tyreese, along with a few other characters, kill other humans without deliberation and with differing degrees of justification. This questionable execution of fellow survivors also occurs in the television adaptation of the comics, where, without trial or justification, Shane kills Otis and Randall, and Rick kills Shane and Tomas.[27] Through a series of murders occurring in the prison, then, *The Walking Dead* foregrounds the suspension of political order and its ethical ramifications.

In the prison of the comic books, Tyreese's daughter and her lover make a suicide pact, agreeing to kill one another at the same time and to "be together forever."[28] The lovers, however, do not pull the trigger at quite the same time, and Tyreese enters the room to find his daughter's corpse, which turns into a zombie and attacks him. After his daughter's lover re-kills her to save Tyreese, Tyreese strangles the lover to death. Rick, ex-police officer and heretofore upholder of justice, law, and political order, sees the murder and does nothing; instead, he is compassionate and complicit. In issue eighteen, after one of his group, Patricia, kills an unstable, murdering inmate in retribution without hesitation, consultation, or trial, Rick explains to his wife: "What **can** I do? It's not like we can **beat** her or just lock her up—we're not **animals**. I'm going to **talk** with her, I guess."[29] Rick's admission that there is nothing to be done, that the Hobbesian world of all against all has made its way inside their sanctum, is startling. He attempts to backpedal, however, claiming a separation from brute, animal life through communication and language. Despite this attempt at a retraction, in the very next issue of *The Walking Dead*, Rick's actions emphasize the discomforting truthfulness of his claims about the diffusion of sovereignty and the lack of a justice system.

At the beginning of issue nineteen, a standoff occurs between Rick and a few mutinous inmates, which is interrupted by a mob of zombies who have been accidentally released.[30] The survivors slaughter the zombies with relish—and the scene emphasizes the reduction of the survivors' life to a bare life, further demonstrating Rick and his group's shift from a biopolitical to a thanatopolitical order.[31] This scene's artwork visually parallels the zombies and their human attackers: a page is filled with sixteen small panels, alternately representing angry or fearful human faces and exploding zombie faces. Hauntingly, the expressions on the faces of the zombies tend to mirror those of the human characters in frames near them, similarly gritting their teeth or opening their mouths. This visual device, then, directly emphasizes the reduction of these human lives to a bare life similar to that of the zombies.

This devaluation of the life of the survivors through security-sanctioned violence is demonstrated by the very character who advocated its use in order to protect life. In the midst of the mass zombie slaughter, Rick shoots and kills the leader of the opposing faction of survivors, framing it as an accident. The history and characterization of Rick and the man he kills further complicate the politics of the security Rick advocates. The criminal, Dexter, is introduced to the reader several issues earlier as a former murderer, but, during his time in the narrative, he never kills any humans or harms anyone in Rick's group. The same, evidently, cannot be said of Rick. In this dramatic reversal, the agent responsible for securing life and political order, the police officer, has attacked life, something Rick does several more times later in the series. The visual layout of the scene further emphasizes its political impact, as Rick's eyes fill a wide frame, glaring ominously before the reader turns the page and sees Dexter's head grotesquely pierced by a bullet.[32] This layout displays Rick's guilt by insinuating premeditation. It also emphasizes Dexter's innocence in the pained and surprised look on his face. In this way, the shift from the farm to the prison represents a shift in the narrative's politics from a biopolitical attempt to secure life and maintain a certain way of life—Aristotle's good life, social life—to its dark reflection: a thanatopolitical destruction of life and political order in an always-already-failing attempt to save life through the slaughter of life. This shift is even registered visually over a number of issues, as the relatively calm and happy domestic arrangement at the farm gives way to the desolate and tense setting of the prison, where the majority of Rick's party will meet an untimely end at the hands of angry humans and the mouths of hungry corpses.

"Night of the Living Dead," Biopolitics and Race

The shift in *The Walking Dead* from a politics aimed simply at securing life to one attempting to secure life by dealing death is not new; rather, it is an established facet of modern zombie narratives. Theoretical and critical developments from the 1980s, and especially after 9/11, have given us a better set of critical tools for identifying and analyzing this representational paradigm. While, as I mentioned earlier, the rise of the autoimmune paradigm in literature and film can be traced to early- and mid-twentieth-century outbreak and invasion narratives, it first became a focal point in Romero's *Night of the Living Dead*. Examining this film after our discussion of *The Walking Dead* reveals a complex interplay between global terror and local security. This interplay serves to intensify questions about the darker side of biosecurity, more specifically the subtle but explicit examination of the conflict between ethics and security.

The tension escalating throughout *Night of the Living Dead* between the cardigan-clad, African American Ben and the testy, tie-wearing Harry is, not least, about the conflict between an ethical call to save as much life as possible (Ben) and a self-preserving logic of security (Harry). At their first encounter, Ben chastises Harry for not coming out of hiding to help at the sound of Barbra's screams. Harry replies that he will not risk his own safety "just because somebody might need help." The encounter reveals Ben's goal of saving as many lives as possible and Harry's goal of securing his own life. The climax of this scene also reveals that, as in *The Walking Dead*, what must be sacrificed for security is a way of living beyond bare life. This is emphasized by the dramatic death of Ben at the end of the film.

Ben's and Harry's argument becomes grounded in the architecture of the farmhouse, where the underground cellar stands as a space of isolated security, and the house above stands as an insecure space of community and society. This distinction is dramatically emphasized when Harry attempts to take Barbra to the cellar with him instead of helping to fortify the house. At this moment, Ben angrily commands Harry to "leave her here. Keep your hands off her and everything else that's up here [above the cellar], too. Because if I stay up here I'm fighting for everything up here; the radio and the food is part of what I'm fighting for." The maintenance of the strict partition between the barren security of the cellar and the rich but riskily-secured house is striking, and the details of Ben's proclamation are telling. Fighting for the radio is an attempt to salvage community since, throughout the film, radio and television connect the survivors to rescue efforts and the world outside. Ultimately, giving up the farmhouse in favor of security is also giving up the home, the family, and all but the barest life, just as it is over forty years later, in the first issues of the comic and the second season of the show *The Walking Dead*. The reduction of the Coopers to bare, zombie life in the secure cellar before the film's climax demonstrates once again the autoimmunitary destruction of the life to be saved. The paradigmatic role of the cellar as the site of security belies its uncanny, double role as the place where bare life is produced: the mechanisms aimed at protecting life are shown to destroy it.

This dual role of the cellar and of security is emphasized in the film's final climactic sequence. When the house is infiltrated by the unruly zombie mob, only Ben survives the ensuing mayhem. With no one left for him to save, Ben forsakes his dream of protecting Barbra, the radio, the food, and a certain way of life, and instead plunges into the cellar and dispatches the reanimated Cooper family. In this moment, Ben embraces the life-diminishing security he has rejected throughout the film. He is transformed after his stay in the cellar, and the previously loud and commanding man appears startlingly silent as he slowly stalks toward the window. As he reaches it, he is shot dead, "right between the eyes," by a posse of local police officers and national guard who are, ironically, searching for survivors. This enigmatic and troubling scene demonstrates the posse's perception of Ben as bare life, implicitly equating him with the zombies. This equality is then visually reinforced and made explicit when Ben is paralleled with the film's first zombie in the corpse-collection-and-burning scene shown behind the credits.

In addition to representing Ben's reduction to bare life through the medium of the cellar, the end of the film reinforces the importance of a communal, political, ethical life and problematically reinscribes the latent issue of race into the film. The organization, cooperation, and effectiveness of the posse is represented clearly in the film, as its members work together, take orders, kill zombies, and cooperate with the culture industry, not only to clear the area of zombies and search for survivors, but also to broadcast their labor on television. This maintenance of social and cultural order is in stark contrast to the chaos that took place in the farmhouse, and it represents the group's salvaging of richer forms of life. The presence of luxuries, such as coffee, the clearly hierarchical nature of the posse, and the production of a news program emphasize the posse's communal life and gesture towards the possible salvation of society. Its killing of Ben, however, simultaneously hints at the maintenance of a more dangerous underside to society and biosecurity.

Autoimmunity and Social Injustice

Ultimately, the group tasked with protecting and maintaining life at the end of *Night of the Living Dead* kills the character attempting to uphold the very same values. In this way, the medicalized figure of the zombie that emerges in Romero's film is already an indicator of an autoimmune reaction, since the mechanisms set in place to secure life lead to its undoing. Simultaneously, the stark racial elements present in the scene of Ben's death demonstrate how the paradigm of autoimmunity I have been interrogating is bound up in a complex interplay with political categories such as race, class, and gender, and the communities formed around them. It is hardly coincidental that the posse at the end of *Night of the Living Dead* consists entirely of white men—or that their leader, like the hero of *The Walking Dead*, is a white male law officer.

Following Foucault's remarks on race, in analyzing the thanatopolitics of Nazi Germany, Esposito explains that racism "performs a double function." First, it "produc[es] a separation within the biological *continuum* between those that need to remain alive and those ... to be killed." Second, it "establish[es] a direct relation between the two conditions," as it is "the deaths of the latter that enable and authorize the survival of the former."[33] This dynamic is precisely what occurs in *The Walking Dead* and many other zombie narratives. The strange continuum between human and zombie is very tenuously replaced by a stark binary. Furthermore, this binary is maintained entirely on the premise that the deaths (or re-deaths) of the zombie-enemy are precisely what enable the survival of the human protagonists. Esposito further explains that "such a conception doesn't concentrate the supreme power of killing only in the hands of the leader," but, instead, following Agamben's claims about the dispersal of the condition of *homo sacer*, the power of killing is "distribute[d] in equal parts to the entire social body."[34] Sovereignty and biopolitics are thus wedded and dispersed evenly across a society that believes that life defends itself and develops through the death of other threatening lives. Rick's flawed survivalist logic in Kirkman and Moore's *The Walking Dead* comics, along with the negligent violence of the posse in *Night of the Living Dead,* may well, then, hint at an issue that is deeper and darker than the already-problematic championing of survival at all costs. These post-apocalyptic portrayals are not merely *symptomatic* of a cultural autoimmune reaction; they are actually *traumatically replicating* the older, more deeply-ingrained cultural conflicts that produce that reaction.

The residue of the diasporic history of the zombie, bound up as it is with colonial, racial, and class violence, pervades current representations of zombies and zombie-like figures—not least, for instance, in the evocation of slavery and lynching at the end of *Night of the Living Dead*. The ways in which this fraught history emerges are manifold, but their continual emergence begs deeper analysis. What are we to make of these recurrences of the historically repressed? Let us return to *The Walking Dead* once again. Michonne, who appears in both the comic and AMC iterations of *The Walking Dead*, eerily echoes colonialism and racism. This tall, cloaked African American woman wielding a sword and leading chained zombies not-so-subtly evokes the slave trade. Initially in the comics, her coldness, cunning, and secrecy make Michonne a stereotypically fraught, strong female character. At one point in the comics, in what appears to be a disgustingly indulgent display of misogyny and racism, Michonne is repeatedly tortured and raped.[35] As if this did not, in and of itself, problematically echo a history of racism, the perpetrator is a malicious white man referred to solely as "the Governor."

A later shift in the representation of Michonne discloses the elided presence of historical conflicts within the zombie narrative. Michonne's abuse in issues twenty-eight and twenty-nine of the comics leaves her face and body visibly scarred.[36] In issue forty-nine, however, all of Michonne's scars are gone. This is very likely related to the artistic difficulty of repeatedly drawing the scars with some accuracy, but their sudden erasure hints at the wiping away of the very history that their presence echoed. Likewise, in the AMC television version of *The Walking Dead*, the punctual removal from the plot of the vocal white supremacist, Merle, signals the erasure of an explicit reference to racial and social conflict. Merle reemerges in season three of the series, but his blatant and overt racism is dampened, and he is removed again before the end of the season. In this way, much like the erasure of Michonne's scars in the comic, the eradication of Merle (and the excesses of his racism) evacuates the character's function as a reminder of racial strife. Just as *Night of the Living Dead* addresses and occludes a history of racial conflict, so too, then, does *The Walking Dead*. This is not to say that all zombie narratives are "about" race, colonialism, and social justice. Rather, it is a reminder that these histories of oppression, however repressed, are nonetheless bound up in and constantly (re)produce the figure of the zombie.

Burying the Living with the Dead: Global Terror and Local Security

In burying the zombie's dark history of slavery, racism, and the exploitation of "other" bodies, we risk burying the lives and histories of oppressed and exploited people who are living. The immune and autoimmune paradigms outlined above are ways of analyzing the political and ethical limitations of security-based reasoning, the logic most prominent in contemporary zombie narratives and, many would argue, in contemporary governance. It is no coincidence that Derrida's theoretical conception of autoimmunity came to the fore after September 11, 2001.[37] In the shadow of 9/11, we have been inundated with messages about the threat of terror and the need for security.[38] Simultaneously, the zombie has become a cultural icon, spawning zombie walks, zombie runs, countless films, comics, novels, and video games. In fact, the figure of the zombie has become so ubiquitous that it has even inspired proposals for investment in a zombie survival theme park, called Z World Detroit.[39]

Perhaps the oversaturation of culture with fears of terrorist threats is what has propelled the current popularity of the zombie. The same generation of people who grew up playing "survival horror" video games like the transmedia *Resident Evil* franchise is now, in the adult world, faced with the implication that everyday life is like survival horror: we must be prepared, we must be secure. The opposition of terror and security and its cultural salience is not so much new as it is reinvigorated and recoded.

The figure of the zombie and its relation to the paradigmatic opposition of terror and security has been at play since before *Night of the Living Dead*. The superimposition of this politically-fraught paradigm upon the zombie narrative has deeper roots than it might seem, going back to such early zombie films as 1941's *King of the Zombies*, which features the nefarious use of voodoo zombies and mesmerism in a Nazi plot. From the beginning, the terror/security paradigm has covered over the racial history and the explicit racial politics of zombie narratives, erasing the historical specificity of the zombie, universalizing its figure, and simultaneously sanctioning its slaughter. At the same time, the historical occlusion at the heart of zombie narrative points to the contemporary elision of race from political issues of terror and security. If recent events have taught us one thing—I began writing this just six months after the death of Trayvon Martin (on February 26, 2012) and days after the shooting in a Sikh temple in Wisconsin (on August 5, 2012)—it is that, in the logic of survival, the drive for security for one group of people often comes at the expense of another group. Let us not delude ourselves into believing that securing a rudimentary, bare life for some is more valuable than tenuously, dangerously maintaining a fuller, fairer life for all. In this era of risk, let us gamble on something that matters, rather than burying the living with the dead.

NOTES

1. The tobacco mosaic virus has played an important part in discovering and understanding the virus. It was the first infecting agent to pass through a porcelain filter that was specifically designed to catch bacteria and fungi. Later, it was one of the first viruses to be identified as primarily a carrier of information. It was identified as a nucleoprotein. It was also most likely the very first virus examined under an electron microscope. I found passages about it in Geddes Smith's *Plague on Us* to be succinct and interesting. For a more in-depth view, see Scholthof et al., *Tobacco Mosaic Virus*.

2. Boycott, "The Transition from Live to Dead," 94.

3. Ibid., 94. Other medical professionals and historians shared this perspective, which was still prevalent and fresh enough in 1941 for Geddes Smith to emphasize it in *Plague on Us*.

4. Seabrook, *The Magic Island,* 12.

5. Cohen examines the evolution of immunity as defense—and, by extension, microbes as invaders and enemies—in *A Body Worth Defending*, which is certainly a book worth reading. Cohen looks to Elie Metchnikoff's work on immunity in the 1880s as the point of intersection between judicial, combative, and biological considerations of immunity.

6. See also Ostherr, *Cinematic Prophylaxis*, and Wald, *Contagious*.

7. Seabrook, *The Magic Island*, 102.

8. Christie, "A Dead New World," 67. Christie also reveals that the staging and plot of the film owed so much to Matheson that he originally thought it was another direct adaptation.

9. Wald, *Contagious*, 2.

10. See Pollock, "Undead is the New Green"; Stratton, "Zombie Trouble"; and Norris, "Giorgio Agamben and the Politics of the Living Dead."

11. Agamben, *Homo Sacer*, 1.

12. Ibid., 8. Emphasis in original.

13. Ibid., 9.

14. Ibid., 9.

15. Ibid., 124.

16. Ibid., 148.

17. This often-overlooked film might be of serious interest to zombie scholars with a biopolitical or critical race interest, since the film features a precursor to the "Nazi zombie" and engages thoughtfully—if still *extremely* problematically—with race and politics at the cusp of World War II.

18. Thacker, "Necrologies," 159.

19. Ibid.

20. Esposito's work—particularly *Bíos*—is a major influence in this analysis, and his use of the language of immunity to address biopolitical issues also serves here to highlight the relation of this discourse to that of viruses and bacteria.

21. Kirkman, Adlard, and Rathburn, *The Walking Dead* #11. Emphasis in original. In this and all future quotes from the comics, I have kept the use of bold lettering intact for emphasis, rather than substituting italics. In the television series, this point is brutally emphasized by Shane, rather than Rick, who repeatedly shoots a zombie in the chest to demonstrate its continued (semi)lifelessness.

22. The incongruity of these statements indicates their emotional rather than logical appeal, much like current political debates surrounding security in the U.S., such as the passionately embattled debates around gun control.

23. Kirkman, Adlard, and Rathburn, *The Walking Dead* #11. Emphasis in original.

24. Ibid.

25. Esposito, *Bíos*, 147.

26. Agamben, *Homo Sacer*, 166–180.

27. The events I am referring to occur in season two, episodes three and twelve, and season three, episode three.

28. Kirkman, Adlard, and Rathburn, *The Walking Dead* #14.

29. Kirkman, Adlard, and Rathburn, *The Walking Dead* #18, emphasis in original.

30. Kirkman, Adlard, and Rathburn, *The Walking Dead* #19, emphasis in original.

31. Following such theorists as Agamben and Esposito, my use of biopolitics is referring to a politics whose object is life, while thanatopolitics is that politics whose object is death.

They are primarily used to indicate a positive (as in life-protecting or life-affirming) and a negative (a life-negating) inflection of similar political apparatuses.

32. Kirkman, Adlard, and Rathburn, *The Walking Dead* #19.

33. Esposito, *Bios*, 110.

34. Ibid.

35. Kirkman, Adlard, and Rathburn, *The Walking Dead* #28, 29.

36. The art is actually annoyingly inconsistent about the scars on her face, which appear and disappear from time to time through issues twenty-nine to forty-nine.

37. See Borradori, "Autoimmunity," 85–89.

38. Clough and Willse go so far as to address the aesthetic impact and branding of security products in "Human Security/National Security."

39. The original proposal for independent investment in Z World Detroit was via indiegogo at: http://www.indiegogo.com/zworlddetroit.

Walking Tall or Walking Dead?

The American Cowboy in the Zombie Apocalypse

P. Ivan Young

A determined Rick Grimes, bag of guns slung over his shoulder, turns the corner of an Atlanta street ironically sign-posted "Do Not Enter" to face what seems an endless mass of zombies ("Days Gone Bye"). The horse rears into the iconic Lone Ranger position, announcing our hero. Only, there's a catch: both hero and horse fall, the latter becoming fodder for the undead, the former scrambling beneath a tank for what appears to be his "last stand." We have, indeed, gone down a street we should not enter. The iconography is quintessentially American—the cowboy on horseback, the big city, the tank, the gun-toter[1]—and, in the tradition of the cowboy, the zombies take on the role of the villain against which the hero defines himself. This villain, however, seems a weak replacement for the bands of Indians, the renegade Mexicans, and the psychopathic gunmen that have long defined the heroes of westerns. Douglas Pye identifies the Lone Ranger as operating on "a simple moral scale of polarized good and evil, with the basic terms and the hero's status never questioned."[2] The moral absolutes such early versions of the western represent become problematic, however, when no villain exists as definitive foil for the hero. In that void, the cowboy becomes introspective, indulging in a self-examination that reveals the cowboy for who he is, a man with a gun seeking to assert his will through violence.

The tension between real and ideal cowboy invokes Stanley Corkin's argument about the western: it grafts "the historical onto the mythic to help audiences adjust to new concepts of national definition."[3] In *The Walking Dead*, where cowboys and zombies collide, the western hero struggles to maintain the illusion of "righteous power," but in the end must watch it erode as he enacts violence almost routinely. As his moral vision of himself collapses, so must his vilification of the zombies. Ultimately, however, the cowboy is forced to recognize that he has become the other, the ruthless killer, and, thus, he must decide whether to cling to definitions of the American landscape that seem irrelevant or find a new way to govern.

Richard Slotkin defines the hero as "the symbolic vessel of the whole culture's collective consciousness."[4] Implicit, then, in Rick Grimes as cowboy is a mythic image of America trying to identify itself in positive moral terms based on an act (killing) that is defined by most belief systems as immoral.[5] Placed as he is in a virtual shooting gallery of the undead, Rick descends into the world of the pure kill: murder without justification. With each kill, *The Walking Dead* asks its audience, ever more insistently, to consider what happens when the easy labels of hero and villain are gone.

The Grimesian cowboy, bedecked in cowboy hat and boots, riding on horseback, carrying a revolver, and enforcing justice has been much written about as an American image.[6] Early visions of the cowboy were integrally connected to authority: *The Great Train Robbery* (1903) championed the sheriff's posse that hunted down robbers; *High Noon* (1952) held as its central hero Marshal Will Kane. Perhaps the most iconic image of the lawman gunslinger is John Wayne in such films as *Rio Bravo* (1959), *Cahill, U.S. Marshall* (1973), and *Rooster Cogburn* (1975). Even when Wayne wasn't an official figure of authority, he was typically (as in the 1939 film *Stagecoach*) enlisted and supported by someone who was.

The cowboy, then, has largely been presented as an enforcer of a "just world." Films such as *The Magnificent Seven* (1960) have presented gunmen as the solution to unjust imbalances of power. The seven men who help defend a small Mexican town represent America as both internal defender of justice and also, on an international scale, as the defender of "weaker" nations. Indeed, a central trope of western justice is the gunman as defender (and often avenger) of the meek. Clint Eastwood built a career upon such an image, although he was far from the traditional image of authority in his "spaghetti westerns." In *The Outlaw Josey Wales* (1976), he not only seeks revenge on the Red Legs who murdered his family, but also comes to the aid of vulnerable women and an elderly Native American.

Certainly, more recent films have complicated the image of the cowboy as morally just. Eastwood (arguably, next to John Wayne, the most recognizable face of the American cowboy) was nominated for an Oscar for his role in *Unforgiven* (1992), a movie that inverts the sheriff/outlaw tradition and questions the justice of revenge. Probably the most recent and daring challenge to cowboy iconography is Ang Lee's *Brokeback Mountain* (2005), which not only subverts traditional masculine and heteronormative visions of the cowboy but also places him in the role reserved for the villain. And Cormac McCarthy's novels have long confounded the myth of the cowboy. *Blood Meridian* (1985) peoples the western landscape with the bloodthirsty and the self-serving; its most provocative character, the Judge, is the embodiment of the modern sociopath. The recent film version of McCarthy's *No Country for Old Men* (2007) places its cowboy figures, both Tommy Lee Jones and Josh Brolin, in a world of extreme violence. Justice does not motivate Brolin's character, though; greed does. The lone lawman, in the figure of Ed Tom Bell (Jones's character), is left ineffectual. There is no justice for the cowboy and violence literally has as much meaning as a coin toss. Cynthia Miller and A. Bowdoin Van Riper, in their introduction to *Undead in the West*, establish that the western hero is "positioned with one foot in the 'wild' and one foot in the civilized world—bearing the responsibility for maintaining the boundaries between order and chaos, civilization and barbarism."[7] Straddling this border space, the cowboy hero has always held the potential to identify with and even immerse himself in savagery. Increasingly, in contemporary iterations of the western, he realizes this potential.

While *The Walking Dead* is rich with interpretive possibilities, this essay proposes that the most illuminating text through which to read the series as western is Stanley Corkin's *Cowboys as Cold Warriors: The Western and U.S. History*, which traces the history of the genre as indicator of American political ethos during the Cold War era. The book is an examination of the American cowboy as a reflection of national attitudes toward expansionist politics after World War II, and, while Corkin doesn't deal with zombies, the role of "the villain" is central to his argument. Clearly, following the 1990 destruction of the Berlin Wall and the subsequent dissolution of the Soviet Union in 1991, the American political atmosphere changed. In the absence of rhetoric that allowed America to reflect itself as white-hatted cowboy against the black-hatted communist threat, a void was left: the cowboy had to seek a villain against which to define himself. *The Walking Dead* provides that "villain" in its hordes of zombies.

In a post-apocalyptic America, Rick Grimes leads a small group trying to survive the omnipresent threat of zombies and "invite[s] us to identify with the good characters against the bad ones and to take voyeuristic—and guiltless pleasure—in the violence."[8] While we can create meaning for the zombies, their very disposability informs the series. Marc Leverette has argued that zombies are a symbolic white space upon which the filmmaker and/or the audience can project value.[9] And, indeed, the zombies of *The Walking Dead* seem less meaningful as entities-in-themselves than as reflections of the human in the act of killing, a mirror of what it means to pull the trigger. This grave doppelgänger vision of the undead is reinforced by scenes in the show, most notably in "Guts," when Rick and Glenn literally don the walking dead by chopping up a zombie corpse and smearing it over their bodies. Zombie and human are to be equated, a point made evident at the end of season two when Rick reveals that everyone already carries the "virus." Slotkin has argued that, at the moment of killing, "there is an exchange of identities or an acknowledgment of kinship between hunter and prey which symbolically reconciles them."[10] *The Walking Dead* suggests a literal kinship, not a reconciliation but a union, between hunter (Rick and his cohort) and prey (zombies).

The western tropes of *The Walking Dead* are pervasive—cowboy hat and boots, six-gun, lynching, saloon showdown—and it was clear even before the series began that the story was steeped in cowboy lore. The original cover for the first comic book, by artist Tony Moore, portrays a man turned in profile, wearing a cowboy hat and revolver and holding a double barrel shotgun broken open.[11] In "Guts," the second episode of the series, Glenn sarcastically compliments Rick Grimes by saying, "nice moves there, Clint Eastwood." Much of the TV series, however, is informed more particularly by one film, George Stevens's *Shane* (1953).[12]

It is no accident that John Bernthal's character on *The Walking Dead* is named Shane. Stevens' Shane (Alan Ladd) is an interloper in the lives of the Starretts, a family struggling to maintain a homestead in Wyoming under threat by cattle baron Rufus Ryker. Ladd's character quickly draws the attention of Mrs. Starrett and her son, Joey. The film makes clear the attraction between Mrs. Starrett and Shane, even in the presence of Mr. Starrett. *The Walking Dead* introduces a similar love triangle: Bernthal's Shane is the interloper in the lives of the Grimes family. And, in this case, the love between Shane and Lori Grimes is quite literal, à la steamy sex scene on the floor of a Georgia forest ("Guts"). While the film keeps the attraction between Starretts's wife and Shane muted, going as far as to have Mrs. Starrett project her denial onto her son when she says, "Don't get to likin' Shane too much," *The Walking Dead* uses Shane's obsessive love for Lori Grimes as a catalyst for much of the violence that erupts, particularly in the second season. AMC's Shane is not the man of restraint that the film offers. Shane will have his woman, and, unlike the chivalric image of the cowboy, he will do so by force, as the confrontation between Shane and Lori in the Centers for Disease Control suggests ("TS-19").

The function of the two Shanes is, then, quite different. The film Shane is the necessary man of action in a world of inaction. Shane acts as foil to Starrett's inability to stand up to the film's villain, Ryker. He is willing to risk his life for the untouchable woman and her family so that they can maintain a lifestyle of which he will never be a part. Shane even says, when asked by Joe Starrett where he's going, "Someplace I've never been." And he never will. Once he fulfills his act of killing, he leaves town. Shane must return to the world of guns and killing he has renounced to do that which Starrett is ultimately incapable of doing. In the film's world, killing has its necessary place, a place that must be kept separate from the Starretts' world. In *The Walking Dead*, on the other hand, where killing is commonplace, Shane acts more as doppelgänger to Rick Grimes. Each is capable of killing, but, while Rick initially moralizes over the kill, Shane is often animalistic and barely restrained. Both are cast in the cowboy image, but Rick is mythic cowboy while Shane is cowboy stripped of moral pretense—or at least his sense of morality is more pragmatic and self-serving. Bernthal's Shane complicates the simplified world of the mythic cowboy that Rick Grimes represents. When Rick struggles in the second season, for instance, over whether to execute Randall, an outsider who knows the location of the farm, Shane tells him again and again that not doing so will most likely result in the death of Rick's family ("18 Miles Out"). And, thus, Shane leads Rick down the path of violence.

Each Shane acts, indeed, as the model of violence for the younger generation. In the western, Joey Starrett is drawn to Shane's gun, stroking it like a new toy and subsequently running about the Starrett farm with a toy pistol. Finally, he can contain himself no longer and asks Shane, "Will you teach me to shoot?" Similarly, *The Walking Dead's* Shane is the expert in weapons and is in charge of training the group in the use of guns. He, too, is ultimately responsible for teaching Carl Grimes how to shoot a pistol. However, embedded in *The Walking Dead* is a commentary on the youthful fascination with violence, illuminated by a scene that contrasts starkly with *Shane*. In the film, on several occasions, Joey Starrett is drawn by the appearance of an elk. Initially, the boy is simply fascinated by the animal, but later, as the boy's attraction to violence increases, he hides behind a corral fence and points a rifle at the elk. We later find out that the boy carries an unloaded rifle, however, and since no violence is enacted, the predominant message is of a harmony between boy and nature. *The Walking Dead's* take is different. Carl Grimes encounters a deer in the forest and is as fascinated with it as his counterpart in the film. While Carl is unarmed, the men behind him are not. As Carl approaches the animal, a shot is heard. Carl is wounded in the stomach and almost dies ("What Lies Ahead"). Nature is, in this case, indifferent to humankind's place in the world—and we find out later that Carl was shot as a result of another man's attempt to kill the deer. Is this an indictment of violence? Alone, Joey Starrett makes gunplay a game, an act of innocence, but in the face of real guns, innocence cannot stand, and child becomes equated with animal— hunted, shot, and almost killed.

Both film and series, indeed, make killing and its justification central to the plot. In *Shane*, the gunfighter tells Joey, "A gun is as good or as bad as the man using it," placing the act within a moral framework. However, he later revises this opinion when he says: "Joey, there's no living with a killing. Right or wrong is in the brain." While film Shane recognizes the need to justify killing through moral interpretation, he ultimately understands that the act itself is beyond morality and has an inevitably corrosive impact. This focus on the meaning of the kill is also introduced early in the TV series. In a montage at the end of "Days Gone Bye," Rick Grimes and Morgan Jones, a survivor who has taken care of Rick, both face the act of killing. Jones must kill his wife, who has become a walker. Rick returns to the site of the "bicycle girl," the first walker he encountered upon leaving the hospital. Both acts are portrayed as mercy killings, but Rick pulls the trigger while Morgan can't. While the series doesn't immediately answer the moral question of who is more humane, it does suggest the dilemma of a society based on violence and "whether a social system defined by its ability and tendency to deal with disruptive elements by annihilating them may be flawed."[13]

Rick Grimes, then, confronts a redefinition of social structure and self. America as he knows it is gone, and he, as the cowboy sheriff, strives to act as figurehead of what America now is—note that he dons his cowboy hat as he emerges from his patrol car in the opening scene of the series ("Days Gone Bye"). Rick must struggle to maintain the mythic vision of America he represents, or he must change, suggesting that whatever moral view America has of itself must be adjusted in this new violent world it has engendered. The series represents the killing of innocence in "Days Gone Bye" when Rick stops at an abandoned gas station to find fuel. In a scene reminiscent of the western hero walking a silent street, Rick Grimes walks through abandoned cars, finally realizing he is not alone. The camera pans across his back as he glances over his shoulder to find the source of the threat. What he finds is a young blonde girl, pink-robed and bunny-slippered, carrying a soiled teddy bear, the epitome of innocence. The sheriff calls out, "Little girl, I'm a policeman." The hero has announced himself; all will be okay. Except, innocence isn't what it seems; the girl turns to reveal the gruesome rotted mouth of a zombie. She charges Grimes, and he shoots her in the head. If, as the series suggests, we are all the walking dead, then our hero has taken the first step toward the loss of his innocence and, by implication, his own self-destruction.

Thus begins Rick Grimes's quest in a landscape that has been stripped of social restraint. American institutions are rife with killing. In "Days Gone Bye," Rick kills a deputy-become-walker. As he drives away from the Sheriff's Department, the central institution for maintaining civil obedience, the American flag flies center screen. In "What Lies Ahead," in season two, the group is drawn to a church where the bell rings. Within the church, Rick and others shoot down walkers gathered in the pews. Clearly, civilizing influence has disappeared, which leads Rick at the end of the episode to ask God if he is doing "the right thing." The bigger question is whether "right" is relevant. He will kill; the zombied world demands it. Who, then, will Rick become? Much of season two concerns this question. Central to the season, for instance, is Rick's struggle with whether to give up the search for Sophia. He is driven to save the young girl who disappears, but he also understands that each time he or others go out to search, they risk being attacked by walkers. The situation is key to Rick's attempt to maintain a distinction between the living and the undead. Is he, as Shane asserts, putting more lives at risk in the fruitless search, and is his persistence in the search an attempt to assuage his guilt over killing the young girl of the first episode? Rick seeks the just solution, but his simplified vision of the world only leads him to crisis.

What exacerbates his crisis is that each decision Rick confronts is challenged by Shane. If Grimes is driven by a sense of morality, Shane, at least initially, seems driven by pragmatism. As Shane says to Rick, "I'm trying to save lives here and you're saving cats from trees" ("Chupacabra"). Shane continuously castigates Rick for putting justice before the safety of the group. And this approach has its takers, particularly Andrea. Rick's own son says of the walkers, "Everything's food for something else" ("Secrets"). The problem is that, at heart, Shane's pragmatism is really atavistic. In season one, he embodies violence barely in check. When he aims his shotgun at Rick early in the season as a way of ridding himself of the obstacle to Lori, his inaction seems less one of moral consternation than one of an incredible act of animal restraint. His face contorts, and he releases a hiss as he lowers the gun ("Wildfire"). But Shane's true transformation into an atavistic being comes in season two when he shoots Otis in the leg so that he can escape walkers ("Save the Last One"). The final vestiges of moral restraint are gone, and Shane signifies this by shaving his head, which in part is to conceal his guilt (it eliminates the patch where Otis had torn out his hair), but which could also be read as an act of mourning for his lost self.[14] His hair also seems the symbol of his physical attractiveness and, in shearing it, he rejects outer appearance, the handsome iconic image of the cowboy and the societal recognition that handsomeness draws. He later admits as much, although his listeners don't understand the significance of his comment when he says of Otis's death, "If any death ever had meaning, it was his." Shane's transformation is complete. He will continue to assert altruistic motives for his actions, but it becomes clear that he is self-serving.

Shane's transformation creates a schism that drives season two. The group now has two fathers[15]: Rick, who doubts both himself and the moral framework that he admits to Lori may be "a way of thinking that doesn't make sense anymore" ("Chupacabra"), and Shane, who pursues all that is important to him: Carl, Lori, the baby she carries that he is certain is his, and control of the group. This is a complete inversion of Stevens's *Shane*. In the film, Shane recognizes his role as killer and seeks to spare Joe Starrett the inevitable stripping effect that killing has on one's humanity. Shane physically fights with Joe only as a way of sparing Joe the trip to town to kill Ryker and his hired gun (played by Jack Palance). *The Walking Dead* erupts in a comparable fistfight—a struggle between Rick and Shane about who is most fit to protect Lori and Carl. Shane makes clear his willingness to kill Rick by trying to hit him with a large machine wrench, but Grimes invites Shane back into the group, albeit by placing a loaded gun in his hand, as if violence is the emblem of belonging ("18 Miles Out"). In *The Walking Dead*, unlike *Shane*, no one is spared the consequences of violence.

The rising battle between two visions of governance intensifies on Hershel's farm, which again has its connections to Stevens's film. In the film, Shane aids the Starretts in protecting the homestead they've established against the interest of cattle baron Ryker, who is connected to the town and particularly the saloon. The westward expansion of America embodied by the western genre is presented here as "a Jeffersonian view of the nobility of the small freeholder and his grassroots democratic institutions."[16] Violence in this context becomes a necessary remedy to forces opposing a harmonic possession of the land. Shane must kill Ryker and his men as the impediment to America's "peaceful westward expansion." In contrast, Hershel's farm stands alone. The city and its institutions—foil to the idyllic farm—no longer exist. Whatever becomes of the homestead is driven internally. And farm life in *The Walking Dead* is challenged by growing dissent: Hershel's ambivalence about letting the group remain, disagreement over the search for Sophia, disagreement over what the walkers represent, growing concerns over Shane's stability, and questions concerning Lori's pregnancy. Arthur Redding asserts that the frontier is the point at which savagery and civilization come together.[17] On Hershel's farm, savagery takes over—literally, at the end of season two, when walkers overrun the farm ("Beside the Dying Fire").

The savagery of the zombies is anticipated, however, by that of the humans. In the shootout in the season two episode, "Nebraska," Rick encounters his definitive moment as a killer. There is no doubt that *The Walking Dead* mirrors *Shane* in this crucial episode. The structure is the same: in the film, Shane stands between Jack Wilson and Ryker, who sits at a table behind him. Wilson goes for his gun, and Shane guns him down, spinning quickly to shoot Ryker, who has also drawn on Shane. Rick Grimes also stands between two strangers whom they've come across in a bar. As in the film, one stands at the bar and confronts Grimes, while the other sits at a table behind him. The strangers insist that Rick reveal the location of the farm, but Rick refuses. Suddenly, the man at the bar draws his gun, but Grimes is quicker, killing first the man who has drawn and then the man at the table behind him who is in the act of drawing his weapon. In the film, this is Shane's defining moment, his return to his role as killer, and he says to Starrett's son, who has been watching, "A man has to be what he is, Joey. You can't break the mold. I tried and it didn't work for me." Rick, too, has become what he is—and it is significant that Rick, not Shane, is the killer in this scene, representing the transfer of violent propensities from one to the other. The shootout in the bar is not an act of killing zombies, nor is it a response to imminent threat. Rick kills not out of moral necessity, but out of self-interest (his family as an extension of self), and he does so even though he warned Daryl in "Wildfire," "We don't kill the living." In "Nebraska," he does. The mask slips: the killer is revealed.

If Rick and Shane constitute a duality of self-definition that represents American authority (both are lawmen cut from the cloth of the western hero), then the rising conflict between them becomes representative of a tension in America's own identity. Shane mocks Dale for being a "moral authority" in "Nebraska," but Rick clearly tries to cling to such a vision of the world. When Rick captures Randall, a member of the group of men he encountered in the bar, he agonizes over whether to kill him in the interest of keeping Hershel's farm hidden. When he decides he must kill him, it is clearly an execution and is couched in western tropes, as Rick ties a noose to hang him ("Judge, Jury, Executioner"). Even though the proposed hanging seems more like a lynching, Rick invokes the rhetoric of state-sanctioned execution when he asks Randall, "Any last words?" He cannot kill Randall in the end, however, because his son watches; he cannot stand to see himself so defined in his son's eyes.

Rick does kill the living again, though. In the penultimate episode of season two, Shane leads Rick into the woods to murder him. Instead, Rick stabs Shane, killing the killer. But Rick's assertion, as he holds Shane, that "this was you. Not me! You did this to us," seems ineffectual ("Better Angels"). To kill Shane is really to become him. Under the weight of finally realizing himself as a killer, Rick cannot maintain the illusion of "moral man." He has killed his best friend and has done so, he discovers, in front of his son. Even worse, Carl has learned the lesson. As Grimes walks away from Shane's corpse, he turns to find his son leveling a gun at his head. Here again are echoes of *Shane*—Joey's admiration of the gunslinger and the internal conflict that this creates for the boy: "I love Shane, I love him almost as much as I love Pa." The boy needs to reconcile the two masculine visions; he needs to know that his father is both just and mighty, so he asks, "Could you whip him, Pa? Could you whip Shane?" In the case of *The Walking Dead*, Pa has indeed whipped Shane, and Carl has born witness. One father is dead at the hand of the other, and the son seems confused. For a moment, we consider the possibility that Carl will shoot Rick. But, when the gun goes off, we discover that Carl has killed Shane-become-walker ("Better Angels"). Here is the most reflective act of killing in the series. Rick turns literally to an image of himself: his son, in essence, is the younger (and more innocent?) version of Grimes. As the audience entertains the possibility that Carl will shoot Rick, we must recognize the corrosive effect that witnessing his father kill has upon the boy. Indeed, Carl mirrors his father's act of violence; he literally kills Shane a second time. He has taken his place within the cycle of violence; he has killed the man who taught him to kill.

The idyllic farm, the American homestead that "resurrects an entire mythic apparatus of American genesis, character, and values," cannot stand when illusions are void, and so walkers descend upon the land *en masse*.[18] Hershel, as representative of the old guard, refuses to leave the land and is forced to leave by the others. The others flee, some are devoured by walkers. Ironically, perhaps the most recognizable symbol of the western homestead, the barn, is set afire by Rick himself ("Beside the Dying Fire"). And, so, the group finds itself again in an unknown wilderness. Walkers surround them, and there seems little hope left. The members of the group have lost faith in Rick as their leader, even though he asserts that there is a new life and that they "just have to find it." Even Lori is unsettled by Rick's admission that he not only killed Shane but that he also "wanted to." A new leader is evolving; Rick is assuming a different mien in his recognition of himself. He turns to the group and announces, "If you're staying, this isn't a democracy anymore" ("Beside the Dying Fire").

In the post–Cold War United States, we still seek to define ourselves as the cowboy against versions of the villain (Al-Qaeda, Taliban, Hispanic immigrants, homosexuals) so that we might conceive of ourselves as morally right. Nothing, however, holds the resonance of the communists of the Cold War era. And in a world of continual violence, how does the cowboy hero survive when stripped of moral authority? Rick Grimes's moral failures leave him aware of what he fundamentally is, a man with a gun. Each act of violence, whether against snarling zombies or his best friend, takes him further from the humanity his golden badge proclaims. If he is to be seen, as the imagery of *The Walking Dead* suggests, as symbolic of American authority, then the message is disturbing. Stripped of moral justification, he is a man wielding influence through guns and acts of violence, and, in this setting, the message is all too clear: "This isn't a democracy anymore."

It is no wonder, then, that the opening episodes of the third season are peopled with sociopaths. Merle Dixon returns; in the prison where Rick's group seeks refuge, they encounter Tomas, who almost kills Rick; and perhaps the most ominous figure, the Governor, is introduced, the charming leader of Woodbury, who keeps a collection of human heads in a private room. The most disturbing transformation of the season, however, may be in Rick and his group. In the first episode of season three ("Seed"), the group enters the prison and goes on a zombie killing spree. Rick stands atop a guard tower, smiling and pulling the trigger. Lori, when asked if she is okay as she kills the zombie in front of her, responds, "Haven't felt this good in weeks." Gone are the days when there was any hesitation in killing. These perhaps understandable kills (they're zombies, after all) are undermined by moments such as when Lori tells Rick, who considers killing the prisoners because they *might* be a threat, "If that's what you think's best." He does, indeed, and when he later kills Tomas, he does so with a smile, a mirror of the moment on the guard tower.

In another ironic commentary, *The Walking Dead* places Rick's group inside prison walls, the residence of the murderer. Gone are the open plains where the film *Shane* locates the family. Instead, the seeming safe harbor for the group is actually the place of their confinement. They are self-imprisoned for what they have become. *The Walking Dead* makes us question whether we too are akin to the zombies, ingesting political rhetoric that creates a facade of humanity. Do we too feed on our own image, numb to the possibilities of violence? Are we imprisoned by our role as killers? Is Rick's transformation ours? We must see through the rhetoric about justice and right and understand the act of killing for what it is. The American system fails as long as the culture of violence prevails. We must recognize the force we wield nationally and internationally for what it is: despotism. Only then can something different arise. Only then can zombies be defeated.

Notes

1. For a discussion of the mythic cowboy, see Henry Nash Smith's "The Western Hero in the Dime Novel," or, more recently, Richard Slotkin's *Gunfighter Nation*.

2. Pye, "The Western (Genre and Movies)," 215.

3. Corkin, *Cowboys as Cold Warriors*, 3.

4. Slotkin, *Regeneration Through Violence*, 28.

5. In a largely Christian society, the nationalistic and patriotic focus on military might presents a moral confusion in which young church-going men and women are instructed against killing but face glorification of state-sanctioned violence. Soldiers and law-enforcement must suspend moral lessons to make "necessary" kills. These contrary demands must have a dramatic impact on the psyche. Slotkin describes such a response in his coverage

of the Frontier Wars: "White troops would become hysterical with rage and massacre the Indian wounded, women, and children with a fury unmatched even by the Indians themselves. To the returning soldier, this hideous lapse from civilized self-restraint would remain a guilty memory, requiring explanation and justification." Slotkin, *Regeneration Through Violence*, 143.

6. For early discussions of the cowboy as hero and antihero, see chapter two of Fenin and Everson's *The Western*. More recent analyses have focused on the role of otherness in opposition to the cowboy, such as in Buscombe and Pearson's collection of essays, *Back in the Saddle Again*.

7. Miller and Van Riper, Introduction, xiii.

8. Rees, "Frontier Values Meet Big City Zombies," 84.

9. Leverette, "The Funk of Forty Thousand Years," 203.

10. Slotkin, *Regeneration Through Violence*, 553.

11. Kirkman and Moore, *The Walking Dead*.

12. As Dawn Keetley was kind enough to point out, in his article on *The Walking Dead*, Gerry Canavan credits in a footnote his colleague, Dale Knickerbocker's suggestion of Shane [Bernthal's character] as a reference to George Steven's 1953 Western *Shane*, which the character echoes in both plot and theme." Canavan, "'We *Are* the Walking Dead,'" 451.

13. Corkin, *Cowboys as Cold Warriors*, 95.

14. The tradition of cutting hair or shaving the head as an act of mourning has a long history. The pagan practice of this tradition is noted in the Bible in passages such as Leviticus 19:27 and Deuteronomy 14:1. The Bible and the Torah may also be the source for the Judaic practice of trimming hair or beards in mourning. Certain Native American tribes, among them Blackfoot and Sioux, cut hair short as an act of mourning.

15. For a discussion of masculine assertion in westerns as a response against femininity and civilization, see Gaylyn Studlar's "Wider Horizons: Douglas Fairbanks and Nostalgic Primitivism."

16. Corkin, *Cowboys as Cold Warriors*, 136.

17. Redding, "Frontier Mythographies," 313.

18. Ibid.

Asserting Law and Order
Over the Mindless

ANGUS NURSE

AMC's *The Walking Dead* provides a continuous narrative of survival in a post-apocalyptic world with changed notions of law and order. Perceptions of lawlessness lie at the center of its ongoing zombie-versus-human narrative and its analysis of the breakdown of society. With its central protagonist a law enforcement officer seeking to make sense of and assert values of law and order in a new social world, *The Walking Dead's* narrative functions as a critique of contemporary law and order policy—in particular, the failure of the reactive policing model to deal with mass lawlessness and the need for alternate law enforcement strategies in the face of rising crime. *The Walking Dead's* zombies represent a threat both physically and philosophically, reflecting the fact that law and order, as socially constructed, construes lawlessness as a force that menaces society and (predominantly western) contemporary notions of acceptable behavior.

Zombie narratives in popular culture reflect social anxiety about the breakdown of societal norms and the threat represented by "otherness," often portrayed as evil. Contemporary zombie narratives have moved on from the paranoia of Cold-War dystopian visions that saw nuclear disaster as the cause of societal breakdown to a more social-realist vision of viral outbreak and super-bug pandemic as causes of the zombie apocalypse. Integral to contemporary cinematic zombie narratives is the aggressive spread of the zombie infection, such that it quickly overwhelms the health, justice, and military apparatus, resulting in rapid societal breakdown so that only small pockets of survivors remain. The narrative, thus, becomes one almost entirely about survival and the search for a safe place with resistance to the zombie outbreak sometimes presenting itself as a secondary theme.

As a small-screen adaptation of a long-running comic/graphic novel series, *The Walking Dead's* serial format—a single story split into weekly episodes—allows for development of a continuous law and order narrative incorporating horror fiction conventions. Crime narratives allow for the interrogation of the criminal justice system and the struggles facing society's protectors, while also addressing societal anxiety about rising crime.[1] With a protagonist who is also a police officer and a central narrative about survival in the face of widespread lawlessness, *The Walking Dead* engages with debates about how best to deal with social threats and the impact of law and order policies (i.e., reactive versus proactive) on different social groups.

This essay argues that *The Walking Dead*, like the best science or horror fiction, raises valid concerns about a perceived social problem in its representations of lawlessness, unthinking violence, intolerance and the use of ultimate force to reassert the power of the state and societal values. The series tackles these issues directly with sub-plots about the consequences of violence and use of force by law officers; it then dramatizes the conflicting merits of using force as a last resort (reactive policing) and preventative (proactive) policing. This essay first considers the nature of the zombie threat within its law and order context and the series' allegorical intentions; secondly, it argues that protagonist Rick Grimes embodies a specific notion of law and order, even as his character adapts to suit the changing social context. The essay then argues how, over the course of its three seasons to date, *The Walking Dead's* shift in its depiction of increasing lawlessness serves both as an allegory for the increasing lawlessness of contemporary society and a critique of the failures of liberal law enforcement, which primarily addresses crime after it has happened (via reactive policing). The essay finally elaborates *The Walking Dead's* conclusion that a reactive non-confrontational crime control approach proves inadequate as a means of dealing with increased and widespread lawlessness and that a more aggressive law enforcement response is required for contemporary crime problems.

Zombie Hordes and Crime

The Walking Dead is set after a zombie apocalypse, in which an unspecified viral outbreak caused an epidemic that has reached pandemic proportions. Andrew Tripp argues that "apocalyptic narratives create spaces for the disenchanted within a larger society," although apocalyptic narratives need not be cataclysmic ones.[2] Instead, narratives that incorporate the challenge of continuing to protect societal norms (such as maintaining and providing for a family) provide a means through which responses to societal problems such as crime can be discussed. Alison Young writes that "the experience of watching, and the ways in which the spectator is thereby implicated in the onscreen image," is an integral part of the affective dimension of visual texts.[3] Intense images of crime, as well as their perceived threat to social norms, is thus an important factor in eliciting the desired response from audiences and is a key aspect of *The Walking Dead's* adaptation from its source comics. The existence of zombies as an ever-present challenge to societal norms—as well as the struggle to re-establish familial bonds after a traumatic event, a key theme of each season—is integral to this audience engagement.

Lars Bang Larsen argues that "the zombie isn't just any monster, but one with a pedigree of social critique."[4] The zombie represents, among other things, alienation and the loss of control (both individual and social), estrangement from oneself and other people, and a dislocation from humanity allowing baser instincts to take control. The first few episodes of *The Walking Dead* clearly establish that its zombies retain no knowledge of their former selves, no ability to organize or reason beyond the basic "mob mentality," and possess only rudimentary motor skills. Their slow-moving, shuffling gait and inability to articulate anything beyond guttural moans and slightly more excitable "attack" tones thus mark them out as deviant. As the walking *dead*, moreover, the zombie poses a threat not only to the normative social order but also to western spiritual ideals of life and death based primarily on Christian notions of faith and what it means to be human. Given normative society's reliance on complying with the principles of the social contract, acceptance of governance by the state for the greater good, and religious ideals that good works on earth are ultimately rewarded, the existence of zombies represents an alarming challenge to orthodox faith and forms of government.

The Walking Dead specifically addresses law and order debates about the attenuated rationality of those who engage in widespread crime and mass deviance. The zombies, indeed, reflect contemporary anxieties about the rise in lawlessness in the West such as the 2010 student riots, the widespread August 2011 riots in the UK, and the 2011 Occupy Wall Street riots in the U.S. Some riots are planned in advance, usually as a means of protesting government policies, whereas others are the spontaneous response of a dispossessed group; however, whatever the causes, the result is often mass arrest, loss of life, and damage to property, raising questions about how such lawlessness should be policed and the nature and legitimacy of state responses to widespread disorder, particularly the use of containment policies. For example, the European Court of Human Rights was asked to assess the legitimacy of the technique of "kettling," a containment strategy used by the police in the 2001 anti-globalization riots. The Court ruled that the technique, which consisted of containing those present within a police cordon for several hours even though some had no affiliation with the protest, was lawful given the circumstances and imminent threat represented by the number of protestors.[5] The NYPD also used kettling as part of its strategy to deal with unrest at the Brooklyn Bridge in October 2011, and it has arguably become a popular U.S. police practice. Through embodying mass lawlessness, the zombies of *The Walking Dead* provide a means through which concerns about mass lawlessness and the militarized role of the police in controlling mass lawlessness can be explored.

There's a New Sheriff in Town

The problem of lawlessness inherent in *The Walking Dead* requires a form of justice. In Rick Grimes, *The Walking Dead* seeks to reassert societal norms and the forces of law and order. On being reunited with his family in "Tell It to the Frogs," Rick automatically assumes the role of protector for his family and the wider group. But he also adopts the role of crime manager, training others in the use of firearms as an enforcement tool. Rick's peace officer persona provides not only a means through which law and order is visibly enforced via the sanctioning of the undead threat to survival, but it is also a means through which ideals of law and order are maintained for other survivors.

P. Ivan Young's essay in this collection identifies Rick as the archetypal cowboy. Initially, however, Rick's and Shane's role as peace officers is to uphold societal values and to employ an accepted policing method of using deadly force only when necessary and as a last resort. This approach quickly proves ineffective not least because the walkers represent a form of deviance that cannot be reasoned with, thus rendering alternatives largely redundant, but also because of the lack of a wider police infrastructure, which places limitations on the tactics that can be used. Rick and Shane, then, are required to implement frontier justice; those perceived as a threat are eliminated, while those whose threat can be avoided are ignored until such time as their threat-level escalates. Thus, the lawlessness threat is contextualized, and walkers are assigned a threat category compatible with the survival needs of the group. Law and order in *The Walking Dead* consists of speedy summary justice—political, oppressive, and absolute.

Despite the demise of familiar social structures, Rick retains his peace officer uniform both as personal identification and as symbol of authority, and he adopts the role of protector, although he frequently fails in his task. Particularly throughout the first two seasons, Rick's uniform becomes a symbol of law and order despite the fact that traditional notions of social control and the operation of a legitimate criminal justice system have broken down. Law enforcement uniforms, however, have social and psychological significance beyond the implication of belonging to the organized police structure, and this significance is integral to Rick as protagonist and authority figure. Citizens recognize police officers by their uniform and may be subconsciously reassured in times of crisis. In addition, the police uniform reveals something about the wearer, notably his identification with upholding the law, social values, and the exercise of judgment over others. Police uniforms attract both respect and trigger compliance towards the wearer as well as eliciting aggression in those challenging the dominant ideology of society or rebelling against authority.[6] Thus, early scenes show Rick as the sole remaining representative of law and order, literally besieged on all sides in the episodes "Days Gone Bye" and "Guts," when he is forced to seek refuge in a tank. When united with other survivors, the lack of respect towards his uniform is exhibited by the working class, represented by Merle and Daryl Dixon, but a level of respect is automatically granted by others of a comparatively middle-class background.

Central to questions of how to deal with crime considered within *The Walking Dead* are the merits of different styles of policing—in particular, whether the police officer role should be that of peacekeeper or crime fighter. By retaining his uniform long after its traditional function has been erased, Rick Grimes adopts not only the role of guardian of the group of survivors but also the authority of traditional values.[7] By contrast, his fellow peace officer Shane abandons his uniform in favor of a more paramilitary style of dress and more readily embraces the notion that early and frequent use of deadly force is the solution to the zombie problem. Thus, two contrasting notions of policing and the role of the police officer are present. Rick adopts a more reactive social-support role, integrating his policing within the community, while Shane adopts a more proactive zero-tolerance approach. The failure of Rick's initially reactive force-as-last-resort approach provides a critique of the continued reliance on this approach, despite the changing nature of contemporary crime problems. The overwhelming nature of the zombie threat renders this approach ineffective as there will always be another group of zombies with which to deal. Likewise, in contemporary society, new offenders continually replace the old, necessitating an escalating program of incarceration, prison building, and growth in police numbers if this approach is to be maintained. In this context, Shane arguably adapts to the changed reality of a world dominated by the lawless, while Rick persists in adherence to an outmoded societal code.

The relationship between the officer who follows the rules and takes responsibility for his actions and the officer who adapts to a new reality and is not bound by the old rules is an important aspect of the law and order debate inherent in *The Walking Dead*. Society requires its police to be accountable even when using lethal force, and citizens need to be assured that force does not become a routine aspect of police practice and that the risk of corrupt officers exercising deadly force is minimized. In this respect, civilian monitoring of police use of force has become a legitimate means of considering whether officers have exceeded their authority. Thus, challenges to the risks taken by Rick and Shane represent legitimate civilian questioning of the use of deadly force against not only the zombie threat but also the wider threat posed by other survivors; yet, the nature of the threat facing society following the zombie apocalypse is such that an escalation in the use of force and a move to the casual use of deadly force quickly becomes a necessity. As Fiona Leverick explains, the right to life is fundamental, thus the moral asymmetry between defender and aggressor can be explained by embracing the notion of forfeiture.[8] The zombie forfeits its right to continued existence by virtue of its posing an unjust and immediate threat to the life of another. So, too, do those humans who threaten the survival of the group.

Shifting Conceptions: Developing the Law and Order Narrative

Conceptions of law and order shift within *The Walking Dead* such that there is a subtle evolution in the manner in which the zombie threat is perceived and dealt with during each of its seasons. Each season comments not only on specific aspects of the failures of crime control policy and of the crime problem, but also on the changing role of law enforcement as applied to its specific context. Season one provides for an examination of law and order away from the confines of the apparatus of home security, while seasons two and three explicitly engage with these ideas. Rick's changing role as law enforcement officer and the direct contrast between his and Shane's approaches are also explicitly examined, inviting viewers to consider the effect of crime on those intimately involved in upholding the law and protecting society.

Season One: Fight for Survival

The narrative of the first season is primarily concerned with survival. After being shot in the line of duty, Rick awakens in hospital to find himself in the aftermath of a zombie apocalypse. His first actions are to establish the whereabouts of his wife and child, but in doing so he must come to terms with the nature of the zombie threat—with the characteristics of the "walkers" and thus the extent of the crime problem. The first episode, "Days Gone Bye," shows Rick's police station deserted, explicitly marking that traditional justice and law enforcement mechanisms have been abandoned, although Rick has yet to learn this lesson. Episode four, "Vatos," highlights the survivalist nature of the post-apocalyptic world and the extent of the law and order breakdown as Rick and his group are attacked by a Latino gang. The episode's commentary on gang culture involves first invoking the stereotype of the Latinos as a street gang, only to disclose soon after that the "gang" is comprised of the former employees of a nursing home who have become a gang in order to protect themselves and the elderly inhabitants. Rick and Shane's lawful use of weapons contrasts with the perceived lawlessness of the gun-wielding Latino "gang." This episode suggests, however, that gang culture is not only socially-constructed but is also a means through which oppressed groups respond to perceived threats from dominant groups within society (which here includes both the walkers and Rick's mostly white group).[9]

Season one also reveals the failure or inadequacy of standard emergency response mechanisms to deal with wider social threats like epidemics, pandemics, and mass riots. The army is shown as inadequate and possibly disbanded, and there are no signs of other police surviving beyond Shane and Rick. Thus, the basic apparatus of social control and law and order maintenance is no longer functioning, and survival needs dominate the response to the societal threat that the walkers represent.

Season Two: Protecting the Family

The second season concerns itself with re-establishing societal norms and protecting the family. Its central metaphor is that of the failure of law-and-order structures to adequately protect the vulnerable, notably children, who suffer from particular forms of violence such as abduction and unwanted sexual attention. Season two also shows how children are often the unintended victims of increased tolerance for aggression in society, with the response to crime resulting in an escalating use of force that has pervasive negative consequences.

Having escaped from the CDC, the survivors, under the protection of Rick and Shane, seek a new shelter at the military base at Fort Benning; however, in the first episode, "What Lies Ahead," they encounter a blocked highway full of abandoned vehicles and a large group of walkers, two of which chase the young girl Sophia into the woods. While Rick reasserts law and order by killing Sophia's pursuers, she goes missing. In the ensuing search for Sophia, Rick, Carl, and Shane encounter a buck in the woods, and Carl is accidentally shot by a hunter.

The two subsequent episodes, "Bloodletting" and "Save the Last One," are concerned with the dual threats to the children, Carl and Sophia. The search for Sophia serves as a device to show how crime, deviance, and lawlessness threaten the innocent and put children at risk, while the attempts to save Carl illustrate the consequences of an increasingly violent and lawless society. Child abduction places particular strains not just on the parents but also on the immediate community, here portrayed by the larger survival group that becomes actively engaged in the search for Sophia. Rick becomes sick himself by providing Carl with a blood transfusion and is unable to prevent Shane from initiating a more aggressive, zero-tolerance approach to the zombie crime problem.

Throughout the season, a contrast is presented between the original group of survivors, who now directly engage with and use force to eliminate the zombie threat under the direction of Rick and Shane, and the survivors on Hershel's farm, who employ a policy of containment and who are seemingly unaffected by the zombie threat. The season contrasts the normalized existence of Hershel's (well-fed) group with the hand-to-mouth existence of Rick's group, which has adopted a reactive liberal approach, responding to the walkers only when they become a threat. Hershel's group arguably fares better through its proactive policy of containment—keeping walkers "alive" and locked in a barn, as revealed in "Chupacabra." This policy in part reflects Hershel's initial belief that the walkers retain their humanity; thus he keeps them alive in the hope of finding a cure. Hershel's preventative strategy, nonetheless, reflects a proactive form of policing similar to "zero tolerance" forms of policing: Hershel's group employs mass imprisonment of the walkers as a preventative tool irrespective of whether individual walkers represent a threat. Ultimately this policy backfires, however, when Rick's group learns of it and Shane releases the walkers against Hershel's wishes, forcing the group to shoot the captured walkers and to confront the necessity of an aggressive approach. Rick's devotion to social norms and the need to protect society from all forms of deviance are firmly established when he finally kills Shane, who had become a direct threat to his personal safety and a perceived threat to the wider group. Thus, Rick's actions confirm that problems of extreme deviance, whether human or walker, require a firm response.

The overwhelming nature of the zombie threat is reinforced in the season's final episode, "Beside the Dying Fire," when an army of walkers overruns the farm—illustrating that once Hershel's containment policy is nullified, the threat resurfaces. Despite being armed and transformed into an effective fighting force, the group is unable to defend its position, and, its reactive response proving inadequate in the face of overwhelming deviance, it is forced to abandon the farm.

Season Three: Passing the Hat

By the third season, the walker threat has become normalized as the small group of survivors has clearly established a means of dealing with them. Norms of law and order have altered, as *active* engagement with the walkers is used as the primary mechanism for dealing with the threat. When groups of walkers are seen as potential threats, a "zero tolerance" approach is routinely adopted, and there is a noticeable increase in the use of deadly force as the core law-and-order response.

The third season also provides for discussion of the use of prison as a means of protecting society from crime. Subverting the common perception of prison as a means of protecting society by incarcerating the deviant, the core group of survivors, now a combined group from Hershel's farm and the remaining members of Rick's original group, decide to make the prison its home. In clearing a prison block of walkers in order to make it safe, it encounters a small group of prisoners trapped in the cafeteria.

The walker threat both within the prison and outside of it represents a more obvious form of threat. The safety of the new prison home is threatened from outside by groups of walkers, but this threat is largely negated by the prison fortifications, high fences, locked gates, and a watchtower serving as an early warning system. Similarly, the town of Woodbury to which Andrea escaped (after surviving the overrunning of the farm but being separated from the rest of the group) is barricaded and defended by the routine elimination of walkers.

Season three thus expressly comments on the individualistic aspects of crime control, in which citizens supplement their reliance on law and order professionals with personal security in the form of home alarms, fences, high security locks and, in the U.S. and Canada, personal firearms. It also comments on the nature of domestic security and the gated community, which resists outside threats via the use of private security, imposing residential requirements and its own rules designed to negate external threats and protect a specific way of life. Sarah Blandy argues that early theory on gated communities considered them a response to "growing disillusionment with the ability of government to provide services and security; and/or a result of the globalization of American taste and aspirations."[10] Subsequent research, however, has suggested that gated communities promote individualism, choice, and the opportunity for individuals to become self-governing or to engage in collective governance contractually agreed upon.[11] Radley Balko notes that Americans have long held that a constitutional right exists to defend the home from invaders.[12] Indeed, by season three, all members of the group, including the child Carl (who adopts Rick's sheriff's hat as a symbol of his new protector role), are routinely armed as a defense against the threat represented by the lawless zombie, while in Woodbury, the Governor's security team adopts the role of private police force.

The third season again demonstrates the conflict between two contrasting notions of law and order. In Rick's group, all members of the community accept protection duties and the use of firearms as a means of self-defense; yet, while both Woodbury and Rick's prison group embrace the regular use of deadly force as a means of subduing the walker threat, the Governor's approach in Woodbury is that of using a paramilitary police force as a solution to the crime problem. Thus, a select group of trained and armed men wield force in order to protect the town, reflecting Tony Jefferson's definition of paramilitary policing as applying "(quasi-)military training, equipment, philosophy and organization to questions of policing."[13] The group engages in raids in select squads to protect the town, notably in "Walk with Me," when a team led by the Governor stages an attack on a group of army survivors to eliminate their perceived threat and recover their weapons, vehicles, and equipment. Ben Bowling and Coretta Phillips argue that paramilitary policing is "part of a vicious circle that contributes to the criminalization of marginalized communities and undermines not only the 'confidence and trust' in the police but also the legitimacy of the state itself."[14] In Woodbury, the state, while legitimately protecting itself against a tangible threat, indeed becomes illegitimate in its use of force. The governor executes those perceived as a threat, actions that are shown to be unlawful even by the rules of the new society.

The Walking Dead's success depends on its ability to adapt the original literary texts to fit the requirements of its television genre conventions. It incorporates crime and horror fiction concerns about lawlessness while exploring different dimensions of the law and order debate. Crime in *The Walking Dead* is a socially-constructed notion that changes according to the situation occupied by its key protagonists; yet, it also serves as a continuous commentary on the need for a proactive response to lawlessness; indeed, the series consistently dramatizes the necessity of employing aggressive law enforcement and deadly force to eliminate not just an actual threat but also the potential threat represented by the zombie. By the third season, this perspective, proactive rather than reactive enforcement, is now the norm. In both Woodbury and the prison home of Rick's group, elimination of the zombies before they become a threat, as well as the use of physical, routinely-monitored barriers and regular eradication, is established practice.

Order Through the Chaos

Liberal law enforcement perspectives dictate that policing should be carried out with the consent of the community. Thus, initiatives like neighborhood policing, problem-oriented policing, and community policing seek to embed the police within the communities they serve.[15] Policing and the specific crime-response activities of the police become part of the whole crime-control apparatus rather than just a reaction to crime and disorder. Community and voluntary agencies also become an active part of crime-control policy, with the community forming voluntary organizations that provide support services aimed at addressing the conditions that cause crime.

Particular crimes of aggression or widespread lawlessness within a community, however, tend to resist such liberal policies. As a result, more forceful forms of policing are required to deal with more extreme or persistent forms of crime and endemic crime problems within a community. Zero-tolerance policing was introduced as a mechanism of preventing more serious forms of crime by aggressively policing minor transgressions with a view to inhibiting major crime. The theory goes that, by implementing a police approach that does not tolerate any crime, even low-level infractions, such as dropping litter, informal and formal social controls will combine to ensure that low-level offending is quickly reported and addressed. In this respect, zero tolerance can be seen as a direct response to liberal perspectives that are considered to be soft on crime; yet, at other times, when the consent of the community is required, for example to deal with lower-level crimes such as graffiti, such an approach may be seen as heavy handed.

Engaging with debates about how best to deal with pervasive lawlessness and threats to society, *The Walking Dead* represents the problems inherent in crime control policy and the perceived failure of reactive approaches that address lawlessness only after it has occurred. Zombies are the lawless mob, intent on destroying society and societal values. They represent a breakdown of personal values and the erosion of law-abiding behavior, characterized by a total lack of adherence to social norms. The zombie's main drive is self-fulfillment and personal gain, albeit an unthinking form of acquisitive behavior predicated on a desire for human flesh. That this minority has become the majority provides for commentary on the extent of perceived lawlessness and attempts to uphold a particular set of social values in the face of challenges from an emergent criminal class. The zombie mob effectively (and literally) consumes everything in its path as its dominant preoccupation with extinguishing norms drives its every action. As *The Walking Dead's* three seasons graphically show, reactive policing, rehabilitation, and community-based reparation are not practical policies to pursue in the face of relentless, persistent violence. Rick's adherence to the reactive approach (killing zombies only when they become a tangible or *direct* threat) is shown to fail time and again because the threat continually resurfaces. Once the kill-or-be-killed proactive approach has been adopted, and the use of force becomes routine, Rick's group arguably fares better, and there are fewer casualties. The series contends, then, that policing the mob requires proactive elimination of the threat—an aggressively-punitive law-and-order approach.

NOTES

1. See Dowler, "Media Consumption and Public Attitudes toward Crime and Justice."
2. Tripp, "Zombie Marches and the Limits of Apocalyptic Space."
3. Young, *The Scene of Violence,* 9.
4. Larsen, "Zombies of Immaterial Labor."
5. See *Austin and Others v United Kingdom* 39692/09 [2012] ECHR 459 Judgment of the European Court of Human Rights, March 2012.
6. See Joseph and Alex, "The Uniform," and Shaw, "The Role of Clothing in the Criminal Justice System."
7. See Bickman, "The Social Power of a Uniform."
8. Leverick, *Killing in Self-Defence,* 45.
9. See Zatz and Portillos, "Voices from the Barrio," and Valdez, *Gangs.*
10. See Blandy, "Gated Communities in England as a Response to Crime and Disorder."
11. See Crawford, "'Contractual Governance' of Deviant Behaviour."
12. Balko, *Overkill,* 1.
13. Jefferson, "Pondering Paramilitarism," 374.
14. Bowling and Phillips, "Policing Ethnic Minority Communities," 549.
15. See Hughes and Rowe, "Neighbourhood Policing and Community Safety"; Buckmeier, "Setting a Higher Standard for the Evaluation of Problem-Oriented Policing Initiatives"; and Bohm, Reynolds, and Holmes, "Perceptions of Neighborhood Problems and Their Solutions."

Rest in Pieces

Violence in Mourning the (Un)Dead

Laura Kremmel

Common enough words are spoken at the modest funeral in the second season of AMC's *The Walking Dead*: "He died, as he lived: in grace." Yet, in a world overrun by zombies, to die is never an end, and one rarely dies as peacefully as these words imply. In the episode, "Cherokee Rose," the service for Otis, who is killed trying to retrieve medical supplies from a walker-infested area, reflects his farm family's adherence to traditional American funerary customs. This task is made incomplete, however, by the absence of the body and of overall closure for his loved ones, who only know vague details about his death. "You were the last one with him," Otis's wife, Patricia, entreats Shane, a member of Rick's "people," as Hershel calls them. "You shared his final moments. Please, I need to hear. I need to know his death had meaning." Dressed in the dead man's oversized clothes, Shane hesitates, murmuring her last word, "meaning," before telling a halting and emotional story of Otis's heroic self-sacrifice. Interspersed throughout Shane's tribute, however, flashes from the previous episode visually render the truth of Otis's death: dark and chaotic scenes in which Shane shoots Otis in the leg, letting walkers overtake and devour him.

These two competing narratives—of closure and violence—reveal a significant and uneasy shift, not only in causes of death in this zombie-infested world but also in treatment of the dead, a classification becoming increasingly difficult to define. The pervasiveness of death in this dangerous new world and the threat that the undead body poses to the living both necessitate and problematize mourning practices, as phrases such as "surviving the death of a loved one" take on a whole new meaning. This essay will trace the ways in which the characters of *The Walking Dead* deal with death, beginning with the disruption of organized traditions. Using the theories of Freud and Kristeva, I will then analyze the new role of violence in the mourning practices of this zombie-filled world. I will end with an assessment of the re-establishment of new rules and order through rituals which solidify the place of violence in society's new customs.

As the dead turn on their distraught and grieving communities, violence against the dead becomes necessary, not only to protect the living community, but also in order to facilitate closure: it offers certainty of death, preservation of the loved one's memory, and separation through accentuated abjection. It also deters the dangers of melancholia, the Freudian concept of maintaining attachment to lost loved ones at the cost of psychic stagnation. Mourning, from the perspective of the melancholic, is already violent since it requires a break with a lost loved one that can often feel physical.[1] Yet, in a world in which nostalgia involves affection for a body that now wants to eat you, getting over the death of a loved one is required for survival. Inclusion of violence into ritual forces this saving separation, thereby actively replacing peaceful mourning traditions that no longer apply and guiding the new rules and rituals for a zombie-human society that must kill for a living.

Ritual Guidance: Clockwork Closure and When the Ticking Stops

The Walking Dead manifests a transformation of the societal system in a world in transition, revealing the implications of testing new options and acting without the safety of rules. The series does not invalidate human rituals themselves—on the contrary, rules and guidelines seem more important than ever—but it suggests, rather, their complete inapplicability, *as they are*, now that the dead walk. The voice of wisdom and morality for *The Walking Dead,* Dale winds his watch every day at the exact same time, an action that, in the midst of turmoil and destruction, the others in his group find entertaining and absurd. Yet, this repeated action creates a ritual for Dale, not only to measure time but to celebrate his survival through another day. Having lost ties to family members, possessions, jobs, and social positions—all stable maintainers of shared time and values—rituals to mark major and minor life experiences have become skewed and confused.

We witness the epitome of this upheaval in season one, episode four, throughout which Andrea painstakingly plans to wrap and present a birthday gift to her sister, salvaging a happy celebration of birth in a world filled with death. Amy dies on her birthday, and the birthday object (a mermaid necklace) instead serves as a funerary object: Andrea insists on the importance of ritual, even though the occasion has changed. When milestones like births/birthdays and deaths occur at the same time—similar to the simultaneous death and rebirth that transform a human into a zombie—participants in such events can suffer anxiety and a loss of the certainty that designated rituals should provide. "Death is not a purely individual act, any more than life is," says Philippe Ariès. "Like every great milestone in life, death is celebrated by a ceremony that is always more or less solemn and whose purpose is to express the individual's solidarity with his family and community."[2] When violence replaces the solemnity of that occasion, however, it can signify rather a forced and damaging break from solidarity, precipitating a distressing sense of ambivalence.

The Walking Dead follows the tradition of zombie fiction and film engaging with the inadequacies of mourning rituals for an undead body. George A. Romero's classic Night of the Living Dead (1968), which opens with a brother and sister performing the memorial act of laying a wreath on their father's grave, explicitly voices anxieties about managing grief. It is worth noting brother Johnny's complaints of the uselessness of their visit to the cemetery. Whether this criticism indicts already-decaying traditions or instigates the return of the un-mourned to life is unclear. Once the dead begin to walk, however, any semblance of custom disappears. Information from the Pittsburgh Medical Center, in regard to how quickly the corpse reanimates, prioritizes violence and protection over mourning traditions: "It doesn't give them time to make funeral arrangements.... The bodies must be carried to the street and burned. They must be burned immediately. Soak them with gasoline and burn them. The bereaved will have to forgo the dubious comforts that a funeral service will give."[3] For the newscaster to whom the scientist speaks, the chaos implicit in neglecting this ritual seems almost on par with the chaos of the dead rising and devouring the grieving relative: the newscaster is shocked. The lack of ceremony with which bodies are thrown on a pyre by the clean-up posse at the end of the film, like Johnny's previous irreverence, might suggest an eagerness to throw over the rituals already in place, catalyzed by this brief zombie attack. Brutality towards the dead comes to serve the purpose that Sigmund Freud assigns to mourning: "to free the memories and expectations of the survivors from the dead."[4] In the case of Night of the Living Dead, the callousness of the armed men and the absence of mourners turn those bodies into mere objects, from which the men certainly do want to be free. The temporary disruption of certainty in Romero's one-night zombie attack allegorizes the enduring and powerful influence of the dead and how we think about death, even while portraying the fragility of deaths rituals.

Set in a world in which zombies are here to stay, The Walking Dead further complicates notions of closure and violence by following the survivors as they are forced to reformulate taboos, rituals, and social structure without precedent or stability. A loved one's death and resurrection simultaneously combines two types of uncertainty in loss that already disrupt the applicability of the old rituals. Pauline Boss's "theory of ambiguous loss" distinguishes two kinds of grief that elude the comfort of mourning: "In the first type, people are perceived by family members as *physically absent* but psychologically present, because it's unclear whether they are dead or alive," which would include Rick's understanding of his wife and son when he woke up and found them missing. "In the second type of ambiguous loss, a person is perceived as physically present but psychologically absent. This condition is illustrated in the extreme by people with Alzheimer's disease, addictions, and other chronic mental illnesses"; this description is embodied in the dead's return as undead before the eyes of their mourners.[5] During a zombie apocalypse, these two types merge into a double ambiguity of both body and mind that disrupts the certainty of death and the closure of mourning: the loved one may be physically missing and also psychologically lost, making it impossible to know whether he or she is living, dead, or undead, as we see with the lost Sophia, who is found transformed into a walker in season two.

Ambiguous loss is a common feature of zombie narratives and is the central concern of Max Brooks's short story, "Closure, Limited," an extension of his bestseller, *World War Z*. In the zombie world Brooks creates, survivors begin to reconstruct their lives and societies but have difficulty abandoning the old rituals. The first-person narrative investigates solutions for those who are faced with missing loved ones: status, unknown. Wealth, in this new world, is not money or material objects but family and friends, and those who have lost them dwell in a state of psychological poverty. Doctor Kiersted, who manages the organization Closure, Limited, describes two different ways of dealing with a lack of closure:

> For a lot of them, not knowing is a gift. It protects them and drives them.... For them, limbo is hope, and sometimes, closure is the death of hope. But what about the other type of survivors, the ones who're paralyzed by limbo? These are the ones who search endlessly through ruins and mass graves and endless, endless lists. They are the survivors who've chosen truth over hope but can't move forward without some physical proof of that truth.[6]

This second method suggests that knowledge of death—or "chosen truth"— is inadequate to initiate the required ritual for closure: you need to have a body. Closure, Limited, produces a facsimile of the lost individual by reconstructing a zombie look-alike, down to matching clothing and accessories. It then allows the mourner to either shoot the zombie or simply observe its twice-dead corpse, thereby providing closure through ritual treatment of the physical body. The zombie is not (and never was) actually the lost loved one, but the painstaking attention to detail—without which "the process simply won't work"—indicates the power and importance of the ritual through not only the actions of the participants but also the symbolic representation of its objects.[7] Most notably, the story ends with an act of violence that solidifies the enactment of closure as the narrator shoots one of these custom-made zombies in the head.

The procedure offered by Closure, Limited, re-affirms customs that inform mourners exactly what to do and how to act towards the undead, a re-establishment that has not yet occurred in the first season of *The Walking Dead*. As Andrea cradles Amy's dying body in "Vatos," she repeats over and over the phrase, "I don't know what to do, I don't know what to do." Mourning rituals, like all rituals, provide a sense of structure and duty during a time when emotion clouds reason and judgment. The anticipation of the body returning to life, however, disrupts the peace and comfort of traditional mourning rituals as the state of becoming a zombie complicates what death is, provoking ever more conflicted reactions of love, loss, fear, devastation, hatred, and repulsion.

Memorializing the Abject: Veneration and Vomit

In her pivotal essay on the abject, Julia Kristeva dissects how repulsion works: abjection refers to "loathing an item of food, a piece of filth, waste, or dung. The spasms and vomiting that protect me. The repugnance, the retching that thrusts me to the side and turns me away from defilement, sewage, and muck."[8] In terms of the corpse, feelings of abjection prevent us from recognizing death as part of life, from recognizing our own connections to it: reverse *memento mori*, in a way. Kristeva says that "corpses show me what I permanently thrust aside in order to live. These body fluids, this defilement, this shit are what life withstands, hardly and with difficulty, on the part of death. There, I am at the border of my condition as a living being."[9] The suggestion that the zombie is us or that we are the zombie—whether that transformation lies in the past or the future—instigates the type of reaction reminiscent of vomiting or some other violence (often against the corpse itself). As Fred Botting says, "Just as one cannot love one's abjection, casting it out in order to survive, so one cannot love one's zombie ... abject, they manifest what is most revolting, abhorrent, and unbearable in living beings, the elements of life and death that must be ejected for life to continue apart from death."[10] Glenn's reaction to chopping up a walker early in the series—to vomit—exemplifies this and commits an involuntary violence against his own body that expels an element that is "not I" suggestive of the group's similar attitude to the zombie corpse.

Many funerary traditions, particularly in the West, take into account the risk of putting mourners in direct confrontation with the abject and deliberately conceal any transformation that a dead body experiences, from the workmanship that goes into preparing it for viewing and burial, to the mortuary procedure of cremation. "In one way or another," says Christine Quigley, "the dead are shielded from view to protect them and us from our natural curiosity. The closed casket forces mourners to rely on their memories, but denies them the opportunity to witness death, if after the fact. Bodies that are exposed in the funeral home are sanitized and don't reveal the real effects of death."[11] What is hidden is the conversion from one state to another, which would reveal to us the frightful notion that the body becomes a thing and, more importantly, that *we* will become a thing. The zombie state of the walker's animated corpse, however, disrupts this protective ignorance by openly displaying the act of decay: a walking transition from us to them, from life to death. More than once *The Walking Dead* shows how easy it is to mistake a human for a walker and vice versa. The distinction between them that allows Rick and Glenn to pass as walkers, for instance, is simply a difference in smell: "They smell dead, we don't," Andrea says, drawing a line that they find unsettlingly easy to cross in the episode "Guts." This odor, an indication of the abject that induces resistance to it, denotes a bodily element that the sterility of funerary or cremation services would never permit to show: its offensive nature would risk turning feelings of mourning and love for the dead into aggression, disgust, and repulsion.

The line between zombie monster and lost loved one becomes even more difficult to distinguish when death and rebirth have been witnessed. Andrea reveals the different stages of mourning these multiple deaths of a lost loved one/reborn zombie in season one. Distressed by the futility of taboos, customs, and rituals, she suffers along with her dying sister. Once Amy has died, Andrea remains with her but appears peaceful and focused, no longer distraught over what to do. She has passed through the period of loss during her sister's death and now performs the traditional mourning ritual of reflection. Rick and Lori both try to persuade Andrea to leave Amy's body. "We'll try to be as gentle as we can," Lori says in "Wildfire," attempting to eliminate violence from the ritual altogether, because "we all cared about her." This view of the situation sees violence as twofold: violence to the corpse/lost loved one and violence to the mourner who is forced to hurt someone he or she loves, thus presenting the possibility for strong feelings of regret, guilt, and self-hatred. Lori's insistence that "you have to let us take her," subscribes to remnants of the anxiety about transformation that Quigley describes. The removal of the body ensures that the mourner witnesses none of the unpleasantries and small violences done to a body that can no longer feel poking, prodding, or chemical treatments, let alone a much messier shot or shovel to the head.

Destruction of the corpse, however, harnesses the disgust and ambivalence inspired by the already-abject zombie, using the effects of the abject for the practical purpose of forcing closure. I would like to suggest, therefore, that one of the reasons mourning practices in *The Walking Dead* necessitate violence is to induce the abject in the extreme. As Kristeva says, an inanimate corpse is already abject, and a zombie merely activates abjection into motion, exposing it and, what's more, moving it closer towards those who are most repulsed by it.[12] A turn to Bataille emphasizes the messiness of the human body, particularly the dead one, and why we fear it:

> We have no greater aversion than the aversion we feel towards those unstable, fetid and lukewarm substances where life ferments ignobly. Those substances where the eggs, germs and maggots swarm not only make our hearts sink, but also turn our stomachs. Death does not come down to the bitter annihilation of being—of all that I am ... but only the anticipation of being, which will be and is not.[13]

In other words, the substances associated with the dead body, more than death itself, cause fear, disgust, and even aggression, making the zombie body the epitome of "the anticipation of being," especially when that zombie used to be a friend or loved one. Performing violence against such creatures can enhance their grotesque nature by augmenting already-open wounds or piercing decayed flesh; the act thus serves to destroy the latent connection between them and us—annihilating the last visual resemblance of the corpse and violently pushing it away so that characters can then destroy it.

Andrea, herself, however, transforms in this moment of grief, adapting what she needs for closure to the new understanding of death and loss with which she is faced. She treats the body as both her sister and not her sister, the way that mourners treat photographs: speaking to it, she directs her thoughts and feelings towards an object that temporarily represents Amy. Particularly in the case of the zombie object, however, this one-sided communication is kept pointedly brief as the abjection of the rebirth quells extended veneration of the representative object. Rather than "I'm sorry," she says, "I'm here now" and "I love you": not only does she need violence in this moment to preserve her sister's memory, to end any potential misery, and to finalize their separation, but she sees it as a measure of sisterly protection to perform that violence *herself*. Her new understanding of the mourning process involves the critical moments between death and rebirth as well as the opportunity with which that rebirth presents her: a second chance to speak to her sister, regardless of her inability to hear. So, when she turns her gun on Rick and the community in order to protect her right to mourn, she is also establishing—with the authority of force—new rules and rituals for mourning this new kind of death.

Violent Love, Hate-Mourning, and Melancholics Who Refuse to Murder

Moments after Lori tells Andrea that they will be as gentle as they can in killing Amy's walker, the camera cuts to a close-up of Daryl as he hacks into a zombie's flesh with the appropriate squish-and-squash sound effects. Daryl might not recognize what he does as an act of mourning, but he would acknowledge it as a duty done to the dead and for the protection of the living: two elements common to mourning. After his suggestion that they kill a member of their group who has been bitten, Shane responds, "Is that what you'd want?" He claims that he would, "and I'd thank you while you did it." Violence can also be a kind of loyalty. It ends the profanation of the host's body by the walker as well as protects the living. Violence against the undead is not the same as violence against the dead, though this is often performed in the series without distinction as a precursor to walker rebirth. The dead and leaking grotesque body may be dangerous to one's sense of self, but it is not always physically threatening, making avoidance a common coping mechanism. When death itself has become violent, however, violence against it becomes absolutely necessary. Daryl, then, illustrates exactly what mourning has become: a hostile battle against the zombie and, for him, the black-and-white duty of destruction, ranging from burial to burning, both after a sharp blow to the brain. Frequently depicted with a shovel, ax, or hammer and rising up into a frame from cutting down into a corpse, Daryl has become the zombie apocalypse's equivalent of the grave-digger, replacing emotion, reflection, and kind words with the sheer labor—sweat and blood and guts—of putting the dead to rest in their many pieces.

Daryl, a hunter, thereby uses violence to protect the living.[14] His actions accentuate the practical aspects of the mourning ritual. We see a much different version of dealing with the dead when he hands off his pickax to Carol, who interrupts his functional violence with a desire for violence of her own. Viewers get a good look at her abusive husband Ed's corpse in this moment: it has already been severely damaged and is unrecognizable, lying prone, pitiful, emaciated, and quite dead in the dirt. "I'll do it. He was my husband,"[15] she says, cleaning up after Ed one last time and combining (marital) responsibility with an element of revenge. In a recap of the episode "Better Angels," Matt Barone coins the term "hate-mourning,"[16] an apt term to describe Carol's form of mourning her husband, who, during his life, humiliated, beat, and restricted both herself and her daughter. In "Wildfire," Carol holds the pick over her shoulder for a moment and begins to cry before the first strike, which cracks down through the head, oozing and spraying blood. The second and third views of the corpse are noticeably different from the first: more life-like, more human, and more Ed, suggesting a change in view from what Daryl sees in this corpse to what Carol sees. Carol projects her memories of suffering onto it, enabling her long-awaited moment of liberation. The scene obviously prioritizes Carol's needs and emotions: even though she swings at the corpse five or six times, the viewer only sees her target twice. Daryl stands by for assistance, more unsettled by the violence erupting from this emotional woman than by any zombie in the series. Carol's violent "hate-mourning" for her husband enacts Freud's release discussed earlier: she is free of his memory and his constraint, and her destruction of his corpse places that action into her hands. Like Andrea's apology to Amy, the destruction of the zombie gives her one last chance to perform the resistance to Ed of which she was incapable while he was alive.

Daryl acknowledges Carol's ownership of her husband's body and her need for violence when he hands her his ax. However, the group does not trust Andrea to do the same. When she refuses to move from her sister's side and protects her right to mourn by raising a gun to the living, the group, in so many words, suspects her of suffering from melancholia, unable to accept her sister's death and just as unable to put that death to rest with violence against the body. They discuss her as a "situation," claiming "We need to deal with it": she is not following the rules under which *not* killing the dead has become taboo. Andrea fulfills her obligation to both the living and the dead, however, handling the "situation" just as required because time, exposure, and community have re-taught her what death is.

The transformation of lost loved ones into walkers causes some other survivors—notably, those more isolated—to stagnate. They either refuse to mourn altogether or refuse to adapt mourning to the new necessity of violence. Freud assigns to mourning the following task: "reality-testing has revealed that the beloved object no longer exists, and demands that the libido as a whole sever its bonds with that object," a long, arduous, and painful task.[17] Mourning involves letting go and finding a replacement love object. Melancholia, on the other hand, is the inability to break that bond, thereby maintaining both the dead and the living in psychological stasis. When Rick meets Morgan, he and his son have already lost their wife/mother. During the first night of attack, she comes to the house, and Morgan's son cries, "It's her!" suggesting that he still associates the walker who resembles his mother to the living person. Both father and son revert to a state of minor denial as they avoid visual, let alone violent, contact with the walker. In other words, they have not found a way to mourn the woman they loved in either the revised violent fashion or even in the old reverent one; they are unable to adapt to new rules, stuck in an isolated state that preserves old feelings and beliefs.

It is the act of raising a gun to the woman he loves that stays the hand of Morgan from freeing them both, however. Fittingly, in her study on the pain of grief, Nancy Berns refers to these kind of melancholics as "the walking wounded," who "believe closure exists, and who want closure, but think they cannot obtain it.... They feel less than whole because they lack closure."[18] Morgan understands why he and his son are stuck, and it takes the presence of an outsider, another member of this new society filled with walkers, to push him slowly towards attempting violence against his walker wife. Freud writes that "in melancholia a series of individual battles for the object begins, in which love and hatred struggle with one another, one to free the libido from the object, the other to maintain the existing libido position against the onslaught."[19] We see Morgan fight this battle in a painful scene in which he aims his gun several times at his wife. Despite the literal onslaught of walkers, his wife among them, Morgan's inability to destroy her speaks to his libido's failure to give up the object in the face of reality, despite his apparent knowledge of that reality. Though he takes promising steps towards mourning and closure in season one—accepting guns and ammo from Rick and showing an investment in teaching his son to shoot—we learn in season three that his ultimate failure to shoot his undead wife costs him the loss of his son and his sanity and turns him into an unstable and dangerous recluse incapable of participating in the developing society.

For melancholics like Morgan, the memory of the walker as a person becomes a curse rather than a blessing, preventing the living from moving beyond the danger in which the undead place them. What they need is a little violence. Perhaps the barn full of walkers on Hershel's farm can best be described as a container of concentrated melancholia, opened only to enact a concentrated form of this violence. When Shane calculatingly shoots a walker in each of its vital organs in order to prove to Hershel that it is not alive, Hershel's expression of pain testifies to the endurance of his psychological connection: he reacts as if he were shot himself. Shane breaks the ultimate taboo of the past in his injury of the dead in front of those who love them: a cruelty to the memory of the person and to the survivor forced to watch violent transformation from animate to object. When told of his daughter Beth's collapse in the episode, "Nebraska," Hershel acknowledges the cause: she should have been mourning her mother. "I robbed her of that.... Annette had been dead long ago, and I was feeding a rotting corpse." Hershel had been sustaining the undead in the barn just as he had been sustaining his lost loved ones in his own psyche, feeding those corpses with his denial and false hope. Violence, in this case, not only puts the walker to final rest, but initiates a process by which melancholia is broken, regardless of how painful that action is. When the walkers burst from the barn, the scene becomes a massacre as they trickle through the doors. The shooters line up, shoulder to shoulder, in more or less the same manner in which they stand before the graves they later dig, with one key difference: the funeral service is peaceful, calm, and somber, and without extreme sorrow. The shooting, on the other hand, is performed with intense emotion, the participants shouting in shock and anger at first, then crying and wailing, visibly crumbling to pieces as their act of violence itself has replaced any other central act of mourning. The moment of violence becomes the funeral; that is when they grieve.

Grieving-violence, then, prioritizes the act of survival, allowing for reflection only afterwards. In their introduction to a book on the politics of loss and the effect of mourning on the community, David Eng and David Kazanjian write that "as soon as the question 'What is lost?' is posed, it invariably slips into the question 'What remains?' That is, loss is inseparable from what remains, for what is lost is known only by what remains of it, by how these remains are produced, read and sustained."[20] Changes in rituals have little bearing on the dead or undead themselves—leaving aside the ongoing discussion about zombie subjectivity—but instead have a profound effect on those who survive them and how they process, remember, and pass on the existence of lost loved ones. The zombie narrative in particular places emphasis on survivors over lost community members, partially because survivors only survive by destroying those lost friends and neighbors. In "Wildfire," Lori Grimes insists on the importance of closure for the survivors after the walker attack: "We haven't had a minute to hold on to anything of our old selves. We need time to mourn, and we need to bury our dead. It's what people do." Dale stresses a similar re-prioritization in describing his wife's death to Andrea. "Did I ever mention how I lost my wife?" he asks, placing all the emphasis and the action on the survivor rather than the deceased.[21] Stressing the connection between selfhood, history, mourning, and humanity, Lori and Dale say little about the dead themselves. Death has more to do with the living than ever.

Restructuring the Living Remains:
A Funeral Fight for the Last Good Man

Participation in rituals as well as shared reconfigurations of rules, customs, and taboos create and shape a cohesive group and its new structure as it decides, through trial and error in this transitional period, what the new walker-infested world will look like. Already, discussion about the consistency of burial practices in the first season leads to debates over authority and responsibility to custom. In disposing of the dead after the first major walker attack, Glenn makes a clear distinction between the bodies of people the group knew and the bodies of strangers, despite the danger and abjection of both categories. As a precaution, several members, most vocally Daryl, want to burn the bodies to dispose of anything that could possibly resurrect. But, just as Quigley describes, Glenn finds the process of burning to be violent and disturbing for a body he and the others once knew as human. "This is for geeks," he says of the fire, classifying the walkers as freakish, grotesque, and monstrous. Recognizing "his people," even through their zombie transformations, Glenn and several others still see a body left to mourn. Daryl asks, "What's the difference? They're all infected." Already a system of segregation between strangers and members of their own community has begun to form on top of the segregation between the living and the (un)dead. "Our people go over there. We don't burn them, we bury them. Understand? Our people go in that row over there," Glenn repeats, laying out a clear and solid rule for the entire community with the pronoun "we" and asking for verification that the others understand.

While Glenn continues to direct him in the placement of bodies, Daryl says to Rick, already the authority figure, "I still think it's a mistake not burning these bodies. It's what we said we'd do. Right? Burn 'em all?" Daryl prioritizes spoken constructions of the law and the new customs, perhaps a mistake in a period during which the rules are still in flux. Yet, Daryl attributes to custom the ability to maintain a stable and orderly society. When Rick answers, "There are no rules," he contradicts himself by claiming some influence in saying it. The sanctity of violence for something as volatile as mourning requires a particularly sensitive amount of authority in order to avoid dangerous mistakes while also offering comfort: authority over the dead has become authority over the living. Rick, in short, underestimates the importance of establishing normalcy in his statement. Mourning practices, particularly the incorporation of something so condemned as violence, have the power to establish rules and instill normalcy. When Lori responds to Rick, "That's a problem," referring to the lack of rules, she justifies her plea for mourning with, "It's what people do." With the whole community gathered around her like children in this scene, she uses their vulnerability in the face of loss to defend humanity, order, and community cohesion. At this juncture, they need rules to know what people do, to verify that they *are* still people. In *The Walking Dead*, Lori calls on the power of custom to define the dead (and, by default, the walker) in relation to "people," and how the dead will be treated according to that relationship, in order to begin reconstruction of the social and political boundaries of her community.

Thus, the questionable area of alive/dead/undead necessitates new kinds of exclusions, new definitions, and new rituals. "The emergence of zombies represents a violent rupture in the understanding of how the universe works," says Greg Pollock in regards to the ecological effects of the walking dead, "but it does not bring time to an end; the bodiliness of the zombie, as opposed to something like the ghost, holds together the paradox of an apocalypse within time, this world as the next world."[22] In other words, adherence to past or temporary customs is not a viable option in this permanently changed world. *The Walking Dead* concentrates management of both loss and remains—to return to Eng and Kazanjian's terminology—on the vehicle of the corpse: the body of the zombie becomes a tool for closure (loss) and also for restructuring rituals and rules (remains). In the second season, we see these new customs beginning to solidify when, after the slaughter of the barn walkers, Maggie asks Glenn, "So what happens now?" and Glenn explains their ritual with confidence. "We bury the ones we love and burn the rest," Andrea clarifies, maintaining that segregation through death. When she suggests a funeral for Sophia—for Carol's sake, T-Dog speaks up, "Yeah, we *all* want that" ("Nebraska"). Mourning has again become a community activity as well as a personal one, with little detection of guilt or uncertainty in regards to the violence involved in the process or what led to it.

I began with an example of the idyllic but obsolete funeral service given for Otis after his dubious death, and I will close with an example that shows the incorporation of new customs near the end of the second season. The mourning ritual for Dale, who has stood for morality and human values for the duration of the first two seasons, involves a service much like Otis's, with kind words and reflections that highlight his memory and his contribution to the community. This scene of tranquility, however, is simultaneously overlaid with other scenes of characters violently but calmly killing walkers, while background music pervades both scenes. Rick's eulogy, in which he highlights the broken group and that "the best way to honor [Dale] is to unbreak it," narrates both the funeral and the hunt, which is itself devoid of language. Thus, the violence has become embedded into the mourning practices without comment, but, in this instance, the degree of violence oversteps the bounds of merely "putting down a walker." This mourning is part revenge, part identity reformation, part communal bonding, all endorsed by Rick's account of Dale's last enduring words of humanity. Yet, the scene of violence has become more unsettling than many of the previous, more practical walker-slayings, as the group surrounds the walkers when they are down. Kicking them furiously, they enact hate-mourning reminiscent of a hate-crime, which is hidden behind the guise of ritual, necessity, and the new customs. Rick will have this same reaction in the episode "Say the Word" in season three when Lori dies without even the remnants of kind words that attempt to give life the meaning that Patricia demands for Otis: his mourning takes the pure form of aggression and violence as he dives back into the zombie-infested prison, solo and with barely a word. Violence has become the only meaning to be had.

The mourning group in season two is notably overseen by Shane, *The Walking Dead's* figure of increasing self-destruction and barbarity. "In the end, he was talking about losing our humanity," Rick says, repeating Dale's words. Yet, it is no coincidence that this double-sided funeral is for Dale in particular, made possible perhaps only because he is dead. Dale, as the spokesman for "humanity," carried with that phrase an adherence to the "old ways"—to the old versions of right and wrong, of ethical judgments and punishments, and of certain strained standards of human decency—that leans dangerously close to Morgan's inability to shoot his wife. Dale himself performs very little violence, even against walkers, despite his normal post on watch-duty. The extreme violence required in his own death may perhaps have been something he, himself, could not perform, as even Rick struggles and leaves it to the gravedigger.[23] Not only the dead must be mourned but also a past way of life, and melancholia for that life is a considerable threat that must be dealt with just as violently. The violence of mourning now structures the community's norms for achieving closure and fulfilling its duty to the dead, allowing it to embrace violence in an official, sanctioned capacity. At the same time, the necessity of violence has begun to escalate beyond the practical and the reverent in this funeral scene, becoming an outlet for the group's aggression in their new society. The menacing walker has replaced the loved one, complicating the fragile distinction between the necessity of violence for closure and the choice of violence for pleasure or control: between what remains and what rests in pieces.

Notes

1. Žižek makes this suggestion when he writes, "Mourning is a kind of betrayal, the second killing of the (lost) object, while the melancholic subject remains faithful to the

lost object, refusing to renounce his or her attachment to it." Žižek, "Melancholy and the Act," 658.

2. Ariès, "The Hour of Our Death," 41.

3. Larkin also mentions this in *"Res Corporealis,"* 22.

4. Freud, *On Murder, Mourning, and Melancholia*, 68.

5. Boss, *Ambiguous Loss*, 8–9.

6. Brooks, "Closure, Limited," 28.

7. Ibid., 22.

8. Kristeva, *Powers of Horror*, 2.

9. Ibid., 3.

10. Botting, "A-ffect-less," 187.

11. Quigley, *The Corpse*, 12. Hertz agrees that the preparation of the body aims to filter the realism of the loved body as it transitions into death, claiming that "the aim of embalmment is precisely to prevent the corruption of the flesh and the transformation of the body into a skeleton; cremation, on the other hand forestalls the spontaneous alteration of the corpse with a rapid and almost complete destruction." Hertz, "A Contribution," 201.

12. Kristeva, *Powers of Horror*, 3.

13. Bataille, "Death," 244.

14. This, rather than saving the dead body from the zombie inhabitant, is Daryl's first priority, despite his comment about wanting to be put down in the case of his own death. We see this when he decides to leave a zombie found hanging in a tree in the second season as it is, as punishment for cowardly suicide. Curiously, in this concept of punishment, he again suggests some thread of consciousness and subjectivity binding the dead and the undead. With the same purpose of protecting the living, he shoots Dale, as well.

15. Carl will later say the same line—"She's my mom. I'll do it."—in reference to shooting Lori when she dies in the third season episode, "Killer Within." This further solidifies the bond of closure and responsibility between the deceased and the mourner and is seen as an act of protection and tribute rather than revenge or aggression.

16. Matt Barone, "'The Walking Dead' Recap: The Not-So-Calm Before The Zombie Storm," *Complex*, March 12, 2012, http://www.complex.com/pop-culture/2012/03/the-walking-dead-recap-better-angels. Barone uses this term in his article in reference to the simultaneous scenes of Dale's funeral and hunting walkers at the end of season two.

17. Freud, *On Murder, Mourning, and Melancholia*, 204.

18. Berns, *Closure*, 40.

19. Freud, *On Murder, Mourning, and Melancholia*, 216.

20. Eng and Kazanjian, "Introduction: Mourning Remains," 2.

21. Unable to move beyond the state of mourning his wife, Dale remained static and angry until finding replacement love objects in these two sisters, thereby acknowledging the pain and danger of melancholia in order to convince Andrea to let her sister go.

22. Pollock, "Undead is the New Green," 179.

23. When Dale is attacked by a walker in "Judge, Jury, Executioner," the group is able to put it down but not to save Dale from painful mortal wounds. Andrea, seeing his suffering, calls for someone to do something, and Rick raises a gun to Dale's head, but it is finally Daryl who is able to pull the trigger, with the words, "Sorry, brother." Interestingly, a similar scene occurs at the end of the season three episode, "This Sorrowful Life," when Daryl comes across his own brother-turned-walker. In this scene, mourning and violence are conflated as he hesitates only for a moment to cry before stabbing his brother in the head more times than necessary.

Roadside "Vigil" for the Dead

Cannibalism, Fossil Fuels and the American Dream

Christine Heckman

RICK: Is this real? Am I here? Wake up! ["Days Gone Bye"].
SHANE: You crazy driving this wailing bastard?
GLENN: Sorry. Got a cool car ["Tell It to the Frogs"].

The automobile is simultaneously one of the most intimate and one of the most public expressions of American identity. Intertwined with memories of childhood past, adolescent stunts, and workaday grinds, the car realizes romantic American rugged individualism in mechanized, industrialized form. Break down the word into its linguistic parts—auto ("self") mobile ("movement")— it means self-movement. But does the auto really propel itself? Are Americans, by association, autonomous?

From the moment Henry Ford famously married the idea of the automobile with mass production, twentieth-century American identity was born. The machines rolling off his mechanized assembly lines shaped and reflected the visage and psyche of the United States. But the automobile made demands, including an entire infrastructure and economy to support this expression of mass individualism. Roads built to accommodate automotive movement cannibalized the landscape and directed (and constrained) mobility. Originally developed for military purposes, the interstate system enabled the very existence of suburbia. The car became a twentieth-century expression of nineteenth-century westward movement and wove itself into the DNA of Americans; it is an integral part of most major life events from cradle to grave. We have become imprisoned by our own Manifest Destiny, however, because one taken-for-granted assumption makes possible this bedrock strand of American identity: unfettered access to fossil fuels, specifically oil. Petrochemical consumption has set in motion a cycle of demand that defines American identity—individual and national.

The Walking Dead (seasons one and two) expresses anxiety about the way in which American identity is simultaneously defined and threatened by a capitalist economic system that runs on fossil fuels, particularly petrochemicals. This essay briefly traces how consumption has historically defined Americans, specifically in terms of the socioeconomic mobility culminating in the middle-class "American dream"—our perceived "unalienable" birthright.[1] First, I will outline the way in which *The Walking Dead* utilizes zombie lore to tie the enslavement, and ultimately consumption, of African Americans to the early American economy. Then, I will chart the ways in which *The Walking Dead* gestures toward the cannibalization of Native American resources, both land and people, in its use of specific vehicles, roads, and Native American histories. In these cases, the economic demands of the white middle class dehumanize, and then consume, both African and Native Americans. Finally, I will discuss how American consumption has evolved, turning a ravenous eye toward the subsequent capture and harnessing of "undead" resources—fossil fuels—to service U.S. economic growth. Access to oil has now become increasingly fraught, however, and the very resource that has enabled American global expansion now threatens to undermine the viability of socioeconomic mobility on which the dream of middle-class American identity rests.

Our Zombie Heritage

> RICK: There are no niggers anymore. No dumb-as-shit-inbred-white-trash fools either. Only dark meat and white meat ["Guts"].

Brought over to the Americas from West and Central Africa, the "zombie concept is essentially one of enslavement by magic, be it of the body or of the soul."[2] This "enslavement," however, is the manipulation of a "supernatural" type of undead, as the "term, nzambi, also designates the creator god of many Bantu peoples. If the dead are given his name, it is because they have acquired superhuman properties."[3] The zombie, then, is a figure with "superhuman properties," harnessed and controlled through magical means. In this context, the zombie is a distorted personification of the fear of enslavement by an economic system or institution; for African Americans, this economic institution was, literally, slavery.[4] Fast forward four hundred years, and Americans are feeling the anxiety of perceived economic and political servitude, particularly in the wake of the attacks of September 11, 2001, and the sustained recession due to the economic collapse of 2008.

Like the zombie, Africans—including both those who had been transported and those subsequently born within the Americas—were held in bondage, traded as chattel, and formed the foundation of colonial and early

American economic growth: "Made to work like a robot in the fields ... the zombie may serve as a watchman, keep the books, steal crops or money for its master, or be rented out or sold to others."[5] While white landowners reaped the benefits of this slave labor, many Americans to this day fail to acknowledge the role forced servitude played in building and sustaining the economic viability of a burgeoning American middle class. This denial permeates popular political discourse, exhumed and resuscitated as recently as the 2012 presidential election. On one side stands the belief that those who are rich should not be penalized for their success because they did it "on their own." The other side argues that no entrepreneur in the U.S. is completely autonomous in his or her success; indeed, the public infrastructure is already in place that enables that success. Despite denials, however, American identity has evolved in part due to the economic and cultural contributions of African Americans, which have been consumed by mainstream America. Jazz, rap, and hip hop all come to mind as twentieth-century instances of African American cultural exploitation and cannibalization through corporatization.

In *The Walking Dead,* the relationship between Rick Grimes and Morgan Jones illustrates the shaping influence of culture and race. Morgan, who is African American, passes on the new world's "cultural knowledge," which is comprised of rules and survival strategies. Morgan also exhibits characteristics similar to those of the lone African American, Ben, in George Romero's 1968 *Night of the Living Dead*. Both Ben and Morgan hole up in houses belonging to others; neither of them knows the previous owners. Rick, however, has "knowledge" of the former owners of Morgan's shelter. From the perspective of critical race theory, whereby "whiteness" simultaneously contains and owns capital, Ben's and Morgan's lack of power, juxtaposed with Rick's efficacy, illustrates the reasons for Rick's successful escape.[6] His power is predicated on the socioeconomic worth of his whiteness, which, in turn, is constructed on Morgan's object position: "The slave status of most African Americans ... resulted in their being objectified as property."[7] Neither Ben nor Morgan carries Rick's intrinsic worth—whiteness; recall that the Constitution originally valued slaves at ⅗ of a person.[8] African Americans in both *Night of the Living Dead* and *The Walking Dead* are not subjects; they are objects, having been transformed into chattel. Ben seeks shelter in the basement—the foundation—of the farmhouse, but when he seeks to emerge of his own volition, transgressing his existence as property, he is mistaken for a threat, a zombie, and is eliminated.

Morgan and his son do not die; they merely disappear from the narrative—but not before an important sequence that depicts Rick and Morgan each trying to kill a zombie. Rick parts with Morgan and heads to the park where he previously encountered the Bicycle Girl zombie. When the viewer next sees Morgan, he has positioned himself in an upper room of the "borrowed" house where he and his son have taken shelter. What follows is a sequence alternately cutting between Rick's and Morgan's individual attempts at killing their respective targets. Armed with the information he receives from Morgan, Rick succeeds in killing the Bicycle Girl with a single bullet to the head. Morgan, however, falters, and when he finally gets his wife in his sights, he breaks down and is unable to kill her. Even with his "cultural knowledge" of this world, he remains unable to sever the bond keeping him in this house, a house in which he is essentially a squatter. Morgan's inability to kill his dead wife, as we find out in season three, leads to the death of his son, who is bitten by his mother. Rick, on the other hand, succeeds, having absorbed the information he needs from Morgan. As Rick says later, when he encounters Morgan again, "You found me, you fed me, you told me what was happening. You saved me" ("Clear").

The next scene begins with the squad car driving down the road; Rick begins the search for his family. This difference in Rick's and Morgan's outcomes seems to lie in socioeconomic mobility. Rick is dressed in full uniform, a personification of social power, embodying middle-class white privilege— and he is able to move forward. Conversely, as of the end of season two, Morgan and Duane have disappeared. Morgan profoundly influences Rick's subsequent decisions, but the "cultural knowledge" Rick gleans from Morgan is not without its traps. While Morgan's information initially helps Rick to survive, it is also the reason Rick ends up face-to-face with a throng of zombies in Atlanta, where Morgan had told him a refugee camp was established. The very knowledge on which his survival is predicated also acts as the very influence that leads him to greatest danger.

The Morgan/ Rick relationship illustrates fundamental aspects of American economic identity that are seldom acknowledged. Whites "consume" African Americans as commodities, marginalize them as full citizens, exploit them for their labor, and absorb them into "mainstream" middle-class, white culture. *The Walking Dead* dramatizes the process by which, until well into the twentieth century, many African Americans were either marginalized (T-Dog has hardly any substantive autonomous action in the first two seasons and is abruptly killed in the third), eradicated (Jacqui chooses her own death at the CDC), or processed and then "consumed" through the dominant white culture (Morgan gives Rick the knowledge he needs, vanishes, then reappears in a clearly mentally unsound state).

While America built its economic power on the backs of African slaves, the young union simultaneously developed in yet another way: westward expansion. And discussion of American expansion and Manifest Destiny cannot take place without acknowledging the dispossession of Native Americans. Significantly, the vehicles that figure prominently in *The Walking Dead* are named for nineteenth-century peoples and events tied to westward movement (primarily Native American tribes). Dale's RV is a Winnebago Chieftain, Carol and Ed's vehicle is a Jeep Cherokee, and Shane drives a Jeep Wrangler. Shane's Wrangler conveys at least two meanings. First, a wrangler is a "person in charge of horses or other livestock," evoking the western frontier; second, it also designates "a person engaged in a lengthy and complicated quarrel or dispute."[9] Shane embodies both of these attributes: physically strong, he feels he is "in charge of" the group, particularly Lori and Carl, but he also serves as the single strongest antagonist to Rick. Like Morgan's relationship to Rick, Shane is in large part the reason Rick survived the outbreak while he was in the hospital; on the other hand, it was arguably Shane's inattentive bravado that led to Rick's injury in the first place. Ultimately, Shane transforms from Rick's lifesaver to his most immediate threat. Like Morgan, Shane's relationship to Rick as both benefactor and antagonist reflects the fraught relationship, dependent and antagonistic, of the United States—specifically the American middle class—to oil.

The make of Dale's vehicle—a Winnebago—references a Native American tribe. And Carol and Ed's Jeep Cherokee is named after one of the tribes most clearly linked to the American Southeast, significant not the least because *The Walking Dead* is set in and around Atlanta, Georgia. Geography and history are crucially linked here, since the economy of the Southeast is rooted not only in the institution of slavery but also in the economic gain from moving Native Americans off of the land. While in the world of *The Walking Dead* the entire world is assumed to have fallen to the zombie apocalypse, the audience only sees the narrative unfolding in this very specific geographic area. The series thus refracts the way in which, although economic health is arguably tied to the global nature of economic oil dependence, most people feel these repercussions on a regional level. In the world of *The Walking Dead*, the zombie is partially the personification of peoples killed and digested to build the U.S. economy, the foundation of the middle-class American dream. This consumptive step facilitating economic growth is articulated by Osteen's interpretation of social mobility as represented by cars in the film *Gun Crazy,* "whereby other humans are merely carcasses serving a cold, hedonistic lifestyle in which ... 'two people[s] [are] dead just so we can live without working.'"[10]

Life Is a Highway

> LORI: We got to turn around ... the highway's back there ["Beside the Dying Fire"].

The allusions to Native Americans encompass more than just the vehicles of the series. The use of roads is bundled in this narrative of socioeconomic identity. *The Walking Dead* nests the relationship of movement and stasis to life and death, respectively. While the characters drive vehicles named for Native American tribes that are either indigenous or connected to the Southeast, the *way* in which they move is equally tied to this history. The first half of season two revolves around the search for twelve-year-old Sophia, the daughter of Carol, the (remaining) owner of the Jeep Cherokee. As the caravan flees Atlanta, it is stopped by a blown radiator hose on the Winnebago, which is caused by an attempt to maneuver the caravan through what is essentially an automotive graveyard on the highway; they are physically blocked by a huge traffic jam of "dead" cars. When the group is overrun by a horde of walkers, Sophia panics and flees as the rest of the group hides under the dead vehicles on the highway ("What Lies Ahead").

During the significantly entitled episode, "Cherokee Rose," Daryl searches for Sophia. Instead, he finds a "Cherokee Rose," presents it to Carol, and recounts the story of the Trail of Tears, the forced movement of Cherokees off ancestral lands. This movement caused the deaths of over four thousand Cherokees, including women and children, all in service of the American government's laying claim to Cherokee land.[11] On the surface, the allusion to the Trail of Tears is connected to Carol's pain over Sophia's loss. There is, however, a deeper link between the forced exodus of the Cherokee Nation and that of *The Walking Dead*'s characters. Native Americans' identities have always been linked to their ancestral lands; this land represented their past and ensured their collective futures. The European settlers and their descendants did not view land in the same way. Howard Zinn points out that, as far back as the Massachusetts Bay Colony, European settlers—John Winthrop among them—argued that, since the Native Americans had failed to "subdue" the land, the tribes had only a "natural," not a "civil," right to the land.[12] This declaration became the justification for annexing Native American lands, as a "natural" right possessed no legal standing.[13] When the Cherokees were ordered off their land, however, they lost ties to their future, both as a result of lands lost and children lost. Similarly, the forced exodus endured by the survivors of *The Walking Dead* costs them their own futurity, symbolized by the loss and subsequent death of Sophia. The fears about a recognizable future expressed in *The Walking Dead* are typical within the apocalyptic genre; in this instance, Sophia's flight, subsequent demise, and ultimate effect on the group within the context of an automotive "Trail of Tears" reflect a loss of faith in those structures so integral and basic to Americans' collective identity and to their future: mobility, oil, and capitalism.

In *The Walking Dead*, survival requires the characters to have an unlimited ability to move. Their automobiles serve two main purposes: as makeshift homes and as a means of transport. While the characters seek stability, death literally comes to them if they stay in one place for too long, not the least because American identity is inextricably intertwined with the automobile: "our emotional and cultural drives have become so blended and confused and so intimately involved with spatial activity that moving and moving again have become almost second nature."[14] When the characters give in to their nostalgic feelings for a time and place rooted in the past, which is arguably a myth, even an illusion, death creeps up on them, and they fall prey to a zombie attack: "the loss of their auto [mobility] adumbrates the loss of liberty and often the loss of life."[15] If the survivors aren't mobile, they cease to be.

The cornerstone of the automobile-turned-home arrangement is, of course, Dale's Chieftain Winnebago, the "symbolic power" of which "lies in its representation as a commodity identified with its owner."[16] Exemplary father figure, Dale stands guard with his binoculars on top of the Winnebago, sitting in a lawn chair shaded by a beach umbrella with a shotgun poised in his lap. The incongruous image is an overt statement: Dale is the "chief" and the "keeper" of the middle-class way of life that affords some creature comforts (like retirement), and he defends himself against anyone who might threaten his perched position. Likewise, the Chieftain, utilitarian and worn, nevertheless possesses an interior warmth because it is a home on wheels and carries with it many of the closest physical echoes of what a middle-class American home would ideally include: a kitchenette with appliances, beds, a dinette area, and a small bathroom. Both Dale and the Chieftain are well-worn nostalgic reminders of some mythical moment when father and home conjured images of safety and comfort.

Dale espouses, though, a view of humanity that has outlived its usefulness in this new world order. As a rift forms in the group, particularly throughout the second season, two distinct worldviews emerge: those who strive to hang on to their ideas of humanity (which the characters seem to equate with democracy) and those who will do anything to survive, even if it means sacrificing their former sense of democratic selfhood. The conflict contains a very similar sentiment to the debates over the existence and role of the Department of Homeland Security: Americans need to be alive to enjoy and defend Constitutionally-defined freedoms, but increasing surveillance, which arguably increasing safety, erodes the very liberties Americans long to preserve. In the world of *The Walking Dead,* after Dale is disemboweled by a zombie, Rick articulates Dale's crucial role within the group, which is one of conscience. He says:

Dale could sure get under your skin…. That kind of honesty is rare and brave…. I couldn't always read him, but he could always read us…. He knew things about us … the truth. Who we really are ["Better Angels"].

"Dale could sure get under your skin" intimates that Dale and his beliefs became a part of the group; there was a common truth he held to be "self-evident," and each and every person in the group shared this common characteristic. Rick states: "Whenever I'd make a decision I'd look at Dale, he'd be looking back at me with that look he had" ("Better Angels"). Dale was a resource to consult, as either a "chief" or a "sage." Indeed, the implicit connection between Dale and a foundational document, such as the U.S. Constitution or the Declaration of Independence, is evident in the line, "I couldn't always read him, but he could always read us … he knew things about us … the truth. Who we really are" ("Better Angels"). The ideals Dale represented have been gutted, however, by relentless consumption of people and resources, reflecting Americans' anxiety about a potential "gutting" of individual freedom and socioeconomic mobility. The last act of Dale's Winnebago is to save Rick and Carl, but the vehicle—the last remaining vestige of "home," the middle-class American dream—has been breached, infected, and destroyed.

Master Becomes Servant

> GLENN: Maybe we should go back. There's an interstate bypass.
> DALE: We can't spare the fuel ["What Lies Ahead"].
> RICK: You're staying, this isn't a democracy anymore ["Beside the Dying Fire"].

What ultimately constrains the characters' movements, threatening stasis and death, is an escalating anxiety about American dependence on fossil fuels. The American dream of most recent memory was manufactured and mass-produced in the industrial age; it is characterized by exponential socioeconomic mobility fueled by petroleum and is materialized in the growth of the American middle class over the past two hundred years. Without oil and access to it, many of the foundational assumptions about middle-class life begin to disintegrate, particularly those surrounding socioeconomic mobility. In "Noir's Cars," Mark Osteen points out: "The material gain encoded in cars, as Ken Mills notes, was thus 'directly connected to acquiring greater agency and social status.' … Exploiting these phenomena, some postwar writers turned road stories into a 'declaration of independence,' creating from highway narratives a 'broader vision of autonomy and mobility for all.'"[17] If the cars cannot move, however, the identity tied to them stagnates. Further, Americans identify themselves with the ideas of the Declaration of Independence and the Constitution, which have in turn been inextricably linked to capital; the degree to which one can be mobile and ultimately "free" depends on wealth. In fact, the U.S. government was created in large part so that property rights—property acquired from Native American tribes (i.e., "wealth")—could be protected.[18] The meanings of "independence," "freedom," and "wealth" have become so intertwined that they seem to be interchangeable; a threat to one is a threat to all and "[w]ealth ensures health, since capital and therefore the means to travel were the most effective (if not the only) preservative."[19] Americans' independence, then, is contingent upon the interdependence of "freedom" and "wealth"—and both of these ideals stand (and fall) on the material ground of oil.

The series illustrates this complex interdependence with the aptly-titled pilot episode, "Days Gone Bye," which opens as a police car drives into the camera's view from a distance. The car stops, and Rick Grimes gets out of the car with a fuel can in his hand and walks down to a deserted gas station littered with abandoned cars and trucks; some are overturned, some are broken, and some are rigged and fitted as makeshift shelters and homes. The vehicles congregate around this gas station as if it was the last bastion of safety and salvation. Clearly, people came to fuel up and flee the zombies; unfortunately, the gas station was out of fuel, as is evidenced by the sign that Rick passes nailed to a support that says, "No Gas." Even if the people who came here for gas had money, it was not the cash that had value; it was the oil. They could no longer access the fuel—the lifeblood—that would allow their cars to move, enabling them to flee death. The empty gas station serves as a trap by luring them with the hope of mobility (access to gas), trapping the refugees, and assimilating them into the horde bereft of autonomy.

The remnants of American middle-class existence litter the frame. The camera pans through the makeshift car camp from Rick's point of view, revealing close-up shots of baby dolls, laundry, and clothing. Among this wreckage are the mundane effects of everyday middle-class life, items packed into cars in the desperate hope of transporting a way of life. While these cars at some point "serve ... as symbols of social mobility and expanded identity," and even as "surrogate homes," they are now eerily abandoned.[20] They are immobile, and there is no human life within or around them. In these broken-down, broken-into, skeletal vehicles are the decayed remains of middle class mobility, a juxtaposition of what Susan Sontag describes as "unremitting banality and inconceivable terror."[21]

The Walking Dead starkly illustrates dwindling confidence in a future propelled by petroleum through its intertwined images of child, automobile, and zombie. While scavenging for gas, Rick's attention is captured by a sound, and he peers underneath a car to see a dirty, worn teddy bear and two small bunny-slippered feet. The chassis frames the feet and the teddy bear, an image that evokes memories of childhood innocence; at the same time, the girl is defined by the car. The shot "frames" conversation about human mobilities: physical (feet) and socioeconomic (cars). The scene continues, showing a girl's hand reaching down for the teddy bear, as if reclaiming possession of the child-hood memories it embodies. The girl is already dead, however, suggestive of a dead future, and Rick is compelled to shoot her squarely between the eyes, throwing her entire body back onto the parking lot asphalt, an area specifically designated for refueling cars.

This confrontation between Rick and the girl illuminates two essential points regarding the links among children, zombies, and a national identity dependent on oil-fueled capitalism. First, the zombies walk among us, and we can no longer distinguish them from the seemingly most innocent, from the "girl next door." Second, the ensuing insecurity indicated by the corruption even of children, the bedrock of futurity, undermines the most basic assump-tion of a capitalist economy: "It is important to note the often missed ... com-ponent of the capitalist phenomenological structuring of time: it presupposes that the world will remain roughly constant and unchanging. Without social stability (i.e., "security"), it is both impossible and futile to make plans about the future."[22] A society that is grounded in an oil-fueled capitalist economy is fundamentally insecure, however, which is why the characters of *The Walking Dead* believe they are facing the end of the world and struggle to make any plans for a future they suspect may be non-existent. Edwin Jenner, the CDC scientist, calls the zombie infection "our extinction event" ("TS-19"), reflecting the fear that, as long as the economy of the United States is based on fossil fuels, Americans face the threat of their own "extinction event."

There seems no future for those in the world of *The Walking Dead*, trying to survive among the wreckage of defunct, fuel-less machinery. Cars without their mobility are a liability. Osteen discusses this claim in the context of *film noir*, but the connection is applicable here as well, since *The Walking Dead's* characters are likewise "rob[bed] of the sense of sovereignty cars are designed to produce. They are now prisoners in their own car ... a Frankenstein's monster assembled from the prized technologies and ideologies of postwar America,"[23] an America that simply no longer exists.

Rick's search for gas in "Days Gone Bye" also presents one of the recurring questions confronting the group of survivors and, by proxy, the viewing audi-ence: "Where do we get more fuel?" Neither the characters nor the viewers can move—literally or figuratively—without gas. Rick must make himself vul-nerable by leaving the safety of his vehicle to find fuel. He not only endangers himself as an individual, but also what he represents—U.S. law and our authority as global "police." A threat to a uniformed Rick signifies an attack on the ideological structures he embodies as "the law." If immobile, the police car becomes a liability—a useless deathtrap; it symbolically places everything at risk—the individual person as well as the societal institutions from which the police car derives its meaning.

Even the military expression of the automobile—the army tank—becomes a sort of sarcophagus. Late in "Days Gone Bye," zombies envelop the tank as Rick takes shelter from almost certain death. The visual is claustrophobic; once again, Rick is enclosed in a vehicle that cannot move, that stifles. Expecting to find safety and shelter within a reinforced military vehicle, Rick finds only stagnation and death.

One could argue that this scene (among others) alludes to military involvement in "national interests" abroad in order to secure and stabilize countries and political regimes on which the U.S. oil supply depends. The U.S. military has suffered a good number of casualties over the last decade, due in large part to multiple, complicated, concurrent military engagements in parts of the world that have a stranglehold on the American oil supply. Arguably, these entanglements have set a global economic stage on which some nations and groups have become impoverished and enraged and, consequently, seek to undermine that which they perceive fuels their plight. Some also contend that the United States is slowly becoming a military state—the establishment of the Department of Homeland Security, the Patriot Act, increasing surveillance, tracking of finances and movements—and that the "men in the white hats" of the twentieth century, along with the archetype of the truth-and-justice-seeking cowboy of the nineteenth century, no longer exist. Others argue that escalating militarization is leading to a death of the very ideals, the very "truths," that "we hold ... to be self-evident."[24] Again, this is reflected in *The Walking Dead*, where Rick's idea of refuge—the tank—becomes an empty coffin. Even as Rick defends himself against the zombie soldier, the gunshot reverberates in the tank chamber, causing Rick disorienting and excruciating pain. Extricating ourselves from this cycle may, as in this instance, prove to be painfully resonant.

Each of the first two seasons of *The Walking Dead* ends with the fallout created by a lack of fuel. The first season culminates in an encounter at the CDC headquarters in Atlanta as the survivors seek shelter and, ultimately, answers. On arrival, the group faces the locked-down and barred doors of the eerily silent and seemingly deserted facility. As the infected corpses close in on them, Rick hurls himself against the door, yelling: "I know you're in there. I know you can hear me. Please, we're desperate. We've got women and children, no food, hardly any gas left, please. You're killing us! You're killing us" ("TS-19"). It is interesting to note the progression of terms in this plea: "women and children," "food," and "gas." The most important items in a list like this, which is essentially an argument, are placed at the end: rhetorically, "gas" has been given the position of greatest import. Rick's desperation, moreover, is in stark contrast to his previously-expressed faith in the institution of the CDC: "If there's any government left—any structure at all—they'd protect the CDC at all costs, wouldn't they? I think it's worth a shot. Shelter, protection" ("Wildfire"). Every other "truth that [he] holds to be self-evident,"[25] truths that comprise his world and his position within it, has disintegrated before his eyes. But he clings to the belief that the "powers that be" would have seen fit to protect a governmental institution of scientific innovation established to preserve and protect American health and well-being.

Unfortunately for Rick and the group, what appears to be scientific salvation is simply a mirage. They spend the night in the CDC, hosted by the single remaining scientist, Edwin Jenner, a name that invokes the ghost of Edward Jenner, pioneer of modern immunology who developed the smallpox vaccine. He treats them to a host of creature comforts from their former life: hot showers, hot food, alcohol, lights, air conditioning, warm and clean beds, and a sense of security. Too soon, however, the group learns that the CDC is within hours of "facility-wide decontamination":

> DALE: That clock is counting down. What happens at zero?
> JENNER: The basement generators—they run out of fuel ["TS-19"].

This exchange prompts Shane, Rick, T-Dog, and Glenn to search the basement for fuel, where they find a graveyard of empty barrels. Jenner explains:

> I've been in the dark almost a month.... The power grid. Ran out of juice. The world runs on fossil fuel, I mean, how stupid is that?! You know what this place *IS?!* We protected the public from very nasty stuff ... stuff you don't want getting out! *EVER!* In the event of a catastrophic power failure and terrorist attack, for example, HITs are deployed to prevent any organisms from getting out.... Sets the air on fire. No pain. An end to sorrow. Grief. Regret. Everything ["TS-19"].

The very institution that is charged with protecting the American way of life via science—specifically, the health and well-being of the physical body—is constructed on the contingency of oil availability. Without it, the mechanisms cannot function, and, ultimately, they cease to exist. The structure designed to protect Americans becomes a source of destruction of that very way of life.

The end of season two similarly confronts the scarcity of fuel. In "Beside the Dying Fire," the car Rick drives runs out of gas. The group stops in the middle of the road and argues over the choices they face. The pressure fractures the group, leading to Rick's announcement, "We're all infected." This revelation is a game-changing one: the firmly held belief that there is a difference between the "walkers" and the "living" proves to be an illusion. Their entire worldview—their identities as individuals, as a group—changes based on this information, and the revelation is precipitated by the pressure imposed by a dry fuel tank. Ultimately, this confrontation illustrates how American identity itself is fractured by foreign policies that pursue oil—policies that shape the economy as well as call into question the morality of America's actions. Everything halts, however, in a world without oil.

What Lies Ahead

> RICK: 125 miles. That's what lies ahead. And I'm trying hard not to lose faith ["What Lies Ahead"].

> LORI: We haven't had one minute to hang onto anything of our old selves. We haven't had time to mourn. We haven't had time to bury our dead. That's what people do" ["Wildfire"].

From the earliest days of European settlement, the United States has been a nation that consumes. Goods are consumed, land is consumed, labor is consumed, and people are consumed. "Everything is food for something else," observes Carl ("Secrets"). The American dream—the belief that individuals, through hard work and perseverance, can achieve a level of socioeconomic security—is the cornerstone of middle-class American identity. Movement, it has been argued, is part of the collective American psyche—movement prompted by Manifest Destiny and by the building of wealth on the acquisition of land and labor. The American dream proliferated in the twentieth century, in large part due to access to oil and fossil fuels.

But consuming fossil fuels, the consumption of the dead, in service of facilitating movement, has poisoned us. Our environment suffers: there is a growing body of evidence that we have altered our biological and environmental processes.[26] Like the snake oil salesmen of the nineteenth century, we have imbibed energy tonic and spread our way of life, through consumption, throughout the world. In doing so, we have infected ourselves with a communicable addiction to dead things—oil among them. Our identities as Americans are tied to gas-guzzling machines; the automobile is fueled by oil and drives the American dream. In our attempts to maintain an identity bound by oil, we have become slaves to it. From travel, to food, to foreign policy, we are losing our ability to define what fuel does for us. Instead, it dictates what we are able to do. Americans are stuck roadside, as Jenner might wryly observe, "out of gas."

Just as Rick wakes from his coma, so too are Americans waking from their individual and collective American dreams only to enter a sort of limbo, a vigil: wakefulness in the dark. Meanings of vigil conjure groups of people waiting in the dark, holding candles, illuminated with small "ripples" of light. Hope, represented by those flames, fuels these vigils, but too often fails to last. In "TS-19," Jenner identifies tiny, random lights in the brain of the infected victim before death as "a person's life. Experiences, memories. It's everything ... all those ripples of light is you. The thing that makes you unique and human" ("TS-19"). Rick watches intently—searching—and asks, "What is this? Some kind of vigil?" ("TS-19"). This individual vigil (Jenner's for his dead wife) allegorizes a cultural "vigil," in which the United States is losing its ability to access the source of its "ripples of light" and "the thing that makes [it] unique." Oil has fueled the American socioeconomic highway and has made the United States the dominant global economic power of the twentieth century. The very thing that has made the U.S. synonymous with economic and military power as well as with social and class mobility has also, however, acted as the catalyst for the nation's socioeconomic zombification.

NOTES

1. *U.S. Declaration of Independence.*
2. Ackermann and Gauthier, "The Ways and Nature of the Zombi," 469.
3. Ibid.
4. Boluk and Lenz, "Infection, Media, and Capitalism," 136.
5. Ackermann and Gauthier, "The Ways and Nature of the Zombi," 474.
6. African American slaves were considered property but could not own property. Whites, however, could legally own both land and slaves, so their "whiteness" served as intrinsic "wealth" and power through which they could hold objects of monetary value (slaves and land). Ladson-Billings and Tate quote Derrick Bell: "the concept of individual rights, unconnected to property rights, was totally foreign to these men [U.S. 'Founding Fathers']." Ladson-Billings and Tate, "Toward a Critical Race Theory," 53–54.
7. Ibid., 53.
8. U. S. Constitution, art. 1, sec. 2.
9. *Oxford Dictionaries Online*, s.v. "wrangler."
10. Osteen, "Noir's Cars," 187.
11. Cherokee Nation, "John Burnett's Story of the Trail of Tears."
12. Zinn, *A People's History of the United States*, 13.
13. Ibid.
14. Pierson, *The Moving American*, 93.
15. Osteen, "Noir's Cars," 185.
16. Ibid.
17. Ibid., 184.
18. Ladson-Billings and Tate, "Toward a Critical Race Theory," 53.
19. Boluk and Lenz, "Infection, Media, and Capitalism," 132.
20. Osteen, "Noir's Cars," 183.

21. Sontag, "The Imagination of Disaster," 224.
22. Datta and MacDonald, "Time for Zombies," 82.
23. Osteen, "Noir's Cars," 189.
24. *U. S. Declaration of Independence.*
25. Ibid.
26. Cederroth et al., "Soy, Phyto-oestrogens," 313.

Mass Shock Therapy for Atlanta's Psych(ot)ic Suburban Legacy

PAUL BOSHEARS

The norm for many today is to kill time in front of a variety of projection screens, whether TV sets, smart phones, computer monitors, and/or tablets. With this explosion of projection, is there not also a concomitant need to understand the therapeutic potential of mass media phenomena such as *The Walking Dead*? Over twenty years ago, Laurence Rickels stated: "TV's constant pull into a self-reflexive interior that is at once its topological surface realizes as 'liveness' or 'timelessness' the self-conscious paradox which the novel endlessly talked about from its origin on and which film would get around only to document."[1] The situation has become exacerbated with the predominance of the algorithms that make social media operational today: we are caught in the paradoxical situation of having more information available to us than ever before, but it is all sifted in ways that suggest the best mode of product placement. Algorithms such as Facebook's EdgeRank and GraphRank filter the level of novelty that can enter users' news feeds so that they feel like they are getting all the information they could want. The world thus comes to be a projection of what the user expects the world to be. Circumscribed and circumcised by this cleaving of the world into "Likes," the work of therapeutic mourning is significantly compromised.

The work of mourning begins with the recognition that we are haunted by our losses. Torn by conflicting feelings of satisfaction at the death of the one whom we cannot consume and the tenderness of our memories for the dead, we engage in projection, which, as Freud described it, displaces our internal dreaded desires onto the external world. These projections are, in themselves, modes of communication between the individual and those he or she mourns. They are modes of telecommunication. According to Rickels, "photography and film project and animate those phantoms which, in *Totem and Taboo*, haunt those who are unable to grant the dead proper burial."[2] We note

110

that, in the pilot episode of *The Walking Dead*, Rick Grimes is sure his wife is alive because the photo albums are missing. In the era of social media, typified by apps like Instagram, the purpose of photos is not to encapsulate and recall a morsel of the world as it actually is, but instead to heed the melancholic call that all memories be externalized rather than metabolized internally. Rick's inference seems to suggest that the only reason a photo album would go missing at the moment of the apocalypse is because the task of collecting photos is to fabricate a collective, totemic, photo archive. These missing photos (conspicuously absent throughout the seasons of *The Walking Dead*) are not in service to sharing the life that Rick and Lori have but are instead calls to witness the deaths that they are experiencing.

Propaganda and its development between and during the World Wars greatly enhanced the field of psychology as it tested the theories of psychoanalysis. The challenge to psychoanalysis became understanding the role of group thinking and the technologies influencing the crowd. Throughout the middle part of the twentieth century, a variety of techniques of harnessing the power of living in groups were developed within psychoanalysis and psychology. Following Rickels's proposition that Sigmund Freud's and Walter Benjamin's theories prove helpful in reading the mass media *socius*,[3] this essay will illuminate a hysterical vision of *The Walking Dead* as a means of group therapy. Atlanta's un-mourned losses have spread, infecting both the nation's domestic and foreign policies. Perhaps these sessions of *The Walking Dead* will awaken us to an understanding of why America is acting out in these ways.

Why Atlanta?

Why not New York, or Los Angeles? They are dream factories and the twin seats of the American cultural empire. Or, why not take the *Simpsons* route and set *The Walking Dead* in a generic "Springfield?" There are economic reasons to film in the state of Georgia: the state legislature passed generous tax programs benefitting film production companies, with no cap to these tax credits.[4] But, the economic incentive is also what motivated Marvel to film *The Avengers* (2012) in Cleveland (a city not only willing to shut down several parts of its downtown for twenty-four hours at a stretch, but generic enough to portray itself as both New York City and Stuttgart, Germany).[5] There must be something peculiar to Atlanta. The prevailing theories about this sprawling city are inconclusive: "Atlanta is not a city, it is a landscape," as Rem Koolhaas stated; it is *the* postmodern city, a center-less city.[6] Culturally, it is marked by its "noplaceness,"[7] and this unique blankness might help us understand why Atlanta and its environs are the location for *The Walking Dead*. Obviously,

Atlanta isn't 'empty; it just frequently appears to be. What do we see in this city's blank stare? Atlanta doesn't just play one on TV; this is a zombie town.

The City of Atlanta's motto, *Resurgens*, is a normative framework: time and again, the buildings, the flows of commerce, and the people are destroyed, and somehow the place comes back to life with a vengeance. Death drives the development of this place, not unlike the walkers' insatiable hunger. The city's first name, Terminus, is frequently attributed to the zero-mile marker of the Western Atlantic Railroad located at what is today called Five Points. But, there is a morbid layer at work here. The name also invokes the termination of William McIntosh, or *Tustunugee Hutke* (White Warrior), a prominent chief of the Creek Nation. On one register, the zombie figure affords us the opportunity to revisit our relationships to the un-mourned, those of our dead incapable of being mourned. In our perpetual battle against melancholia, the zombie shuffles towards us, reminding us of a primal scene of murder and unspeakable disappearance.

There would not be a City of Atlanta were it not for the Indian Springs Treaty of 1821 that McIntosh engineered. Because it was this instrument that alienated the entire Creek Nation from their maternal lands, McIntosh was condemned to death by the Creek Nation Council. Consider that scene: a nation alienated from the actual grounds of its origins, thrown into a state of anarchy by the actions of its slave-trading half-brother[8]; the murder of the traitorous McIntosh by the police force that he himself called into existence. Viewers of season three of *The Walking Dead* will recognize the birthplace of William McIntosh, present-day Senoia, Georgia, but known as Woodbury on that looking-glass version of our lives called TV. The Governor rules Woodbury through the careful manipulation of murderous spectacle while hiding his melancholic inability to let his daughter, Penny, die. A violent and tense period of ten years followed the execution of McIntosh, with the crescendo of this decade being the brief battle between the United States and the Creeks in 1836 that resulted in the removal of the Creek Nation to present-day Oklahoma. Daryl, in season two, tries to provide succor to Carol by sharing the fable of the Cherokee Rose, a Native American symbol for the tears of the mothers who lost their children on the Trail of Tears on the way to Oklahoma. These murderous plots by land speculators led to the creation of Terminus at the intersection of the two Creek Nation trails, Sandtown and Peachtree (one of the ubiquitous Peachtree streets that mark the Atlanta region; there are seventy-one). This is the end of the line for a nation at the hands of a former debtors' prison colony, whose collective payback reverberates today in the national psyche.

Less than one generation after the murder of McIntosh and the forced exodus of the Creek Nation, the City of Atlanta was burned to the ground by the Union Army forces led by William Tecumseh Sherman. The city would rebuild only to experience two more major fires in 1908 and 1917. What cannot be destroyed in Atlanta is the legacy of its forefathers and, it seems, the traumatic events that guide the future of Atlanta. Given this incendiary history and stolid regrowth, the phoenix has come to be the totemic emblem of the City of Atlanta. The phoenix is a zombie bird. According to Ovid, the phoenix flies with the nest in which it was born. It carries with it the sepulcher of its father, its cradle.[9] Atlanta's totemic zombie bird, then, serves as a constant reminder of an un-mournable violence—a perpetual melancholic state.

ATLienated

The zombie was a slave figure born of Haitian plantations before George Romero turned it into a shuffling, decaying cannibal. The zombie, more specifically, was a figure that embodied the fear experienced by plantation slaves, the fear, as Kieran Murphy puts it, "of the first modern industrial workers who were stripped of human dignity as they were turned into the instrument of a master's whim."[10] This fear of the master's whim has now become folded into the repetitive actions demanded by mechanical means of reproduction. We fear becoming only the extension of some Other's will, an automaton rather than possessing autonomy. From Walter Benjamin's perspective, it is the absence of movement toward craftsmanship, zombie work, that is responsible for our debilitated state in the world. Given the mechanical and inhuman rhythms by which the human environments were produced, to live in the modern era is to live in a state of constant shock. In film, Benjamin saw that, "perception conditioned by shock [*chockförmige Wahrnehmung*] was established as a formal principle."[11] Humans are trained by these technologies. They shape human actions. One's body is no longer one's own; it is an *unheimlich* container, like the familiar landscapes of Atlanta and its suburbs, where *The Walking Dead* unfolds. These homes, these cities, these towns are no longer ours (perhaps some bank has acquired the second mortgage and bundled, with a thousand others, our collective insurance policies annulled in a bad trade that sank some massive company like Lehman Brothers). We are terrified to learn that, not only do our bodies exist to do the work of others, but so do our appliances purchased on credit, and so do our home mortgages,[12] and our children's student loans. All of these entities seem to exist only to consume, like walkers. Unable to bury these debts—not even dischargeable in the event of our deaths—we have become a nation of unceasing, un-mournable consumers, shambling, hungry ghosts in a panorama of blinking LED lights and high-definition television screens.

On Benjamin's reading of Freud, the protection of the psyche from over-stimulation is more important than the reception of stimuli. We must shield ourselves from the traumatic shocks that inevitably will impinge upon us. These shocks are not only from the inundation of startling messages or provocative imagery but also from seeing burgeoning numbers of people. Benjamin reports that "fear, revulsion, and horror were the emotions which the big-city crowd aroused in those who first observed it."[13] One becomes only a number in a throng. We see this moment of shock acted out by Rick and Glenn in the episode "Guts," from season one. The only way for Rick and Glenn to walk through the city of Atlanta is to cover themselves in the gore and festering putrescence of a recently-killed walker.

Shock marks a moment of recognizing something that is Other and unknown, but prolonged exposure to shock desensitizes one to the information onslaught. Stunning shocks can be quarantined into *Erlebnis* (what is lived through), and in so doing, the psyche protects the more integrative form of memory that one develops into a vision of self over time, *Erfahrung* (what is experienced). Without this shock-defense capacity, the person is reduced to a dumb screen across whom things happen.[14] Without the rich associations that are afforded through *Erfahrung*, the "auratic experience" is not possible. For Benjamin, the proximity to an encounter is central to "aura" and authentic living—precisely what mechanical reproductions, like photographs, cannot provide.[15] Anticipating what is today called Posttraumatic Stress Disorder (PTSD), if a perception is experienced (*Erlebnis*) and constantly remembered, then this experience cannot be metabolized through the unconscious operations of *Erfahrung*. The core experience of PTSD is the inability to integrate the reality of particular experiences and the resulting repetitive replay of the trauma in images, behaviors, feelings, physiological states, and interpersonal relationships. Dissociated as an inaccessible double, in the absence of the integration of one's traumatic experience, the potential for PTSD becomes possible. As Bessel van der Kolk and Alexander McFarlane put it, "posttraumatic syndrome is the result of a failure of time to heal all wounds."[16] Here, Benjamin's notion of *Erfahrung* may be informative for understanding the therapeutic potential of watching zombie and other horror films.

Thomas Elsaesser points out that *fahren* (to travel) is the root of the verb *Erfahrung*, typifying an integrated journey narrative with character-centered cohesion and biographical closure.[17] This is also the structure of cinematic storytelling: "a cathartic progress from *hamartia* (ignorance) and miscognition, to *anagnorisis* (recognition) and the narrational play of different gradients of knowledge towards their eventual convergence."[18] The operation of cinema is to transform the discontinuous experience (*Erlebnis*—the cinematic techniques of the jump cut and montage) into transmissible experience (*Erfahrung*). By viewing *The Walking Dead* together, whether in collective viewing parties at bars or friends' homes or asynchronously communicating (via Twitter or Facebook), are we not creating a group journey narrative?

Escape the City

Atlanta is the site of Techwood Homes, the first public housing project in the United States. Whereas in the early twentieth century audiences were haunted by the figure of the zombie as a phantom of industrial slavery, the last half of that century was haunted by a less obvious menace in the form of the welfare mother. This phantasmagorical figure was purported to be the next barbarian at the gates of American civilization. Georgia Congressman Ben Blackburn's words make clear the threat: "Suburbanites have invested their lives in their houses and they don't want to see them ruined." Blackburn saw the heart of the problem as "the welfare mother and her numerous kids," pouring out from the city center.[19]

A central concern of *The Walking Dead* is palpating the psychology driving the suburban secessionism that has come to dominate American politics since the 1970s. A simple question leads us: where are the safest places on Earth after the zombie apocalypse? The trajectory for the survivors' journey begins with a foray into the city of Atlanta, then to the suburbs of that sprawling metropolis, then further from the city center into the exurbs (literally, to Henry County), and then to the twin hells of prisons and pre-planned communities (Woodbury).

The 1968 presidential election was the first in which votes from the suburbs outnumbered the votes of either rural or urban areas, and the Republican Party had done its best to capitalize on the demographic changes, collectively known as white flight. Richard Nixon courted this suburban vote through his selection of Spiro Agnew as his running mate. While governor of Maryland, Agnew had gained fame for his tough law-and-order response to rioting in Baltimore, enabling Nixon to introduce Agnew as an expert on "urban problems." But Agnew's real experience lay in the suburbs: having served as chief executive officer of suburban Baltimore County, a booming area that was less than three percent black by the end of the 1960s. According to Garry Wills, Agnew's main contribution to the Nixon campaign was that he "early grasped and overcame what white suburbanites take to be their main city problem—how to escape the city."[20]

Atlanta, somehow, managed to avoid the negative associations stemming from the Civil Rights era that seemed to stick to other southern cities. Atlanta was the "city too busy to hate," as former mayor William B. Hartsfield advertised. The city may have avoided some of the more egregious violence broadcast from other southern cities during the era of desegregation; the experience of racial avoidance that came to be known as white flight across all the major cities in the U.S. gave Atlanta the more apt nickname, "the city too busy moving to hate." While white flight is typically understood as the result of a post–World War II housing boom, this explanation fails to recognize the market psychology that drove up the demand for housing in the suburbs. The reality is that (primarily white) people were moving away from urban centers in response to federally-mandated racial integration laws.[21] This exodus of upwardly-mobile white people has had lasting impacts not only on the physical character of Atlanta but also on the trajectory of United States domestic and foreign policy over the last forty years. Atlanta's experience is a proxy for the rest of the United States.

A surprisingly large number of the Atlanta scenes filmed in the first season of *The Walking Dead* are in areas where many Atlanta citizens would not notice the difference. Large swathes of the city's core are typically empty during daylight hours. This is the legacy of white flight and the abandonment of public space by whites living in Atlanta. While many African Americans from across the South looked to Atlanta as a site of opportunity, many whites were actively seeking legal means by which to ensure the separation of the races. Today the city's streets continue to be divided by race: on one side of the line, the streets have their "whites only" names, and on the other side are the names for the "colored" sections of town.[22] Neighborhoods where the working-class whites were closest to historically black neighborhoods were able to address their integration fears through the construction of interstate highways across their previously informal racial dividing lines. Sweet Auburn, birthplace and long-time residence of Martin Luther King, Jr., the locus of African American power and wealth, was shattered during the 1970s by the construction of not only one but three intersecting interstate highways (I-20, I-85, and I-75).[23] When rezoning (now-integrated) residential neighborhoods to include heavy industrial concerns or sixteen lanes of commercial interstate traffic was not enough to soothe the anxieties of panicking middle-class whites, there were the real estate developers, luring city dwellers to the pastoral fantasies of the suburbs.

Suburbs, which housed only a fourth of the country's population in 1950 and still just a third in 1960, encompassed more than half of America by 1990. While the U.S. population grew increasingly metropolitan each decade of the twentieth century, from twenty-eight percent in 1910 to eighty percent in

2000, it was the suburbs, rather than central cities, that accounted for most of the metropolitan growth.[24] Atlanta led the country in suburbanization. During the 1980s, Cobb and Gwinnett counties were among the fastest-growing in the United States. Again, during the 1990s, three more Atlanta suburban counties led the U. S.: Forsyth (with an increase of 123 percent, making it the second fastest-growing county for the decade), Paulding (the fourth), and Henry (seventh in the country). Like the earlier waves of white flight, this latest explosion of the population was primarily white.[25]

Fueling this sea of change was a heady combination of an individualistic interpretation of "freedom of association," a zealous but untested faith in free enterprise, and a vocal hostility to the federal government. This new suburban conservatism, which developed during the 1970s and 80s, took the now-familiar themes of isolation, individualism, and privatization to unprecedented levels. Atlanta led the U.S. not only in this demographic shift but also in a corollary new form of secessionist thinking that massively changed the political posture of the United States. So significant was this political change that, in 1992, political analyst William Schneider announced, "The third century of American history is shaping up to be the suburban century."[26] Season one of *The Walking Dead* presents Atlanta's northern suburbs as the last bastion of humanity in the wake of a zombie apocalypse. This staging speaks to a particular orientation not only geographically but also culturally. It also hints at some of the pernicious struggles with which we grapple today.

White Eschaton

Watching "Tell It to the Frogs," we view the last of humanity huddled on the northwestern perimeter of the city of Atlanta, at Bellwood Quarry, arranging a pillaging raid on the urban core. There are no people in Atlanta, only faceless, threatening bodies between the suburbanites (now apocalyptic survivors) and what they want. This is a metaphor for the relationship between Atlanta and its north suburban neighbors. Were one to continue northwest from Bellwood Quarry along nearby Interstate 75, one arrives at Cobb County, which has long been a conservative force in national politics. During the 1980s and 90s, Atlanta's northern suburbs were represented by some of the most influential conservative politicians in the country. The lineage of suburban secessionist conservatism in Congressional District 7 begins with former president of the John Birch Society and congressman Larry McDonald. Bob Barr, first to lead the impeachment charges against Bill Clinton in response to the Monica Lewinsky affair, was elected to represent District 7 in the mid–1990s. Barr was then succeeded by John Linder, head of the Republican National

Congressional Committee. To the west of these archconservatives, representing Cobb County, sat Speaker of the House Newt Gingrich.

Cobb is one of the wealthiest counties in the United States and historically has looked to the City of Atlanta as a menacing vision on its horizon. While the 1968 presidential election was the first in which suburban votes exceeded either the urban or the rural vote, it was during the 1994 congressional election that the suburban vote first exceeded the combined votes of the urban and rural votes. One can get a sense of the psychology of this massive block of voters from Newt Gingrich's description of his constituency just before the watershed 1994 election that secured him Speaker of the House:

> These people want safety, and they believe big cities have failed and are controlled by people who are incapable of delivering goods and services.... People in Cobb don't object to upper-middle-class neighbors who keep their lawn cut and move to the area to avoid crime.... What people worry about is the bus line gradually destroying one apartment complex after another, bringing people out for public housing who have no middle-class values and whose kids as they become teenagers often are centers of robbery and where the schools collapse because the parents that live in the apartment complexes don't care that the kids don't do well in school and the whole school collapses.[27]

The politics of Atlanta's northern suburbs have been dominated by a fear of an imaginary criminal urban denizen. This hysterical vision manifests in the constant refusal to allow the MARTA transit system to enter their borders for fear of a rise in crime.[28] Unable, or unwilling, to recognize past patterns that led to both the rise of suburbia and the decline of inner cities, suburbanites came to see their isolation as normal and harmless. The suburban secessionist interpretation of "freedom of association" slips into a freely dissociative state. It is from this dissociated state that *The Walking Dead* presents its mass psychotherapeutic potential.

In season one, where is it that the last human beings alive on earth—those who are allowed to kill without fear of murdering—are heading? Where is the safest place on earth? They are heading for the Centers for Disease Control (CDC). But, those of us who live in Atlanta know where the campuses of the CDC actually are: they're downtown (which is no man's land, according to the logic of the show's script). Operating as a work of cultural therapy, the logic of *The Walking Dead* is not about representing Atlanta as it is but as how it feels to live in a place like the northern suburbs of Atlanta. Those who live in Atlanta can understand why "the CDC" is the only safe place on Earth: because in reality that building is the Cobb Energy Center, nothing less than the very cultural center of Cobb County. Of course, all that is found when the survivors attempt to identify with the dissociated suburbanite lifestyle is suicide—along with the terrifying revelation that we are all already infected ("TS-19"). In trying to reason-out a truly revolutionary violence that would redeem human suffering, Benjamin came to the conclusion that the baroque eschatological vision left only emptiness. "The hereafter is emptied of everything that contains the slightest breath of this world," writes Giorgio Agamben. This "white eschatology" consigns humanity to a white sky of nothingness[29]: total divorce from a Divine Will and utter disconnect between any notion of sovereignty and a transcendental firmament upon which to establish Truth.

Throughout *The Walking Dead*, there is a consistent attempt to identify the form of violence that will lead to the cessation of violence. The practice of white eschatology can be seen in the trajectory of violence visited upon the survivors over the course of the first three seasons. As they flee the city and then its closest suburbs, the survivors seek refuge in the exurban idyll of Hershel's farm. Swarmed by a tsunami of walkers, the survivors flee the farm to secure themselves in a prison (demonstrating Gingrich's comment that the suburbanites of Cobb want security above all else). Season three presents viewers with two models of how society can operate in the post-apocalyptic era. Future survivors, we assess, in weekly doses of *The Walking Dead*, the merits of securing freedom within the confines of a prison versus the charismatic violence that the Governor visits upon those outside his direct sphere of control. This is our current white eschaton, presented in safe-to-use, over-the-counter suspensions and titrations.

Massive Trauma

If *The Walking Dead* were a therapeutic exercise, what would it be treating? The 2010 Census shows that the South has become a rapidly diversifying and developing region. A significant change for Atlanta has been so-called "bright flight" or the inverse movement of white populations from the suburbs into the urban centers.[30] With these demographic shifts come the shocks associated with exposure to unknown people and folkways. The future of Atlanta requires a more closely-linked infrastructure, and there will continue to be waves of demographic shifts. But, what sort of future does Atlanta have in the face of this intractable suburban secessionist political legacy? The demand for national safety before all else in the wake of the 9/11 attacks on the World Trade Center ushered in sweeping changes to the United States' domestic and foreign policy.

On first blush, it would seem that the United States entered something of a state of exception in the wake of the terrorist attacks on September 11,

2001. The original Latin term for the state of exception, *iustitium*, referred to a standstill of law itself. As Rick Grimes says during season one, "Those rules don't apply anymore." As Agamben clarifies, "The crucial problem connected to the suspension of the law is that of the acts committed during the *iustitium*.... They are neither transgressive, executive, nor legislative, they seem to be situated in an absolute non-place with respect to the law."[31] It is this crisis of sovereignty that is at the heart of the drama in every episode of *The Walking Dead*, and it is this quality of non-placeness that Atlanta lends to human activities and that enables the story to unfold from the perspective of Atlanta's suburbs. Agamben points out a troubling memory problem for the state of exception, however. At some point in Roman history, *iustitium* ceased to carry its technical meaning of the suspension of law and instead became an act of public mourning for the death of the sovereign or his close relatives.[32] We must ask ourselves, what happened in Atlanta that shifted its position from its "noplaceness," as diagnosed by Koolhaas in the late–1980s, to the place of public mourning that serves as the backdrop for *The Walking Dead*? Allow me to hazard a guess. It might have something to do with the children that came into adulthood in the 1970s and 80s—the folks who would be the architects and city planners and congresspersons of today.

Fifty years before *The Walking Dead* would be produced in Atlanta, the city experienced a catastrophic shock whose traumatic effects continue to be grappled with today: the Orly crash. In the summer of 1962, almost the entirety of Atlanta's white power elite was killed in the crash of Air France flight 007 at Paris Orly airport. There were only two survivors of the 132 passengers, the vast majority of whom (106) were the most significant arts patrons of Atlanta.[33] A national push to fund and build a memorial arts center for those who died at Orly began so that Atlantans could bury their dead and do the work of mourning. What is today known as the Woodruff Arts Center opened its doors in 1968, just a few months after the burial of Martin Luther King, Jr., who is arguably the most visible figure of the black power elite. In the absence of these authority figures, Atlanta's suburban population exploded in a frenzy to secure safety from a perceived urban menace, sowing blight along their exit routes.

Despite the erection of this monument, the people of Atlanta struggled to process the loss of their powerful socialites, as evidenced by the largely-unnoticed disappearance of Rodin's "The Shade," a gift given by the people of France at the opening ceremonies of the Woodruff. The statue would re-materialize during the early 1980s, but, as Ann Uhry Abrams claims, "Atlanta's amnesia was so complete, it took several years for anyone other than relatives of the Orly victims to notice it was gone."[34] The Woodruff Arts Center dominates cultural life in the southeastern United States. In addition to amnesia, Abrams diagnoses a violent streak in the city's cultural ambassador: "The Woodruff Center is brash, ambitious, and aggressive."[35] Is there another diagnosis that might also explain why, psychically, Atlanta found itself at the center of *The Walking Dead*? Given this history of sporadic violence, a trenchant insistence on asocial living at the margins of its own economic engine, lack of memory, and an exaggerated watchfulness, might we better diagnose the metro Atlanta region as suffering from Posttraumatic Stress Disorder? PTSD brought on by not only the modern conditions of massively alienated city life and the anomie induced by ubiquitous technological apparatuses but a very basic and fundamental loss of the primal relationships between the city and its parental authorities?

Preemptive Attack

We live in times characterized by profound anxiety toward uncertainty. One century earlier, Freud, and later Benjamin, attempted to develop prophylactic measures by prescribing exposure to trauma as a means to grow a resilience to impingements. But, the world of knowable threatening things is no longer with us. We've experienced a shift: "Threat in today's world is not objective. It is potential."[36] Living under these affective parameters, what are the techniques available to us that afford us the potential to process the inevitable traumatic futures ahead of us? Benjamin looked to Baudelaire and saw a strategy for metabolizing the shock of experience [*Chockerlebnis*] by imbuing this *Erlebnis* with "the weight of an experience [*einer Erfahrung*],"[37] and it is through this active experiencing together that living is possible. It is precisely this affective experiencing together that is possible in the movie-going experience and the weekly dosage of *The Walking Dead*.

A constant component of the show's trauma sessions is the moment of undecidability. Are walkers people, too? Is Shane wrong to beat Carol's abusive husband? Is it wrong to preemptively kill non-group members? The moment of undecidability is a jolting shock to our well-regulated lives. Rather than focus on the absence of sovereignty or decidability every week, *The Walking Dead* coats this ubiquitous facet of contemporary life with ultra-violence and just unbelievable-enough zombie gore to gloss over the horror of our political crisis. We understand *The Walking Dead* as a form of mass traumatic shock therapy: regularly scheduled intensive trauma sessions shifting the audience from the victims of their traumatic pasts to survivors of their future-lived traumas. Atlanta prepares for its future.

NOTES

1. Rickels, "Psychoanalysis on TV," 45.
2. Rickels, "Subliminalation," 22.
3. Rickels, "Endopsychic Allegories."
4. Rodney Ho, "Georgia Film/TV Tax Incentives Revisions Pass House and Senate," Access Atlanta, March 29, 2012, http://blogs.ajc.com/radio-tv-talk/2012/03/29/filmtv-tax-incentives-revisions-pass-house-and-senate/.
5. Nick Groundry, "Filming Incentives and Location Flexibility Won Marvel's Avengers for Ohio," The Location Guide, May 8, 2012, http://www.thelocationguide.com/blog/2012/05/filming-incentives-and-location-flexibility-won-marvel's-avengers-for-ohio/.
6. Koolhaas, "Atlanta."
7. See Cullum, Fox, Hicks, and Oliver, eds., *Noplaceness: Art in a Post-Urban Landscape*.
8. McIntosh was implicated in the smuggling of African slaves into the United States during the *Miguel de Castro v. Ninety-five African Negros* trial of 1820. In response to McIntosh's execution, the United States voided the treaty, yet the State of Georgia continued to operate under the provisions of the treaty, despite warnings from President John Quincy Adams. See Frank, "The Rise and Fall of William McIntosh."
9. We learn of this curious Assyrian bird in Book 15 of Ovid's *Metamorphoses*.
10. Murphy, "White Zombie," 47–48.
11. Benjamin, "On Some Motifs in Baudelaire," 177.
12. Atlanta has led the United States in home foreclosures throughout the subprime crisis unfolding since 2006.
13. Benjamin, "On Some Motifs in Baudelaire," 174.
14. Ibid., 319.
15. Benjamin, "The Work of Art in the Age of Mechanical Reproduction," 222.
16. van der Kolk and McFarlane, "The Black Hole of Trauma," 7.
17. Elsaesser, "Between *Erlebnis* and *Erfahrung*," 294.
18. Ibid., 295.
19. Kruse, *White Flight*, 252.
20. Wills, *Nixon Agonistes*, 278.
21. The debate about the role of federally-mandated desegregation and the white flight phenomenon is a long one, but the literature tends to suggest that white flight followed the *Brown v. Board of Education* ruling. Exemplary texts in the debate include: Rossell, "School Desegregation and White Flight"; Clark, "School Desegregation and White Flight"; and George Judson, "Expert Links Mandatory Desegregation to 'White Flight,'" *New York Times*, February 6, 1993, http://www.nytimes.com/1993/02/06/nyregion/expert-links-mandatory-desegregation-to-white-flight.html.
22. Ponce De Leon Avenue is that dividing line for several miles heading east from downtown, where Juniper (white) becomes Courtland (Black), Boulevard (Black) becomes Monroe (white), and Moreland (Black) becomes Briarcliff (white). See Jones, *Atlanta's Ponce de Leon Avenue*.
23. For an introduction to these phenomena, see Baylor, *Race and the Shaping of Twentieth-Century Atlanta*.
24. Hobbs and Stoops, *Demographic Trends in the 20th Century*.
25. Smith, Ahmed, and Sink, *An Analysis of State and County Population Changes by Characteristics*.
26. William Schneider, "The Suburban Century Begins," *The Atlantic Monthly* 270.1 (July 1992): 33–34, http://www.theatlantic.com/past/politics/ecbig/schnsub.htm.

27. Peter Applebome, "A Suburban Eden Where the Right Rules," *The New York Times*, August 1, 1994, http://www.nytimes.com/1994/08/01/us/a-suburban-eden-where-the-right-rules.html.

28. According to reports from a Cobb County Town Hall meeting concerning a proposed tax referendum that would support public transit expansion connecting MARTA to Cobb, one Cobb citizen objected that there would not be adequate police presence to contain "the crime issues that automatically come in with mass transit." Jon Gillooly, "Citizens Blast Light-rail Proposal at Town Hall," *Marietta Daily Journal*, September 1, 2011, http://mdjonline.com/view/full_story/15286106/article-Citizens-blast-light-rail-proposal-at-town-hall.

29. Agamben, *State of Exception*, 56–57.

30. Hope Yen, "Suburbs Losing Young Whites to Cities, Brookings Institution Finds," *The Huffington Post*, July 9, 2010, http://www.huffingtonpost.com/2010/05/09/suburbs-losing-young-whit_n_569226.html.

31. Agamben, *State of Exception*, 51.

32. Ibid., 65.

33. Telegrams came from around the world—from Pope John XXIII, Charles de Gaulle, and German Chancellor Konrad Adenauer—many of these forwarded from the White House itself. Also an eerie note: twenty years later, it would be Korean Air Lines flight 007 in which Georgia Congressman Larry McDonald would die.

34. Abrams, *Explosion at Orly*, 223.

35. Ibid., 224.

36. Massumi, "Potential Politics and the Primacy of Preemption," paragraph 17.

37. Benjamin, "On Some Motifs in Baudelaire," 194.

Part II

Posthumanity

Apocalyptic Utopia
The Zombie and the (r)Evolution of Subjectivity

CHRIS BOEHM

AMC's *The Walking Dead* is the latest in a long line of zombie narratives to emerge in the last decade. Adapted from the graphic novel series of the same name by Robert Kirkman and Tony Moore, *The Walking Dead* explores the reconstitution of social order after the old models of order are destroyed by the eruption of "walkers." Unlike the grislier, misanthropic zombie narratives of George A. Romero, *The Walking Dead* depicts the post-apocalyptic world as one of utopian potentiality, if still traumatic at every turn. Indeed, there seems to be an "un-burdening" quality to losing the old way of life, if not for the characters then certainly for Kirkman and Moore:

> The world we knew is gone. The world of commerce and frivolous necessity has been replaced by a world of survival and responsibility.... In a matter of months society has crumbled[,] no government, no grocery stores, no mail delivery, no cable TV. In a world ruled by the dead, we are forced to finally start living.[1]

This quotation appears on the back of the first graphic novel, *Days Gone Bye*, and might be considered a thesis statement for both the television series and the graphic novels. Kirkman and Moore suggest that in our late capitalist world we are already zombies. Unbeknownst to us, we have been "bitten" and turned to "walkers" by our "frivolous" wants and by "infectious" cable television (ironically, *The Walking Dead* is a cable television program). Far from serving as the means of our survival, the conveniences of modern life have prevented us from living according to Kirkman and Moore. Consequently, it is only when we acknowledge our death in the zombie apocalypse that we begin to live. In this essay, I will take up this thesis as my own, examining Frank Darabont's television adaptation and bringing the "apocalyptic utopia" of the show into focus through the lens of the psychoanalytic notion of "death drive" and its relationship to Alain Badiou's ethics. *The Walking Dead* and numerous other contemporary manifestations of the disaster/apocalypse movie articulate a latent (death-drive) wish to "blow it all up" and start over, to start better in a more progressive, socio-political sense. Ultimately, it is only when we realize our "inner zombie" capacity for destruction (at the conceptual level, of course) as the first act of creation that we realize the potential in the zombie apocalypse, not as a full-stop end, but as a beginning.

Same Town, Different Place

In order to understand how the zombie is a transitional step toward a utopian re-imagining of social organization, it is necessary to distinguish between the psychoanalytic notions of desire and drive and their relationship to fantasy. Desire and drive are two poles at which we can place, respectively, the human and the zombie. Whereas the zombie embodies the destructive potential of drive, the human belongs within the socio-symbolic network underpinned by desire. Drive and desire, however, are not simply polar opposites. Like a parasite, desire requires drive as a host to redistribute its otherwise destructive energy according to some fantasmatic schematic. As Slavoj Žižek puts it in *The Plague of Fantasies*:

> In this precise sense, *fantasy is the very screen that separates desire from drive*: it tells the story which allows the subject to (mis)perceive the void around which drive circulates as the primordial loss constitutive of desire. In other words, fantasy provides a *rationale* for the inherent deadlock of desire: it constructs a scene in which the *jouissance* we are deprived of is concentrated in the other who stole it from us.[2]

Desire is the socially acceptable model of enjoyment within any social order, insofar as it acknowledges a set of prohibitions (like the incest taboo) and offers surrogate objects in place of those prohibited things. Drive, on the other hand, is the perpetual circulation around some central void or structural impossibility (the Real). It is fantasy's job in conjunction with the Law, or the symbolic, to conceal that void or structural impossibility with some object of desire. Interjecting itself between the object and drive, fantasy explains (and consequently redirects) drive's endless circulation as grounded in a "primordial loss"; in other words, the object that would satisfy us was long ago taken by some other, and we are left to search for it in a series of surrogate objects.

If in a typical, desire-oriented society we locate otherness with any number of racial, ethnic, religious or sexual identities that belong to the essentially rational, self-interested world, then the zombie stands in for the absolute otherness of drive's irrational disinterestedness. Unlike in the normal order of things, where fantasy identifies the other's otherness by his/her unspeakable pleasure, there is no mysterious desire when it comes to the zombie, no strange rationale behind his peculiar *jouissance*. By openly and unself-consciously consuming human flesh, the zombie closes the distance created by fantasy between normal, respectable society and the other. In making explicit what was hitherto implicit, the zombie forces a dissolution of the fantasmatic narrative and the socio-symbolic network that it tenuously holds together. This shift from a desire-oriented world to that of drive is what Žižek would call a "parallax," in which something occurs (like the zombie apocalypse) that forces a dramatic perspective shift; we can no longer see and understand the world the same as before.

This symbolic dissolution of the familiar perspective is evident in the opening of AMC's *The Walking Dead* when protagonist Rick Grimes awakens from a coma ("Days Gone Bye"). Grimes's coma, insofar as his role as a deputy sheriff makes him a symbol for the law, indicates the "blacking out" of the old order meant to sustain the world as a safe, contained realm of meaning. While the "big Other" sleeps, the other in the figure of the zombie emerges to wreak havoc on those left unprotected, transforming the world into a traumatic wasteland. If this world deprived of fantasy is, as Žižek claims, "an 'irreal' nightmarish universe with no firm ontological foundation," then it must bear a stark resemblance to the bleak world that Grimes discovers both within and immediately surrounding the hospital.[3] Bodies litter the hallways in the hospital, and a chained cafeteria door bulges with "walkers" inside. The words "DONT OPEN DEAD INSIDE" appear on the door, introducing the upheaval of meaning in this world, where the otherwise definitive line between life and death has dissolved along with social order. The play of light and dark as Grimes leaves the hospital emphasizes the incomprehensibility of the post-apocalyptic zombie world. Both the stairwell leading out of the hospital, which is pitch-black, and the harsh light that erupts into the stairwell when Grimes opens the door are blinding. Like life and death, what were opposites (dark and light) collapse to produce a common effect, disorientation and confusion.

Outside of the hospital the scene is no less confusing for Grimes, whose ignorance of the situation is a reflection of the effect of fantasmatic dissolution; the familiarity of the surroundings emphasizes the normalizing force of fantasy. While it may suddenly appear terrifyingly alien to him, the small town Grimes discovers outside the hospital is his home. Drawing upon the stereotypical associations of the small town as a place of comfort, familiarity, and stable identity, the initial setting in *The Walking Dead* further highlights the discrepancy between meaningful perspective provided by fantasy and the sudden perspective transformation of home through its disintegration. As Žižek claims, "the nightmarish universe is not 'pure fantasy' but, on the contrary, *that which remains of reality after reality is deprived of its support in fantasy.*"[4] This traversal, this loss of fantasy, makes the once familiar place suddenly and traumatically different. While one certainly does not expect to see the dead strolling through a hospital, the grislier aspects of corporeality are expected within a hospital setting. Outside the hospital, however, Grimes has no choice but to confront the nightmarish ramifications of the zombie apocalypse. He is initially overwhelmed by the volume of carnage—by the lines of executed walkers. Ostensibly, he is still "home," but his small town is dramatically transformed by the eruption of a traumatic event that has rendered foreign the most homely of homes.

"Days Gone Bye" follows Rick Grimes's discovery of what we might call the "zombie event" after waking up from a coma. Like Jim in *28 Days Later* (2002), who also emerges from a coma into a post-apocalyptic world, Grimes staggers through his small town discovering a wasteland of dead bodies, abandoned homes, and the occasional "walker." In his state of traumatized stupefaction, Grimes is initially mistaken for a zombie by the young Duane Jones; the easy stratification of the pre-zombie world once again blurred in what Duane's father, Morgan, calls "these crazy" times. While the line between dead and living was definitive prior to the zombie event, in the aftermath it is easily confused. From the moment Rick wakes up in his hospital bed, *The Walking Dead* presents us with an apocalyptic fantasy that is at the heart of the death drive. Evident in the zombie's stubbornly undead persistence, the death drive is not simply the movement towards a physical death. Quite the contrary; for psychoanalysis it is an essential component of creation. Žižek explains this crucial distinction in *For They Know Not What They Do*: "the death-drive does the negative work of destruction, of suspending the existing order of Law, thereby, as it were, clearing the table, opening up the space for sublimation, which can (re)start the work of creation."[5] One of the jobs of the death drive is to clear away outmoded symbolic forms that have failed to conceal the disturbing "gaps" in the socio-symbolic network.

Like the zombies in Romero's *Dead* series, the walkers have overrun the late capitalist order and left a chaotic social abyss in which rational order had once existed. Consequently, it becomes imperative for those remaining to engage in the work of reconstruction. Given the totality of the destruction wrought by the zombies, this process is more complex than simply determining a new "sublime object of ideology" against which to reconstitute an old mode of social order. This strategy would be akin to plugging a finger in the leaky dike of civilization. The zombies have destroyed the dike and flooded the old order. The re-constitution of society thus involves determining what will be the appropriate new system of norms and laws going forward. While the scene outside of the hospital as well as numerous other vignettes of carnage in *The Walking Dead* are traumatic for those within the narrative and unsettling for viewers, the zombies accomplish the first step in the possible recreation of a better social order.

The Death of the Future

It might seem strange to consider the zombie apocalypse in *The Walking Dead* to be a potentially utopian event. Indeed, the term "dystopia" may seem more appropriate for what Dr. Edwin Jenner in the final episode of season one calls "our extinction event" ("TS-19"). Despite the bleak imagery, carnage, social disintegration, and infighting among the survivors, *The Walking Dead* engages in a utopian envisioning of the future, a future where significant socio-political change is not only possible but necessary for survival. Consequently, we need a parallax shift in perspective regarding the zombie's function and significance. Just as the shift to drive designates the first step towards creation, the apocalypse is not the end for the survivors in *The Walking Dead* but a beginning. This re-imagining of the end as a new beginning is precisely what Robert Kirkman had in mind when he began work on the graphic novel series from which the television series is adapted: "for me the worst part of every zombie movie is the end. I always want to know what happens next. Even when all the characters die at the end.... I just want it to keep going."[6] The ellipsis in Kirkman's writing is particularly significant; it corresponds to his desire for the story to go on despite all the characters' deaths: the ellipsis represents the potential of the event that opens a hitherto closed situation. Against the backdrop of a bleak economic future, political stalemating, the seeming eventuality of catastrophic climate change, and the hopelessness of proposing an alternative socio-political project that might effectively respond to the daunting challenges of our late capitalist world, the zombie apocalypse in *The Walking Dead* offers the far-flung hope of real, substantial change. The utopian vision is, as Dale claims, "a great opportunity for a fresh start" ("TS-19").

In "The Space of Apocalypse in Zombie Cinema," David Pagano argues that the apocalyptic visions of zombie cinema are a reflection of the disillusionment we feel as subjects of (post)modernity. Citing Simon Critchley, Pagano claims that in our "postreligious" world, seeking any transcendental meaning in life leads ultimately to frustration; I would argue that this is also true of seeking meaningful socio-politico-economic reform. Rick and Shane's conversation in the opening moments of the series, about their respective relationships with women, illustrates a fundamental frustration with modernity.

In a pop-psychology exchange about the differences between men and women, Rick and Shane crudely characterize the emotional particularities of sexual difference that are the focus of talk shows and self-help books. Shane puts the appropriate touch of postmodern ironic inflection (never to be taken too seriously) on his question to Rick: "Do you tell her your feelings? Do you express your thoughts? *Those types* of things?" ("Days Gone Bye"). This moment, evocative of a male-oriented *The View*, is violently interrupted by a dispatch call to a police chase, which ends in Rick being shot in the chest. The juxtaposition of the pop-psychologizing moment between the two reluctantly open male friends and the grisly crime suggests a double frustration with modern society. One is either stymied by the petty demand to express one's "thoughts and feelings" in a compulsory, performative manner (which Rick certainly finds problematic), or one reacts violently to this modern malaise with criminal activity.

While Pagano argues that the apocalyptic visions of zombie cinema are a response to "historical trauma,"[7] Shane and Rick's conversation and the criminals they encounter indicate that the apocalypse is as much a response to a lack of historical significance as it is to significant historical shifts. Unlike Romero's Vietnam-era characters in *Night of the Living Dead*, the characters in *The Walking Dead* are not particularly traumatized by history. Rick and Shane are Nietzschean "Last Men" who talk about marital strife over fast food in the iconic American small town, passing time until the apocalypse. Even the criminals Rick and Shane take down seem to be of the grungy, petty sort; they are stock "bad guys" in a "stock" world. The fact that we do not know the nature of the thugs' crimes deepens the relationship between frustration and the condition of postmodernity. That is, in the malaise of the postmodern world, violence emerges out of nowhere, irrationally, providing some momentary distraction from the compulsory performance of expressing one's feelings.

A response to the ultimate insignificance of modern existence, the opening and closing scenes of the first season of *The Walking Dead* depict a death-drive-influenced apocalyptic fantasy. Emphasizing the confusion wrought by the traumatic intrusion of the "zombie-event," the opening scene of the series deviates from linear narrative continuity, as if the scene were a kind of prophetic, apocalyptic dream prior to the actual event itself ("Days Gone Bye"). In it, we see Rick Grimes stopped along a highway for gasoline at a service station littered with defunct vehicles, decaying corpses, and the detritus of an abandoned survivor camp. The camera emphasizes our imaginary link to this scene by utilizing first-person point-of-view filming. Not only do we not yet know who this character is, we also do not know what has caused the carnage through which Grimes weaves on his way to the gasoline pumps. Both the bobbling of the hand-held camera and the limitations caused by the anchoring of the frame to Rick's perspective do not allow for a stable or encompassing vision. These unmooring limitations are further emphasized by the lack of an establishing shot of the gas station. The absence of this shot and tight camera angles are staples of the horror genre, used to maximize suspense, but they serve double duty here as a reflection of the confusing, dangerous conditions of the post-apocalyptic world. If the opening scene is a kind of "establishing shot" for the series, then it emphasizes the "disestablishment" and confusion wrought by the zombies, which is further jumbled by the discontinuity of the scene in relation to the otherwise linear narrative. Not only does the subjective camera serve to disorient the viewer, but it also suggests that this vision of the world run amok is not just confined to the fictional narrative but seeps into our imagination: Rick's view of this world in the opening moments of the show is notably our view as well. Indeed, from *Night of the Living Dead* (1968) to *2012* (2009), the proliferation of zombie and disaster/apocalypse films over the course of the last forty years makes Grimes's view uncannily familiar; we have for some time been half in love with our own demise.

The content of the sequence also speaks to the disruption of the normal order of things brought about through the zombie apocalypse. While searching for gas, Rick finds what he believes to be a young girl, who has somehow survived whatever force burned out or devoured the camp. When Grimes calls out to the little girl, she turns to reveal that she has not, in fact, survived, at least not in the traditional sense; she is a zombie. As she slowly charges the troubled police officer, Grimes is forced to shoot her in the head. This grisly image of a child zombie, clutching a teddy bear and being shot in the head, is our introduction to the universe of *The Walking Dead*, which is a place where the future is guaranteed only if one is willing to make the kind of quick, disturbing decision that Grimes does. In other words, the apocalypse introduces an end to any imaginary pretenses about the future, embodied doubly by the dead girl. As a child, she stands for a certain continuation of life associated with youth—for all the redemptive hopes that a parent may have when looking at his or her son or daughter. Grimes quickly ends any belief that things may be better with the next generation. As a female, moreover, she also stands for the potentiality of begetting another generation that may sustain the belief that things will eventually progress. There is no "future" in the clichéd, campaign-advertisement sense of the term any longer; or, as Shane succinctly claims later in the series at the survivor camp, "we're living day to day here" ("Guts"). It is undoubtedly a harsh lesson, but the future belongs to those like Grimes, who do not have the luxury of postponing hope and change to the next generation.

If *The Walking Dead* begins the series with a symbolic destruction of the "future," then the final scene accomplishes a similar destruction at the socio-political level. The CDC in Atlanta represents the remaining shred of hope for the survivors, who expect to find some lingering, functional branch of government that will restore their lost society. This utopian hope of social order, which fails to materialize, is a common trope in the zombie film. Both Romero in *Day of the Dead* (1985) and Boyle in *28 Days Later* present a corrupt or dysfunctional government, primarily military-based, for those seeking "the answer to infection," as Major West puts it in *28 Days Later*. The CDC in *The Walking Dead* proves to be as much of a letdown as its counterparts in these films. The lone remaining scientist, Jenner, is well-intentioned but ultimately incompetent. As he explains to the survivors, the real hope, his wife, has already perished as a "test patient" after contracting the zombie virus ("TS-19"). Time, as an objective means of order, becomes a symbolic embodiment of governmental order in the final episode; both are ultimately bound together and negated. Operating on stored energy, the underground CDC station is essentially a large bomb counting down to expiration. Jenner explains to the group that the clock on the wall that Dale, the "Father Time" figure in the show, notices is counting down the time left on the station's generator. When the clock reaches zero, the building will "decontaminate," or, in other words, it will become a massive fire bomb. Time, in this case, is an analog for institutional order. The CDC's self-destruction demarcates the completion of the zombie apocalypse, which culminates in the negation of time as an objective means of organizing the world. The hope invested in the CDC was for time to matter again in the post-apocalyptic world, a time when Dale's wristwatch would not seem ridiculous or a painful reminder of what had been lost. If the opening scene deprives the viewer and survivors of a fantasmatic narrative to make sense of the world, then the closing scene erases the symbolic means of organizing the world into a meaningful realm. With the fall of the CDC, the work of the death drive is complete.

Utopian Visions

When Kyle Bishop's comprehensive cultural history of the zombie *American Zombie Gothic* was published in 2010, AMC's adaption of Kirkman and Moore's comic had just been announced. Bishop rightly acknowledges that the graphic novels and the show are about "the struggles of Rick Grimes as he works with others to rebuild some kind of community after the world has collapsed around him. In essence," he continues, "*The Walking Dead* isn't about zombies at all; it's about human character."[8] *The Walking Dead*, specifically, is more concerned with the reconstitution of society than its fall—a luxury afforded by the serial nature of television drama. Indeed, the series dramatizes what Alain Badiou calls an "event" and its resulting "truth process." In his short work, *Ethics*, Badiou identifies the "event" as "something" that has happened and that "cannot be reduced to its ordinary inscription in 'what there is.'"[9] The event designates a traumatic shift in perspective, much like the Žižekian parallax, which we lack the means to situate in any comprehensible manner. Since we cannot use any previous rationale to understand and situate the traumatic impact of the event, it calls upon us to "invent a new way of being."[10] This "new way" is the process of "truth" in which the event compels us to participate. Our ethical mandate requires us not to reduce the singularity of the event to previous means of understanding (the symbolic or fantasy) and to think our situation going forward from the opening created by its impact. Badiou calls this willingness to engage in a radical reconsideration of our socio-symbolic situation a "fidelity," and it is only when we accept this arduous labor that we truly become "subjects."

If, in Badiouan terms, zombie cinema is more interested in depicting the immediacy of the zombie event, then *The Walking Dead* is the continued depiction of a "fidelity" to that event, which forces survivors to determine how they will live and re-establish order in a post-apocalyptic world. As Kirkman writes in his introduction to the comic series:

> The idea behind *The Walking Dead* is to stay with the character, in this case, Rick Grimes for as long as humanly possible. I want *The Walking Dead* to be a chronicle of Rick's life. We will NEVER wonder what happens to Rick next, we will see it. *The Walking Dead* will be the zombie movie that never ends.[11]

Kirkman's commitment to chronicling Grimes's experience in rebuilding social order is akin to the work of fidelity to the event—an ability to think of a situation as open at all times, always ready for a possible re-ordering. Fidelity, to borrow Kirkman's terms, means to "just keep going on."[12] In other words, the revolution (or apocalypse in this case) does not define a society, but, instead, the social order that emerges in the wake of the revolution retroactively determines the meaning of that revolution.

If the work of reconstruction taken up by Grimes and the remaining survivors might be considered what Badiou calls a "truth process," the tenuous, makeshift socio-symbolic orders that spring up in the post-apocalyptic world are uniquely "fortunate" in their ability to sustain the radical openness of fidelity. From the perspective of the truth process, the zombie is not just a traumatic monster serving an apocalyptic function. Quite the contrary, the zombie becomes a necessary evolutionary step in the re-organization of society. The zombie embodies the death drive's destructive energy, doing the necessary work of clearing away an outmoded, frustrating way of life; at the same time, it creates the path for epochal shifts hitherto unthinkable within the parameters of late capitalism. Fidelity to the event—the potentiality for utopian epochal shifts—is grounded in the figure of Rick Grimes. Despite protestations from his wife, Lori, and from Shane, at no point during the first season does officer Grimes avoid an ethical obligation. From refusing to leave the violent and uncooperative Merle handcuffed to the roof of a building at the mercy of the zombies, to his deal with the Latino gang for the return of Glenn, Rick has a seemingly incorruptible moral center. If the world prior to the zombie apocalypse was characterized as a place of unapologetic self-interest, then Grimes recognizes that self-interest is an unproductive, potentially deadly way of being A.Z. (After Zombies).

Grimes's "fidelity to the zombie event" and the utopian potential created by that event are evident in his introduction to Merle. Camera position becomes a means of distinguishing between obsolete ways of social organization and the new way of being indicative of fidelity. Following a conflict between Merle and T-Dog, in which Merle calls T-Dog a "nigger" and assaults him, Merle claims control over the group ("Guts"). Presiding over a farce of democracy, Merle takes a vote to establish the new leader of the group—a vote coerced by the gun that Merle wields. As he is calling for the vote, the camera frames him from an extremely low angle, presumably from the submissive position into which he forces T-Dog. The (barely) lesser of two evils (Merle or death), Merle takes "office" by unanimous vote. Jacqui notably votes in protest with her middle finger. Merle's political platform is one of harsh "demographics," separating the world out into the whites with authority and the "niggers" and "taco benders," who not only know their place but are forced to vote for it.

Grimes emerges to teach Merle a lesson in politics in the world A.Z., handcuffing him to a pipe on the roof of the building and explaining, "Look here, Merle, things are different now. There are no niggers anymore. No inbred, dumb-as-shit, white-trash fools either. There's only dark meat and white meat. There's us and the dead. We survive this by pulling together, not apart" ("Guts"). Standing for absolute difference, the zombies negate all otherness, which had hitherto divided the world in terms of identitarian politics, and, consequently, they motivate a radical reconsideration of social classification. Cutting across old differences, the universality of the event promises an equality that only existed in socio-political discourse as a dream of some idealistic future. As with Merle, camera position indicates Grimes's worldview. Unlike Merle, who looks down on his subjugated "citizens," Grimes is framed at eye level with the stubborn racist. Equality is not simply political doublespeak for

Grimes; it is his mode of being. Grimes comes down to Merle, for instance, squatting in order to relate to him. Unlike Merle who classifies and situates according to visible differences, Grimes, in his fidelity, is a force of negation that undermines not only Merle's racial epithets but also Merle's own reduction to "inbred, white-trash fool." This act of negation is precisely what Badiou means by fidelity to the event, insofar as Grimes starts to bring about a new order by refusing the limited, reductive means of classifying left over from the pre-apocalyptic world.

Try Again. Fail Again. Fail Better

The ethical orientation of the post-apocalyptic world, grounded in the figure of Grimes, is the primary focus of season two of *The Walking Dead*. The battle between the obscene, ruthless pragmatism of Shane and the idyllic justice embodied in Rick plays out over the course of the season against the pastoral backdrop of Hershel Greene's family farm. In the absence of any prevailing legal authority, Rick becomes the oft-questioned leader for his small group of survivors. For the better part of the season, Rick's lofty ethical engagements are underpinned by the "dirty but necessary" things that Shane must do to keep Rick's family and the group safe, most notably sacrificing Otis to a horde of zombies so that Carl may survive ("Save the Last One"). Establishing the ideological pillars of their new community, Rick negotiates with Hershel, privileging diplomacy over weaponry, saves a young man who had on two occasions tried to kill him, and, at Hershel's request, attempts to regard the "walkers" as sick (not dead) people. Shane, on the other hand, saves both Carl and Lori, executes the prisoner posing a threat to the group, and exterminates the zombies that Hershel keeps locked in the barn. Safety at all costs is Shane's only and often ruthless ethic. If Rick embodies some utopian potential in the post-apocalyptic world, then what do we make of the grisly work that Shane does to keep the group afloat?

One way of reading Shane's "regression" is as an ethical lesson that Grimes must learn as a leader. Throughout season two, Shane regards himself and Andrea as "outcasts" of the group. What seems to place Andrea and Shane on the outskirts of the community is an inability to surrender pathological, self-interest. Shane refuses diplomacy, compromise, and subjugating his ideal ("protecting Lori and Carl") to the needs of the group, unlike Rick who is able to synthesize the needs of the group with the same ideal, even if he needs Shane from time to time to pick up his slack. Andrea subverts the otherwise patriarchal gender roles at the farm by becoming proficient with a gun and serving watch duty rather than washing clothes and cooking. Both Shane and Andrea are incapable of integrating themselves within the organic community at the farm—even Dale, the liberal, rabble-rouser has a place as the outspoken moral conscience of the group. Shane's attempt to usurp Rick's authority, both as head of the group and head of the Grimes family, ultimately results in his "double death," once as a man (Rick kills him) and once as a zombie (Carl kills him) ("Better Angels"). It is no coincidence that this collapse of the human "other," Shane, against which the new social order was establishing itself, conjures the zombies. Shane's death is immediately followed by the emergence of a horde of zombies, which overruns their makeshift community. Ostensibly, Shane was correct in asserting that he was protecting the group from the zombies, but he was mistaken in exactly how he was doing so. As an embodiment of otherness, Shane was a liminal figure, inserted between the burgeoning community and the zombie as the absolute, destructive other. Over the course of the season, Shane increasingly pushes himself to the margins, momentarily serving the same purpose as the zombie, and, consequently, forging a conceptual barrier between the walkers and the group. With the collapse of the other/Shane, the zombies come crawling out of the woodwork to resume the work of destruction.

Ultimately, *The Walking Dead's* second season illustrates the complexities of Rick's utopian vision in the post-apocalyptic world. Not predicated solely on Rick's ideal justice, the possibility of utopian social organization occurs in response to some threat. While the makeshift human societies that spring up in response to the zombie "emergency" are often more selfish and dystopian than harmonious, the zombie offers an absolute other against which a more organic, united society can organize. The first season's survivor group, whose primary concern is fending off "walkers," is more harmonious in their Edenic garden than the community at the farmhouse. Despite a few dust-ups mixed in for maximum suspense, the better part of season two of *The Walking Dead* depicts a world where zombies pose less of a threat than the humans do. The season ends, however, with the re-emergence of the "walkers" as the primary threat to the group, which not coincidentally corresponds to Shane's death. Following his death, the group is forced to remember Rick's central utopian message from the first season regarding the equality afforded by the absolute otherness of the zombie: "There's only us and the dead." In other words, the second season depicts the re-visiting of mistakes of past social organization, disclosing how self-interest emerges to undermine the liberating virtues of justice and equality, albeit a justice and equality that is predicated upon the exclusion of the zombie.

However, this exclusion takes on a new level of complexity when the group learns, as Rick does from Jenner at the end of season one, that everyone is a carrier of the zombie virus. If utopian projects, as Žižek argues, do not so much eliminate "evil" as convert it into some "mythic threat" against which the community establishes itself, then the community in *The Walking Dead* presents a twist on this transformation. The position of the other or "mythic threat" within the utopian order is integral to the maintenance of its tenuous harmony.[13] In the utopian ideological fantasy, the other is identified as an obstacle to some idealized future; once the obstacle is eliminated, social harmony will erupt spontaneously. The obstacle/other, however, is merely a displaced embodiment of social antagonisms already within the existing order—a displacement that perpetuates the illusion that some postponed harmony is possible. Much like the zombie disease that we learn everyone carries, we rediscover in season two that we are all "others to ourselves." Like Shane, who turns when Rick stabs him, we are all inherently zombies undermined from within by our deceptive, self-interested desire and the self-destructive drive lurking not far beneath. If one of the shortcomings of utopian imagining is the exclusion of others—perceived as the only obstacle to utopia and thus the ultimate guarantor of utopia's illusory presence—then *The Walking Dead* makes this exclusion in some way impossible. The antagonistic split between the social order and the other is already incorporated within the "normal" order of things vis-à-vis the zombie virus. In other words, the social order that Grimes will attempt to reconstruct must acknowledge that it is already somehow split from within, already divided between pathological self-interest and the destructive nature of drive.

Recognizing the other already within the subject of a social order, even if only at the potential level, announces a new kind of utopia pursued in *The Walking Dead*. Neither the zombie/human split nor the collapse of the group's initial social project signals the end or folly of utopian potential; the initial failure motivates a renewal of that original project. This failure is not an indication of an inherent corruption in the underlying idea (Rick's justice and collectivity), but, instead, follows from the inherent split (the inner zombie drive) that provides the renewing potential of negativity. In the comfort of our "late capitalist" historical moment, it is easy to be suspicious of radical political change, given the catastrophic failings and gruesome effects of numerous political projects of the twentieth century. For Rick Grimes, this is a suspicion neutralized by the zombie apocalypse, which makes the work for positive, productive change a necessity. Fidelity to the event is unconcerned with potential failure, as Žižek notes: "one has to take the risk of fidelity to an Event, even if that Event ends up in an 'obscure disaster.'"[14] What the dire circumstances afford the citizens of a post-apocalyptic universe is the ability to see "obscure disaster" as a chance to start fresh. In other words, the close proximity of the death drive to everyday life in *The Walking Dead* forces the arduous work of social reconstitution according to indispensable ideals. Perhaps, then, at a theoretical level, we can reconsider the zombie not necessarily as an enemy other against which Rick must organize society, but as a positive evolutionary step in the movement towards the kind of socio-political change hitherto unthinkable.

This shift from other to evolution is the parallax shift necessary to understand the zombie virus in *The Walking Dead*. Ultimately, the evolution from an exclusionary "Us versus Them" worldview that has hitherto tainted all social organization, utopian or not, to a more inclusive model is located at the individual level. In the revelation that "we are already them!" lies the potential to see from what has hitherto been our blind spot, and, consequently, it maintains the possibility for positive change at any point. The crucial distinction here is between being "them" on the physical level, which is tantamount to being a destructive machine without consciousness, and being "them" at the conceptual level. Here Badiou's notion of the "immortal" potential in humanity may be helpful:

> But Man, as immortal, is sustained by non-being. To forbid him to imagine the Good, to devote his collective powers to it, to work towards the realization of unknown possibilities, to think what might be in terms that break radically with what is, is quite simply to forbid him humanity as such.[15]

Badiou's definition of immortality is evident in the ethical battle that plays out between Shane and Rick. Shane's pragmatic desire, which is fixated on Lori and Carl, limits him to an outmoded existence that passed with the zombie apocalypse. In a world of drive, Shane still operates as an agent of desire. Rick, on the other hand, sees the potential in the situation for reconsidering what "is" and what "could be," or, to put it another way, Rick sees the possibility of becoming the immortal by pursuing an existence that is not grounded primarily in pathological self-interest. To put this in terms of the zombie infection, Badiou's "non-being" is a force of negation that is ready to "tear it all apart" and start over again and again when necessary. At the conceptual level, the zombie virus (non-being) is an evolved position where social order can be broken apart, attempted again. To borrow a quote from Beckett that Žižek often cites, "Try again. Fail again. Fail Better." At the narrative level the "walkers" are still a perpetual threat against which the survivors organize their new society. However, carrying the zombie virus makes the humans in *The Walking Dead* "like-zombie," capable of more easily (than us) accomplishing the parallax shift from desire to drive constitutive of a movement towards some disavowed truth. Zombie, as the virus of drive, is not an inhuman monster threatening the socio-symbolic network, but is instead the name for an ethical mode of being that allows a radical re-conception of the fundamental underpinnings of that order.

Like most horror-show monsters, zombies serve a dual function of terrifying and edifying us by exposing some horrifying, disavowed truth about our world or ourselves. Be it the eviscerated body on the evening news during the Vietnam War or the mindless consumption of goods in late capitalist society, the zombie has frequently embodied our socio-politico-ethical shortcomings. What we see in Romero's zombies, in *Night of the Living Dead* and *Dawn of the Dead* (1978), are our flaws embodied in the mindless walking dead; we are the zombie with slightly more consciousness. The zombie is essentially a figure of desire taken to its extreme point, burned out, and passed over into the realm of non-pathological, destructive drive. Still, drive is not simply destructive, but the necessary emptying of some cumbersome means of structuring social order: the first step in creation. In *Land of the Dead* (2005), Romero shifts his depiction of the zombie from one of simple, destructive monstrosity to something more sympathetic, organized around the figure of "Big Daddy." Big Daddy leads a zombie revolution against the "gated community" of Fiddler's Green where the wealthy elite close themselves off to the horrors of the post-apocalyptic world. Ultimately, the zombie revolution allows for the impoverished, exploited humans living in the city surrounding Fiddler's Green to attempt to rebuild society in a more equitable fashion. While *The Walking Dead* does not quite literalize the function of the death-drive the way Romero does in *Land*, a similar parallax shift occurs *vis-à-vis* the zombie virus for which everyone is a carrier. These humans do not necessarily need the zombies to start a revolution because they are already zombies. No longer reliant upon figures like Big Daddy to clear the way, the survivors in *The Walking Dead* carry that potential with them, in their blood. Unlike in Romero's post-apocalyptic societies, humans in *The Walking Dead* seem to be more selfless and cooperative, particularly Rick Grimes, and, consequently, the show is less a dystopian vision of our end than a hopeful, if terrifying, reboot. *The Walking Dead* illustrates that utopia is not necessarily a materially-constituted social order (the dream of a "city on the hill" or a lost Eden), but, like Badiou's truth process, a perpetual willingness to become zombie, to see from the point of exclusion, in order to start over again and build it better the next time.

NOTES

1. Kirkman and Moore, *Days Gone Bye*, Back Cover.
2. Žižek, *The Plague of Fantasies*, 32.

3. Ibid., 66.
4. Ibid.
5. Žižek, *For They Know Not What They Do*, lxxxiii.
6. Kirkman and Moore, *Days Gone Bye,* Introduction.
7. Pagano, "The Space of Apocalypse," 84.
8. Bishop, *American Zombie Gothic*, 209.
9. Badiou, *Ethics*, 41.
10. Ibid.
11. Kirkman and Moore, *Days Gone Bye,* Introduction.
12. Ibid.
13. Žižek, *Violence*, 26.
14. Žižek, *First as Tragedy, Then as Farce*, 76.
15. Badiou, *Ethics*, 14.

Nothing But the Meat

Posthuman Bodies and the Dying Undead

Xavier Aldana Reyes

Despite *The Walking Dead's* being only two years old, its opening episode has already reached iconic status.[1] Its "bicycle girl," reaching out for help or in hunger to sheriff Rick Grimes, appears soon after Grimes's escape from a derelict hospital and sets the nihilistic tone that has come to define the series. Her face twists and contorts, perhaps in an attempt to express the pain her lipless mouth is incapable of putting into words, as she lurches on, little more than a rotting bust. This peripheral character, accessory as the rest of the hordes of walkers are to the show, nevertheless carries all the import of a new kind of zombie that seems to have reached its biomedical climax. Films like *28 Days Later* (2002), *28 Weeks Later* (2007), *I Am Legend* (2007), and *Quarantine* (2008), all successful Hollywood blockbusters, have taken the nuclear warfare connections of *Night of the Living Dead* (1968) and *Return of the Living Dead* (1985) into new extremes of paranoid infection. Their reliance on a rational scientific discourse and the immense speed of their creatures, as well as their apparent refusal to stand for "the inertial lurch of mechanical mass," has led critics like Fred Botting to argue that these films do not technically belong to the zombie genre.[2] In this essay I read the figure of the walker precisely as a response to these viral rethinkings of the zombie myth and argue that it needs to be understood as a secular reading of embodiment in direct opposition to the strand of posthumanism that has often colored the study of zombies. Thus, I view the walkers in the first two seasons of *The Walking Dead* as challenging notions of traditional zombiehood; they celebrate or declaim, depending on one's view, the corporeal and decaying nature of life understood as an organic process.

The shift from the zombie as corpse, possessed by a magical force through voodoo, to an infected "enraged" individual "coded as [a] disease carrier" is significant and one that has not gone unnoticed.³ As has been suggested, the Haitian formulation of the zombie as either a spirit governed by the *bokor* priest or as a reanimated dead corpse to be manipulated—evident in films like *White Zombie* (1932), *Revolt of the Zombies* (1936), *King of the Zombies* (1941), and the parodic *Zombies on Broadway* (1945)—changed drastically as a consequence of the new horrors suggested by the coming of the atomic age.⁴ The 1950s, 60s and 70s situated the zombie in the context of his/her embodied nature and, to a certain extent, replaced the prevailing master-slave power dynamics with a latent visceral awareness that, at least in George A. Romero's films, led the creature to start decomposing. The zombie narrative thus gained a new corporeal dimension, and the undead turned into something more than a collection of drives or instincts. Because inherently carnal, the zombie was suddenly faced, through its own material presence, with the pain and despair of decay. Without this theoretical move it would have been impossible to conceive of films like *I, Zombie: The Chronicles of Pain* (1999) that establish clear connections between the status of the zombie and that of sufferers of life-changing diseases like AIDS. The new viral zombies have gone as far as to completely eschew the concept of death itself, becoming fast creatures who are infected through character-altering viruses and need not die to become zombies.

Critics have been quick to acknowledge the reliance of contemporary horror films on science, medicine, and biopower, but little has been written on the philosophical implications of the embrace of what I would like to term the "dying undead." This neologism insists on a distinction between the zombie who can be seen to be both dead and alive (the "living dead") and the zombie who is slowly decomposing to extinction through a species of resurrected life (the "dying undead").⁵ This nuance is important: it communicates the difference between a dualist and a materialist approach to the zombie. As Gwyneth Peaty has explained, "biomedical intervention [has] supplant[ed] supernatural possession for the infected zombie" in such a way that the latter has "retain[ed] and revis[ed] the principle of mind/body separation embodied by previous incarnations through the frame of posthuman dualism."⁶ These new zombies may be read as material vessels devoid of social meaning and in direct opposition to their living counterparts who remain human due to their capacity to think. Theorists have used the visceral corporeality of zombies, which makes them incapable of social functioning, to champion a Cartesian understanding of consciousness. For example, in an article that uses the "p-zombie" model developed by David J. Chalmers, Gordon Hawkes asks:

> Is consciousness more than just a physical function of the brain? Is there some part of us that can't be eaten by the walkers? I, for one, am going to side with Rick Grimes and his affirmation that we are more than just our body. He may

very well be mistaken—he is in opposition to most philosophers today—but, for me, when it comes down to it, the possibility of zombies just seems obvious.[7]

Hawkes's view of consciousness resonates with Hans Moravec's and Ray Kurzweil's transhumanist theories of the mind's imminent ability to transcend the body, which will be explored later. For now, my contention is that the undead should be read not as an endorsement of how human consciousness must be more than mere material existence but rather as a critique of the possibility of pure disembodied consciousness. The dualistic model ignores the materiality of consciousness itself, which is what the dying undead seem ready to reclaim. The figures that populate *The Walking Dead* posit a more interesting reading of the zombie as sentient meat. As I will show, this is not a revision of the mind/body division but rather its collapse into a form of existence that acknowledges the organic or biological as constitutive of the human.

The Zombie as Posthuman, the Posthuman as Zombie

It is perfectly understandable, even predictable, that the zombie should have been chosen as "an apt icon for the post-human."[8] From an economic angle, the zombie can be read as "present[ing] the 'human face' of capitalist monstrosity" in its atomization within a larger group of alienated individuals.[9] From a philosophical point of view, these creatures serve as models through which to study the relation between consciousness and physicality in an age where the differences between the machine and the human have gradually been elided.[10] From a political perspective, zombies "manifest the (internal) excess that biopolitics produces and needs" and become "ambivalent, un-civil, un-living, un-dead, destructive figures of fear situated along the crossing of the categories out of which the new world emerges and on which it legitimates itself."[11] But it is perhaps their humanity (or lack of it) as constructed through the mind that I think has been influential in the alignment of the zombie with the posthuman condition as well as in the reading of the capitalist subject as agentless zombie. This is a tactical move that cannot be countenanced unless we first trace the shedding of the soul in contemporary formulations of the posthuman and the subsequent embrace of the idea of a personality or set of embodied "human" characteristics that has come to replace it. It is an understanding of what constitutes modern life that, as I will show later, has gained popularity and is at the heart of *The Walking Dead*.

One strand of posthumanism, the one to receive the fiercest critiques from scholars in the field, contemplates the idealist dream of what Ingrid

Richardson and Carly Harper have called the "fleshless ontology" of cyberspace that "is all about the final non-necessity of the body, or achieving a mode of existence that can do without the body."[12] This strand of thinking is evident in the work of transhumanist critics like Marvin Minsky or Nick Bostrom, but it has perhaps been most famously articulated in the work of Hans Moravec and Ray Kurzweil. In their fantasies of a posthuman world where consciousness is capable of transcending the body (understood as matter), they revisit the territory that William Gibson once explored through his cyberpunk novel *Necromancer* (1984). According to such futuristic writings, man-made machines will eventually take over, and robots will become humanity's progeny after the discovery that consciousness is not anchored to the carnal. Moravec calls this form of transhumanist life "Mind" and describes it as a form of existence that, "unlike life alone, which learns from its past, but is blind to its future, ... can choose among alternatives to imperfectly select its own destiny—even to amplify that very ability."[13] We can see how such a discourse of life follows a Cartesian model that prioritizes the mind over the body. When Moravec suggests that it will soon be possible to download human consciousness into a computer only to retrieve it later, the implication is that consciousness itself is a process that may take place in isolation from biology.[14]

Even Katherine N. Hayles, who herself vouches for a form of extension of the human through technology, argues that posthumanism of the fleshless type could be seen as "antihuman."[15] Her qualm is precisely with the nature of this disembodiment and the perceptual inability to understand the intricate workings of consciousness, which she sees as forming part of a more complex system that cannot be understood as separate from the body. Similarly, Cary Wolfe has been quick to separate his own definition of the term from those that came before: "posthumanism, in my sense isn't posthuman at all—in the sense of being 'after' our embodiment has been transcended—but is only posthuman*ist*, in the sense that it opposes the fantasies of disembodiment and autonomy, inherited from humanism itself, that Hayles rightly criticizes."[16] Whilst the essence and strength of these works lie outside the remit of this article in that they are imbricated in the role of technology in the creation of the posthuman subject, it is important to note that posthumanism has come virulently to reject any thought of the subject that does not conceive of its radical materialism. In like manner, *The Walking Dead* goes to great lengths both to situate its zombies in a geographically sound and realistic manner and to depict them as physical presences. The viral zombie, which the show returns to its Romerian decomposing dead/alive self, thus lays bare the critical challenge to disembodiment raised by Wolfe.

As a creature that is pure body and guts, although also residually cognitive, the zombie naturally forces us to consider the main thrust of human life, if perhaps not existence, as nothing but organic; for if zombies are a product of alterity, always constructed by and through opposition, their standing with regard to the soul has been crucial in their dehumanization. This is precisely why they have become interesting to critics of the postmodern and posthuman condition. For example, in a recent article by Sean Moreland, zombies are described as "interrogat[ing] the convenient distinction between human beings and 'soul-less' animals and/or machines, dramatically re-presenting the element of Darwinian thought that has always been the most troubling to Platonists, creationists, and essentialists of all stripes."[17] In fact, it is the critical import of the soullessness of zombies that has animated important arguments for their typification of modernity. Marina Warner has even traced the history of the zombie, at the end of her influential *Phantasmagoria* (2006), alongside the development of Western secularity. For her, secularization sets posthuman zombies in opposition to the spiritual world as they gradually abandon the slave condition of their Caribbean origins and their proletarian connections in films like *White Zombie*. This modern zombie acts less as a social or ethnic other and more as an abject part of the self through a process of internalization that becomes "a mirror of a certain common fear of numbness and loss."[18] According to this paradigm shift, a film like *The Matrix* (1998) may be read as an exploration of the dispossession of the posthuman subject who is, in this particular film, because comatose and unable to interact in real life, a literal zombie-victim.

The epitome of such a critical repositioning of the zombie is Sarah Juliet Lauro and Karen Embry's "antisubject," or "zombie," proposed in the first instance as a response to the inevitability of the posthuman future and as an antidote to Donna Haraway's liberating but improbable cyborgian model.[19] For Lauro and Embry, the figure of the zombie becomes an extreme species of human embodiment that reminds us of the physical limits of our bodies or, as the authors put it, of our own "inescapable mortality":

> The vulnerability of the flesh and the instinctual fear of its decay, as well as the dissolution of consciousness—all things that happen as we approach death—are suggested in the monstrous hyperbolic of the zombie as living corpse.... The corpse itself has the ability to terrify by implication, but the animate corpse, a walking contradiction, may frighten most deeply because it represents not only our future but our present.[20]

As Lauro and Embry themselves acknowledge, the zombie as body poses a direct challenge to the empowering but impossible fantasy of posthumanist disembodiment. This is not purely to accept that we might be, in a sense, already walking corpses (since we must inevitably return to that state) but, more crucially, that what is terrifying about the zombie is that s/he acts as reminder of the "lived human condition."[21] The zombie as a contemporary analogy for the postmodern subject shies away from the limitations of socio-historical, economical, and cultural readings of fantastic creatures and instead points towards the real threat of being simply a body. Little more than an anti-cathartic and truculent *memento mori*, the zombie, as Lauro and Embry envision it, is a depressing yet beneficial image of the posthuman body, aware of both his/her own transient material nature and its lack of transcendence. The illusion of a liberation from matter, under this particular light, morphs into a flesh nightmare that we cannot escape because flight may only be effected through destruction. This brief account should hopefully show just how profoundly different the embodied reading of the zombie is from the fleshless ontological landscapes of the transhumanists. In what remains of this essay, I will refine this emphasis on embodiment through a study of the walker to show that the negation of a separate consciousness must not necessarily end with an acceptance of carnal despair but rather can and should culminate in an engagement with the somatic level of being.

In a sense, the current conceptualization and portrayal of the zombie, at least in *The Walking Dead*, seems to align itself with Lauro and Embry's embodied "zombie." Walkers are radically incarnate zombies that may be understood not as experiments in the lack of consciousness—as I will show, this is a position difficult to sustain in itself—but as the process of extreme embodiment through which contemporary body theory is currently asking us to reconsider existence. I would like to suggest the possibility that the zombie might not be set in opposition to the human but could, instead, be seen to reflect him/her. The fact that the "zombie" is being positioned as a figure that defines the posthuman condition is telling in itself: it is not that we are scared of becoming zombies but that we might inadvertently already be "them." If films like *28 Days Later* or *I Am Legend* subscribe to this idea by not necessarily featuring "dead" zombies (i.e., contagion is the essence of procreation, and no decay is necessary), *The Walking Dead* expands this corporeal mythology by turning its zombies into sentient and, although only residually, thinking meat. That the zombies die only to resurrect and live a second life in death, one in which their flesh starts corrupting almost immediately, may signal social anxieties about beauty, aging, or widespread and contagious diseases, but it is first and foremost about the fact that these corpses are effectively alive. *The Walking Dead* seems to encourage a new image of the zombie, a composite of Romero and the viral zombie, steeped in materialist embodied responses to the fleshless ontological project.

First, the divide between mind and body is one that I find entirely absent from the series if not downright denied. In "TS-19," Dr. Edwin Jenner describes the origin of walkers, and his choice of the words "microbial, parasitic, fungal" is significant: they define zombiedom as an inherently biological state of being, as a type of disease or illness that needs a period of incubation. According to this logic, the cause only matters insofar as it situates the zombie within the natural order: whether caused by bacteria or parasites, humans are vulnerable to it. The series drives this point home in "Chupacabra," in which a distinction is established between superstitious beliefs in the American cryptid and the hard evidence of the rotting walker. There is no mention of souls or of an afterlife, and suicide is increasingly seen as "opting out" rather than as some form of Christian damnation to eternal suffering. Second, if the concept of the human is still built through difference—as Duane in "Days Gone Bye" explains, the zombie simply "[i]sn't a man"—the difference between walkers and humans inheres in the apparent capacity of the latter to be ontologically aware: the living continue to live *de facto* and are only made conscious of this very same "aliveness" by being threatened with becoming "other-than-life."

Walkers, in contrast, seem oblivious to the fact that they are ceasing to exist through gradual erosion and physical decay. The series takes great pains, however, to make a point of their suffering and often exploits this possibility to show differences between the main characters and their attitudes to life. To illustrate this point, some of the characters express the need to kill walkers found in what would be construed as agony or torture. In "Save the Last One," after Andrea finds a walker hanging from a tree, it becomes obvious that she is witness to a man who attempted suicide but forgot that the brain is the essence of zombie life. Daryl refuses to "waste" a good arrow on the walker because weapons are scarce, and he does not think death would make a difference to the ontological status of this creature. For Andrea, though, this becomes a mercy killing, a gesture of good will, and something that signals to the viewer the disturbing possibility that walkers may suffer and, hence, "feel."

Such an empathic approach to the walkers is further elaborated through the introduction of Hershel Greene. His compassion often leads to irate discussions about the nature of walkers and establishes a division between characters (like Shane) who judge the walkers' humanity on the basis of their physical endurance (no human is capable of sustaining massive chest injuries) and those (like Hershel) who see in walkers the remainder of the humans they once were. Closing the divide requires a strategic move from apprehending walkers as "others" bereft of consciousness to a system of thought that understands them as "sick people" ("Pretty Much Dead Already"). Hershel's hoarding of zombies in his barn constitutes another highly sympathetic act of hope or faith in the connections between humans and walkers. This is not purely because Hershel insists on the possibility that they might eventually find an antidote for the walker condition, something the series has so far not disproven, but because it is set in opposition to the aggressive alternative that Shane has come to represent by this point. His subsequent death at the hands of Rick after a failed murder attempt further distances the spectator from Shane's vision of the world. Whilst I would not want to suggest that we wholeheartedly accept Hershel's view—for one thing, it is largely impractical—such moments in the series are meant to instill a thorough questioning of the intrinsic nature and value of walkers as subjects, of their consciousness and their bodies.

Such scenes are testimony to the fact that, far from a form of death that refuses to be human, these creatures are more akin to a relentless and voiceless organic form of dying undeath. I class them as "dying" (rather than dead) because walkers eventually cease to physically exist—because they can die a second death (through the bullet in the forehead). They are alive in a different way than humans. Walkers do not sit uncomfortably somewhere between a disembodied human essence and an infected embodiment but rather challenge the very existence of this divide. As Deborah Christie argues, "If we are to consider whether the zombie is or can be representative of the post-human state, we must first purge ourselves of the very binaries that define the old Cartesian model."[22] This is why it is important that we turn to this notion of dying undeath and the theoretical and critical complications that may arise from refusing to acknowledge the biological side of zombies in the context of *The Walking Dead*. When Sheriff Rick Grimes explains that they (humans) "don't kill the living," what is he actually saying, and how does his understanding of life contradict the show's? This seems relevant if we consider that, at times, even some of the characters confuse humans with walkers, as Rick does at the beginning of "TS-19," or that other characters manage to play dead convincingly, as Daryl does in "Chupacabra." It would appear that the problem stems from a reluctance to accept that the differences between walker and human may be largely categorical and not axiomatic.

Walkers and the Dying Undead

Walkers seem to act like animals: they bite and scratch, pursue the scent of blood, move toward loud sounds, and, even more specifically, move in "herds" and "wandering packs" ("What Lies Ahead"). They may be tricked into thinking a survivor is dead if the stench of viscera is strong enough to mask that of human skin ("Guts") or may be distracted with lights ("Bloodletting"). All of this should not lead us to think, however, that walkers have an underdeveloped animal consciousness or even no consciousness at all. Although they do not speak, they have some form of residual memory. They try to open doors, as Jenny does in "Days Gone Bye." They go back to places they know and, most significantly, are capable of complex cognitive and psycho-motive processes, like picking up a brick to smash a glass window or going up emergency ladders ("Guts"). They are far removed from the zombies in George A. Romero's *Land of the Dead* (2005): they do not demonstrate a clear rational agency like that of the undead revolutionary Big Daddy. One cannot help but wonder, however, how far walkers might be from mastering guns or performing mercy killings. If, as Craig Derksen and Darren Hudson Hick (after John Locke) have argued, personal identity is developed from a sense of continuity in consciousness,[23] then walkers are at the threshold: marginal subjects incapable of full cognitive or retentive faculties. Whilst it is appealing to say that humans "become a body" upon death and that, therefore, the zombie is little but a shell without consciousness, this seems to go against the more basic argument that all forms of consciousness must needs be embodied. Walkers are subjects, not because they have an inherent sense of who they are, but rather because their bodies are positioned within a biomedical context that recognizes their animation through an internal force.

Walkers are challenging precisely because of that something in the brain that, although latent and not expressly rational, still impels them into basic locomotion. This, and their rotting, seems, at least initially, to distance them from humans, but the differences between the two become less apparent as the series advances. In "Beside the Dying Fire," we are told that all the characters are already dead insofar as "natural" death has been evacuated from the order of reality, and all humans are infected carriers of the walker pathogen. Such a move is relevant in a number of ways. First, it short-circuits the "us against them" divide, positing the walker as removed from the human by a mere formality. This is perhaps best portrayed in "Vatos," when Andrea waits a whole night for the bitten and feverish Amy to transition. The process here is largely symbolic since Amy's status as a human only ends when her zombie self begins, although figuratively this passage is shown through a change in Amy's eyes and the cessation of life "as we know it" via rigor mortis. Technically, as soon as she is infected, the walker in Amy has won the battle, but Andrea decides to wait until everything that she deems "human" is evacuated from her sister's body. Second, this situation reads human resistance to its destiny as foolhardy and ultimately futile; many of the characters, in fact, struggle to find reasons not to kill themselves and have to be persuaded that there might still be hope of a future. Third, the fact that all characters are always already walkers, at least potentially, institutes death not as an endpoint but as a second life or extension of it. Death is possible insofar as it physically occurs, but what matters to human characters is the cessation of human intellect and the subsequent retardation of the rational or social component.

The only way out of this solipsistic nightmare, as I have already pointed out, is to destroy the brain itself. This is significant because it would seem to support the idea that life relies on the synaptic processes that create intelligibility and the phenomenological lived-in body. A key scene in "TS-19" does much to situate the walker within biomedical and ontological discourses, dispelling transhuman disembodiment. When the "Enhanced Internal View" of the MRI virtual camera is activated half-way through the episode, the computer takes us, quite literally, inside the head of a zombie. This is a pivotal moment in the series, and the only one so far to give firm clues about the nature of walkers. Dr. Jenner's comments on the entropic process through which the human dies and is reborn as a zombie, illustrated here in all its anatomic detail, serve not only as a reminder of the differences between humans and walkers but also of the differences between walkers and the dead. The ultimate marker of ontological difference in this case is, not surprisingly, the brain. Described by Jenner as "a person's life," the brain defines the structural kernel of the human as a form of ineluctable life: "Experiences, memories, it's everything. Somewhere in all that organic wiring, all those ripples of light, is you. The thing that makes you unique and human." When one of the characters inquires about the points of light in the scanner, Jenner explains that "those are synapses, electric impulses in the brain that carry all the messages," and that they "determine everything a person says, does or thinks from the moment of birth to the moment of death." Upon death, this is all gone: "The frontal lobes, the human part, that doesn't come back. The 'you' part." Upon death, walkers return as little more than "a shell driven by mindless instinct."

Yet this is not technically true. We have to accept that there is a human residue in the raw instinct and the shreds of memory that seem to have survived in walkers. The idea of latent cognition further complicates the matter since synaptic connections cannot lie dormant or, as seems to be suggested, die completely yet still manage to sustain movement. It is telling that, even though invasion of the body by the foreign agent leads to a shutdown of the brain and of the major organs through a hemorrhaging of the adrenal glands, the brain still returns after resurrection. In fact, the series supports its "us against them" logic precisely through the fact that the foreign agent in this context "restarts not the brain, but the brain stem," so that "[i]t's nothing like before," and the person becomes, in Jenner's words, "dark. Lifeless. Dead." Most interestingly, however, upon further questioning and prodding from Rick about the ontological status of such a creature, the doctor seems unable to conclude that walkers are not technically alive. To sustain the possibility that the walker is intrinsically alien and "other" to the human, we would need to accept that the body can live independently of the mind or that the brain stem is capable of functioning without further cognitive involvement. Jenner's helplessness, the cul-de-sac his investigations seem to have reached, signals, in my view, the series' acceptance that walkers, for all the human efforts to turn them into abject beings, lie incomprehensibly and disturbingly close to life itself.

But to accept Jenner's proposition has further implications, the most important of which is the surrender to the possibility that the body can live on without consciousness. Jenner's position, which I explored in the second part of this article, is one riddled with complications that are contradicted by the main thrust of *The Walking Dead*. Derksen and Hick have traced the consequences of maintaining a "strict Cartesian distinction between mind and body":

> On such a view, it seems either *always* possible that the zombie is Uncle Rege (because no amount of harm to the body—including death—is going to have any effect on the mind), or seems utterly *impossible* that it is Uncle Rege because on such a view none of us *are* our bodies, or are even connected to them in any substantial fashion.[24]

The logical problem here is that, to sustain either of Derksen and Hick's premises, we would have to maintain the posthuman illusion that consciousness might be free from the body, that it is possible to have a mind without a body. While it is possible for Rick Grimes to exclaim before lodging a bullet in Leon Basset's brain that he just "can't leave him like that" ("Days Gone Bye"), thus revealing that he feels there is some of Leon left in his body, most characters refer to walkers as "not people" ("Secrets"). In its denial of any form of afterlife that is not dying undeath, *The Walking Dead* would seem to propose that what is at stake here is how we actually choose to envision life itself. If death leads to an extension of existence, or even a second life of a different order, then reflecting upon the similarities and differences between the two reveals the message hidden between the lines: life is intrinsically embodied, and death is only possible with the destruction of consciousness that is inevitably material. That the latter is inextricably linked to the annihilation of the brain as the center of organic life is only logical.

This seems to me to pose a problem to the binaristic system that has rekindled the posthuman debate and that has led to conclusions like Christie and Lauro's: "Just as the post-human will always assert what the human is by that which it supposes itself to be beyond, the zombie both is, and is not, dead and alive."[25] The zombies in *The Walking Dead* "come back" ("Days Gone

Bye"). That is, they do not remain dead. Instead, their brain stems are reactivated, and this is what, in the first instance, makes their decay and their eventual final annihilation possible. This has two implications. First, walkers are capable of dying an additional, and perhaps true, death. Second, the process of decomposition that they are subjected to is a direct result of their first life. Their second life is therefore a life lived in death with all its concomitant viscous inconveniences and not a "dead and alive" state. Put simply, the zombie can only be alive and dead if we understand these processes as concomitant or inclusive of each other. Walkers are no more alive and dead than the humans are alive and dead, in that each ontology encapsulates the other. There is no possibility of death in the world of *The Walking Dead* that does not lead to this second life in death unless we count the bullet through the head that precludes it. Total or final death is only apprehended through the cessation of all life in the dead walker, which would seem to presuppose that walkers cannot be truly dead in the first instance. That their actual death relies on their capacity to "act," understood here as a locomo-cognitive process, is crucial, as it marks the difference between a walker who appears dead because s/he is not moving (and may, therefore, jump when approached) and one who is "alive" and moving. The only way to tell a dead zombie apart from a dying zombie is our capacity to connect movement with being. Even in the escapist scenario of the final bullet, humans are reduced to the brain, to their cognitive selves; yet this should not be equated with an acceptance of the disembodied understanding of consciousness. Rather, in its very dependence on the synaptic connections that make us who we are, it reminds us that being is a totally biological process.

The Walking Dead, thus, totally short-circuits the idea that zombies may stand in for a potential exploration of the non-physical reality of the mind,[26] since that mind and its degenerative corruption are merely replicating the process of death and the eventual collapse of the subject as a sentient and organic body. What seems to be taking place instead is a process whereby the zombie does not lose his/her consciousness but only his/her social qualities or capacity to interact successfully with human beings. In a sense, such a view entails a return to a pre-symbolic state that would seem to come closer to, although it is not interchangeable with, the animal. Walkers are not without consciousness but merely incapable of social interaction with humans—let us remember, they do not eat or attack each other. Walkers run mostly, but not totally, on instinct and have thus lost the capacity to interact or self-reflect. They are a residue condemned to a gradual wasting-away, to a shedding of equal layers of flesh and sociality. In their dying undeath, they represent a thorough challenge to what we understand as human.

Conclusion: Us and Them and "Viscera" Versa

When Carol tells herself that Sophia is no longer "[her] little girl, it's some other thing," in "Nebraska," we can hardly blame her for refusing to acknowledge as a close relation the walker that lumbers out of Hershel's barn with a twisted rictus on her absent face. Similarly, it is difficult to conceive of the pile of exposed viscera that forms our first encounter with "bicycle girl" as a human subject. This rejection of the walker is entirely justified, for these creatures are a direct threat and come coated in a layer of abjection that is hard to shake off. What I hope to have clarified, however, is that, ultimately, walkers problematize the neat divide between us and them, and they do so more thoroughly than the traditional Romero zombie or the bio-zombie. Their collapse of both categories (us and them) into a new figure that is latently conscious (s/he has a residue of memory that impacts on his/her present) poses a challenge to posthumanist conceptions of a fleshless ontology and of the zombie as a valid example of its theoretical possibility. It is important to note that I am not suggesting that walkers cannot be read socially or that they may fail to signify outside their thorough revision of materialist understandings of the body. To do so would be to establish embodiment as a master-discourse for the zombie myth.[27] Much like the somatic body is governed by socio-political, economic, cultural (gendered, sexual) and medical discourses, so the zombie's numbness, retardation, or sedation may come to signify a number of similar positions of repression or marginalization. Similarly, the aggression and destruction inherent to walkers, and zombies more generally, may come to represent a number of practices of resistance, particularly at a time when we seem keen to learn to love (or at least live with) our zombies. This essay does not take issue with these critical approaches.

Instead, what I am suggesting is that we should bring base corporeality back into our reading of zombies, for, underlying all those social inscriptions lies a somatically-felt body. Ignoring how the case of walkers forces us to reconsider notions of embodiment and feeling is tantamount to closing the door to the possibility that the meanings we ascribe to them might ultimately erase the biological investment of contemporary horror. The new dying dead, the walkers in *The Walking Dead*, may still cause fear and horror, but they are one step closer to being humanized, if only because they problematize the differences between life and death as we currently understand them. Perhaps we should read the process of encountering the rotting, latently conscious body as a recognition that, against the transhumanist model, we now contemplate the possibility of being nothing but meat. This is not to say that we are reduced to our bodies, but rather that we are finally apprehending our nature as biological organisms. That we might be nothing but walking, sentient, and socially constructed meat should not come as an existentialist cry of despair, but as a liberation from strains of thought that deny the materialism at the heart of human experience.

NOTES

1. See, for example, Landis, *Monsters in the Movies*, 105.
2. Botting, "Zombie Death Drive," 36, 42.
3. Muntean and Payne, "Attack of the Livid Dead," 246–247.
4. McIntosh, "The Evolution of the Zombie," 7; Dendle, *The Zombie Movie Encyclopedia*, 5.
5. This term will be developed later, but it is important to note that the use of "dying undead" envisions the zombie as residually conscious.
6. Peaty, "Infected with Life," 114.
7. Hawkes, "Are You Just Braaaiiinnnsss or Something More?," 15. "P-zombie" stands for philosophical zombie. See Kirk, *Zombies and Consciousness*, 31–33.
8. Christie and Lauro, Introduction, 2. It is important to note that I am not using the term "zombie" in the same sense that philosophers like Daniel C. Dennett or Robert Kirk have used it. These creatures have been used as models through which to study the relation between consciousness and physicality and are more machinic in nature—and they don't rot.
9. Shaviro, "Capitalist Monsters," 288.
10. Peaty, "Infected with Life," 114. See also Chalmers, *The Conscious Mind*, 94–99.
11. Botting, "Zombie London," 166.
12. Richardson and Harper, "Corporeal Virtuality."
13. Moravec, *Robot*, 12.
14. Moravec, *Mind Children*, 123.
15. Hayles, *How We Became Posthuman*, 286.
16. Wolfe, *What Is Posthumanism?*, xv.
17. Moreland, "Shambling Towards Mount Improbable to Be Born," 85.
18. Warner, *Phantasmagoria*, 368.
19. Lauro and Embry, "A Zombie Manifesto," 87. The different spelling indicates the authors' distinction between the zombie as a physical body and the zombii as a theoretical construct. For Haraway's cyborgian model, see "A Cyborg Manifesto."
20. Ibid., 101.
21. Ibid., 102.
22. Christie, "A Dead New World," 68.
23. Derksen and Hick, "Your Zombie and You," 18.
24. Ibid. Emphasis in the original.
25. Christie and Lauro, Introduction, 2.
26. See, for example, Hawkes, "Are You Just Braaaiiinnnsss or Something More?," 9–10.
27. This is an argument that body theorists are aware of and that they have also addressed. See, for example, Atkinson, Introduction, 9.

Human Choice and Zombie Consciousness

DAWN KEETLEY

Since their cinematic inception in the 1930s, zombies have represented an inner lack: the horrifying evacuation of interiority. Steven Shaviro writes that zombies are "empty shells of life that scandalously continue to function in the absence of any rationale and of any interiority" and that they embody "an ecstatic emptying out of the self."[1] Marina Warner agrees, describing the zombie as "a body which has been hollowed out, emptied of selfhood," going on to assert that the modern zombie has become the sign of "human existential diminishment," the very figure of modernity's loss of the soul.[2] Most recently, Sarah Juliet Lauro and Karen Embry argue that the zombie has "completely lost its mind, becoming a blank—animate, but wholly devoid of consciousness." The terror provoked by the zombie, they contend, is thus "primarily a fear of the loss of consciousness."[3]

The zombies of *The Walking Dead*, however, embody a different fear. They allegorize, this essay argues, not an absence, not loss or emptiness, but instead the overwhelming presence of a de-individualizing and determining corporeality. Peter Dendle has astutely noted that in "an increasingly disembodied—virtual generation, the zombie is becoming increasingly biological." "In their own features," he writes, zombies wear "the biological anatomy of the human animal."[4] So while Kevin Boon writes of the terrifying possibility that "we could look into the body and find only an absence,"[5] *The Walking Dead* suggests that we could look into the body and find, well, the body. And that look inside does not necessarily produce what Boon calls a "loss of internal reliability."[6] Indeed, to look inside and find only matter risks a certain *overdetermination* of who we are: biological conviction replaces existential uncertainty, and this possibility can be just as frightening.[7]

The walkers of *The Walking Dead* signify a particular "inside" that I call "zombie consciousness"—a realm of automatism produced by our bodies (our

156

neurons and our muscles) and over which we have scant conscious control.[8] Zombie consciousness encompasses our reflexes and drives along with the multitude of other functions that scientists of various disciplines argue inhere in our bodies. As psychologists John Bargh and Tanya Chartrand wrote in 1999, "most of daily life is driven by automatic, nonconscious mental processes"[9]— and work in psychology and neuroscience devoted to uncovering what Bargh and Chartrand call "the unbearable automaticity of being"[10] has only proliferated in the more than a decade since they wrote those words. Some scientists have even begun referring to "automatic" systems as "zombie" systems. Neuroscientists Francis Crik and Christof Koch, for instance, have described an "army" of "zombie agents" that carries out specialized sensory-motor processes subserving most of what we do.[11] *The Walking Dead*, then, evokes what has become, in the early twenty-first century, an intensified fear of our own "automaticity," produced by proliferating popularized iterations of the human neurological unconscious.

The fear is an old fear, though, and a persistent fear. Roberto Esposito has traced back to Xavier Bichat, a late eighteenth-century French physiologist, the notion that we have a double life, that "life never breaks its biological link with nature." We are and always have been inextricably bound to our organic, "vegetal" part, a part that co-exists uneasily with the conscious, reasoning actor, the "person" of social, political, and economic life. As Esposito articulates it, "the person is traversed by a power that is foreign to it, which shapes its instincts, emotions, and desires into a form that can no longer be ascribed to a single element. It is as if," he continues, "a non-human— something different from and earlier than animal nature itself—had taken up residence in the human being; or as if it had always been there, with dissolutive effects on the personal modality of this being."[12] The zombie is not only the externalized embodiment of this "non-human" force within us, but it is at the same time, in *The Walking Dead*, clearly internalized too. "We're all infected," Rick tells his group ("Beside the Dying Fire"). The zombie virus has already "taken up residence" within. Indeed, since the virus is expressly given no origin, it has, perhaps, "always been there," and it most certainly has "dissolutive effects" on the "personhood" of the survivors. *The Walking Dead* is inevitably biopolitical, then, in that it is crucially about exploring the "frontier" between "what is human and what, inside the human itself, is other than human."[13] The series maps this "frontier" most visibly, I argue, in its interrogation of choices—choices consciously made and choices impelled by our "zombie consciousness," the paradoxically "non-human" implanted within the human.

This essay will first map the series' hyperbolic repetition of "choice" as a mark of the survivors' humanity. The belief in our status as freely-choosing, rational beings (manifest most clearly in Rick Grimes) is consistently eroded, however, by the turn to bodies. Bodies answer questions; bodies tell us who we are. In this turn to the body, *The Walking Dead* bears the indelible mark of a particular early twenty-first century manifestation of biological determinism—of all the proliferating popular expositions of the "neurological unconscious." Three facets of what I earlier define as zombie consciousness are evident in *The Walking Dead*—in Shane Walsh in particular: the drive to survive, muscle memory, and mimetic desire. All three bodily drives underlie apparent choices, undermining the status of those choices as free, rational, conscious, or even fully "human."

My Choice

Because it ceaselessly evokes the fear of "automaticity," *The Walking Dead* also tries to allay it, and, before exploring the series' representations of "zombie consciousness," I will point out how the series seeks to dispel its own anxious preoccupation with the "non-human" component of the human. The series reiterates *choice* as the humanist principle that marks our ontological difference from the walking dead. We can choose our actions, we can make deliberative decisions, and thus we are not reducible to the reflexes and drives immanent in our bodies. Craig Derksen and Darren Hudson Hick articulate a crucial point of distinction between conscious choice and a physiological reflex: "in philosophy, rational agency is described as the capacity for a thing to make and act according to reasoned choices. Such an agent does not simply respond to stimuli according to innate biological imperatives, but rather *decides* which desires to act on and how. The agent acts on *reasons*."[14] This same distinction manifests itself in *The Walking Dead*. Humans have the capacity for rational agency. Humans can choose their course of action, against the impulsions of instinct, biological imperative, and reflex, and they can do so alone, against the pull of the horde. In contrast, the walkers avidly, thoughtlessly, pursue food—their movement a physiological reflex, an automatic response to stimuli. They flock, mindlessly following each other.

Beginning in the last episode of season one and throughout season two, there are recurring exchanges in the series that foreground "choice." In "TS-19," when the group realizes that Edwin Jenner plans to incinerate the CDC along with everyone in it, Rick appeals to him to let them leave: "That's all we want. A choice. A chance." Andrea wants to stay, but Dale refuses to leave without her, coercing her to flee with the others. Then, in the first episode of season two, Andrea confronts Dale: "Jenner gave us an option. I chose to stay," she tells him angrily. "You chose suicide," he responds. "That was my choice," repeats Andrea. "You took my choice away" ("What Lies Ahead"). In the same episode, Rick and Lori confront the possibility of Carl's death from a gunshot wound and Hershel tells them: "You have to make a choice"—about whether he should go ahead with the surgery to remove the bullet fragments or wait till Shane and Otis come back with crucial equipment. Lori and Rick agonize over their choice, and underlying it is Lori's fear that the better choice may be for Carl to die. In episode six, having discovered that she is pregnant, Lori asks Glenn to get her some abortion pills from the pharmacy. He also gets her prenatal vitamins. "That's a hell of a choice," she tells him. "Glad it's not mine," responds Glenn, adding, "It's your choice" ("Secrets"). In episode ten, Hershel's daughter, Beth, wants to kill herself, and the characters debate whether they should stop her. After Beth cuts herself only superficially, Andrea says: "She wants to live. She made her decision." Lori agrees: "Beth has made her choice and now she wants to live and she knows it" ("18 Miles Out"). Finally, in the debate over whether to kill Randall, Rick and Shane say "We have no choice," but Dale insists: "Keeping our humanity. That's a choice" ("Judge, Jury, Executioner"). Dale thus articulates what the series as a whole dramatizes: "humanity" hinges on "choice."

The repetition of "choice" and *The Walking Dead's* strategy of dramatizing agonizing choices for its characters are a part of the series' creation of an existential world, one that has been stripped of familiar meaning and values, the crutches on which we typically (and often unthinkingly) rely to guide our choices. In this world, it is Rick who most consistently asserts the value of a humanity realized in the act of making free and ethical choices. Brandon Kempner calls him "existentialist Rick,"[15] and, indeed, Rick does seem to embody Sartre's "first principle" of existentialism: "man is nothing else but what he makes of himself."[16] Jen Webb and Sam Byrnand have noted that in most zombie films, the survivors "do so little to distinguish themselves from zombies." In "the horror of their changed world," they continue, "they become like zombies, 'all dark inside.'"[17] Rick, perhaps more than any other character, recognizes this danger, saying to Hershel that the new world they're living in "changes you—either into one of them or a lot less than the person you were" ("Pretty Much Dead Already"). And the series makes it clear that one need not die to become "one of them." Rick continually strives to act in a fully human, ethical way even though (or perhaps because) the world is devoid of rules. As he says to Shane: "Stop acting like you know the rules. There are no rules, man. We're lost" ("18 Miles Out"). Giving up the illusion that there are predetermined rules, recognizing that they're "lost," Rick also recognizes that he makes his own rules, and makes himself, through acts of mindful choice.

An important instance of Rick's willfully choosing an ethical way is when he tells the group that he is going back for Merle Dixon, whom they left handcuffed to a pipe on the roof of a building in Atlanta ("Guts"). Although it was Rick who handcuffed Merle to the pipe, he clearly did not intend to leave him there: they ended up doing so out of necessity (they were being pursued by walkers) and accident (T-Dog dropped the key to the handcuffs down a drain). Rick wants to rectify something he would not have chosen, did not, in fact, choose. After Rick says he's going back for Merle, Shane immediately confronts him: "Why would you risk your life for a douchebag like Merle Dixon.... Merle Dixon—guy wouldn't give you a glass of water if you were dying of thirst." Rick responds: "What he would or wouldn't do doesn't interest me. *I* can't let a man die of thirst. *Me*. Thirst and exposure. We left him like an animal caught in a trap. That's no way for anything to die, let alone a human being" ("Tell It to the Frogs"). Rick responds by insisting that he will adopt no one else's value system—that he will choose his own ("*I* can't let a man die of thirst. *Me*"). By insisting on Merle's humanity, and by making his own conscious choice, Rick asserts his *own* humanity, responding to Merle's desperate cry to T-Dog who, at the end of the prior episode, was alone on the rooftop with him, with the key: "You can't leave me here. It's not human."[18]

Except for Something in the Brain

The Walking Dead undercuts its own hyperbolic reiterations of choice, however, suggesting that not all our choices are conscious and that they are not, in the end, *reliable* markers of our difference from zombies. The series can't free itself (just as we can't) of zombie consciousness, of the immanent non-human. It's significant, for instance, that in the highly-politicized moment when Lori faces her "choice" between pre-natal vitamins and abortion pills, she "chooses" to take the abortion pills but then reflexively vomits them back up ("Secrets"). Who, or what, "chooses" here? And the fact that Lori may well have tried to make the rational "choice" when she took the abortion pills is emphasized when she dies in a horribly painful childbirth scene in the aptly named season three episode, "Killer Within."

All zombie narratives inevitably evoke a materialism that attenuates our choice: we live in dangerous proximity to the zombie body, not least because zombies are creatures of purely biological drives, notably the drive to consume, which we undoubtedly share. *The Walking Dead*, though, seems particularly preoccupied with the interiors of bodies—and not just as spectacle. The insides of bodies answer questions. A notable example of this is when

Rick and Daryl are looking for Sophia in the woods and run across a walker. They are afraid that it might have eaten Sophia, so in an extended gut-churning scene, they dig in the contents of its stomach to find the missing girl ("What Lies Ahead"). This search in the literal insides of a zombie is ironically juxtaposed with Rick's asking God, later, for a sign that Sophia is still alive. The hope for the transcendent sign, however, has dissolved, in *The Walking Dead*, into a search for a masticated body part inside a walking corpse. The search for truth, for a miraculous "sign," seems always to turn back to the body.

The final episode of season one ("TS-19") articulates the series' anxious preoccupation with the determining force of the body, offering another instance of the group's ending up at bodily interiors when they seek answers. At the CDC, Jenner first shows the survivors the fMRI of his wife's living brain, explaining to them that the lights they see *are* "a person's life." "Somewhere in all that organic wiring," he continues, "all those ripples of light, is you—the thing that makes you unique and human." The lights, he continues, the synapses of the brain, "*determine* everything a person says, does, or thinks from the moment of birth to the moment of death" (emphasis mine). Jenner then shows the group an fMRI of the "test subject" dying and reanimating, light returning (partially) to her brain. In response to Lori's question—"It re-starts the brain?"—he replies "No. Just the brain stem. Basically it gets them up and moving." Rick comments on the obvious difference of the post-death fMRI: "It's nothing like before. Most of that brain is dark." Jenner agrees: "Dark, lifeless, dead," evoking philosopher David Chalmers' description of the zombie as "all dark inside."[19] "The frontal lobe," Jenner continues, "the neo-cortex, the human part, that doesn't come back. The you-part."[20] Instead, after the "resurrection," we see "[j]ust a shell driven by mindless instinct." Jenner draws a line, then, between human (the "you-part") and what gets reanimated ("a shell driven by mindless instinct"), but it's a line not very easily held since human and zombie alike are the product of activity in the brain. In fact, when Rick asks, "But they're not alive ...?," Jenner pointedly does not answer the question. "You tell me," he responds. His conception of life as inhering in the brain, produced by the brain's "organic wiring," does not easily allow him to say that a creature similarly animated is not, in fact, alive.

Much current research in psychology, neuroscience, and cognitive science suggests that who we are may indeed come down to what's in the brain, our "organic wiring," fundamentally questioning the extent to which we are free agents. As philosopher Todd Moody writes: "Increasingly, scientists are finding that what happens in consciousness is not essential for understanding mental functioning. We recognize each other, solve problems, use language, and although all these things have 'conscious accompaniments' it seems that the real work is not done consciously at all."[21] This insight is repeated over and over in books and articles written in the last two decades. "Given one's understandable desire to believe in free will and self-determination," write Bargh and Chartrand, "it may be hard to bear that most of daily life is driven by automatic, nonconscious mental processes."[22] Unbearable indeed—especially when the human is defined, and distinguished from other animals, in large part by our ability to make reasoned choices.

Numerous scientists have been illuminating our neurological unconscious—our "zombie consciousness"—an unacknowledged, often inaccessible, physiological bedrock underlying (and attenuating) our conscious selves. The neurological unconscious is not synonymous with the ineffable "psyche" but is constituted by and in the body; it is the very tangible ground of our choices, yet it is terrain that eludes our conscious grasp. Neuroscientist Antonio Damasio imagines the conscious mind connected by a "long umbilical cord" to the "depths of very elementary and very *un*-conscious regulators" of the mind and continues with the inevitable conclusion that our conscious selves "are not in control of every decision."[23] Psychologist Daniel Kahneman's recent book describes the "automatic operations" and the "unconscious operations" that form one part of the two-part system, which, he argues, determines our choices and judgments beyond the reach of conscious deliberation. Most "impressions and thoughts," he writes, arise in your conscious experience without your knowing how they got there." "Much of our mental work," he continues, that "produces impressions, intuitions, and many decisions goes on in silence in our minds."[24] In a chapter tellingly entitled, "There's Someone in My Head, But It's Not Me," neuroscientist David Eagleman sums up the argument of his book *Incognito*: "most of what we do and think and feel is not under our conscious control. The vast jungle of neurons," he further explains, "operate their own programs."[25] And in his recent book, *Consciousness*, neuroscientist Christof Koch argues for his slow conversion to the belief that we are largely shaped by unconscious processes: "the actions of the sovereign 'I' are determined by habit, instincts, and impulses that largely bypass conscious inspection."[26] In all these accounts, the neurological unconscious is a version of the foreign power that, according to Esposito, traverses the human, shaping "its instincts, emotions, and desires"—a "non-human" yet organic "something," "different from and earlier than animal nature itself."[27] This neurological unconscious is granted an autonomy, moreover, yet it is distinctly not the autonomy of the conscious human actor; it is a non-conscious, non-reasoning, "elementary" (as Damasio puts it) autonomy—and thus it is well embodied in the zombie, incarnation of the neurological unconscious.

Zombie Consciousness i: Survival

If conscious choice is exemplified particularly by Rick Grimes, zombie consciousness is embodied in Shane Walsh, and it drives him toward increasingly violent conflict with Rick. Derksen and Hick contrast the capacity to act "according to reasoned choices" with the response "to stimuli according to innate biological imperatives."[28] One particularly powerful form of an "innate biological imperative" in *The Walking Dead* (in all zombie narratives in fact) is the mandate of survival. This mandate is incarnate in the walkers themselves—in their ferocious drive to eat at all costs that, in *The Walking Dead*, seems at least in part to be about staving off starvation. Early in season one, the survivors speculate that the walkers are leaving Atlanta and will be encroaching on their camp because they are searching for food. In season three, the Governor's scientist, Milton Mamet, studies Michonne's two zombie slaves, whose jaws she removed, and he reports to the Governor: "They are starving; they just do it slower than we do" ("Walk with Me"). In *The Walking Dead*, walker and human alike are driven by the biological mandate to find food in order to survive.

While Rick, exemplar of rational decision-making, very rarely makes arguments based on doing what it takes to survive, Shane does so in virtually every episode, and his claims about the necessity of survival come with a corollary claim about the evacuation of choice, as in "I had no choice" or "We have no choice." Shane articulates perfectly in "18 Miles Out" the stance he invariably adopts. He and Rick drive Randall (stray member of another, potentially dangerous group) eighteen miles from the farm, blindfolded, to abandon him in a place from where he'll be unable to return (they fear his finding his group again and leading a raid on the farm). They end up discovering, though, that Randall went to school with Maggie and knows exactly where her farm is, so Shane immediately proclaims that they must kill him—for the survival of their group: "The right choice is the one that keeps us alive," he insists. This demand prompts Rick to say: "Stop acting like you know the rules. There are no rules, man," and, undoubtedly, Shane's continual insistence that his way, the way of survival, is the *only choice* suggests he is following some unspoken but absolute rule, as if he knows the play-book of the post-apocalyptic world. Shane tends to eschew thought and deliberation—jumping always to the single choice that he claims is the one, the only one, that will enable them to survive. When Rick says that, yes, they'll probably have to kill Randall, but he needs at least one night to "think about it," Shane is baffled—because he *just knows* Randall must die, that it's "the right choice." For him, the law of survival pre-exists him. It is a kind of instinctive knowledge rooted not in the mind but in the body, in the organism's habit of living. Indeed, Shane never needs to think about the "choices" he makes because for him, despite what Rick says, there *are* rules (not really choices at all), and he knows what they are. They are embodied rules, the rules of nature and of instinct.

Shane's imperative of survival involves not only choices that in the end are not choices at all, but it also typically involves abandoning someone (something Rick never does, through the end of season two at least). The most dramatic instance of Shane's mandate of survival is his horrifying action in "Save the Last One." He and Otis go to the high school near Hershel's farm to get medical supplies necessary to save Carl's life after Otis accidentally shoots him. Pursued by a horde of walkers, Otis and Shane are limping toward their car, and it becomes apparent that they will not make it. Confronted with what he believes is a choice to live or die, Shane shoots Otis in the leg and leaves him for the walkers, a distraction so he can escape. Shane is motivated in part to save Carl—but presumably Otis could have delivered the supplies just as well if Shane had left himself for bait. Although he doesn't admit it, Shane leaves Otis to be eaten by zombies so *he can survive*. It's a "choice" that happens at a relatively unconscious level—a choice he makes through and with his body, his gut, his instinct. The only time Shane talks about it honestly is with Rick, who asks him: "Was it to survive?" Shane responds: "If one of us wasn't going to make it out, it had to be him. Reality is, he had no business being here—or there" ("18 Miles Out"). As in other moments, Shane's imperative of survival—that *he* must survive, that such is the dictate of "reality"—involves choices that are no choice at all and that diminish other lives.

Zombie Consciousness ii: Muscle Memory

Shane embodies not only the instinct of survival, but also "muscle memory," a notion that the body—flesh, nerves, muscle, and sinews—contains its own form of knowledge, instilled through routine and habit. Shane voices this view on the two occasions he's teaching Andrea to shoot: someone has to die, he tells her, "and you better hope you're the one making that decision." These moments of "decision" pointedly exclude conscious cognition. He tells her, when confronting her target, to "use your instinct.... Turn off a switch—the switch—the one that makes you scared, or angry, or sympathetic—whatever. You don't think. You just act" ("Cherokee Rose"). Then, again, the next time they're at target practice, he tells her she's too emotional and that she needs "to shut it down. Do not think about it," he continues. "I'm talking about muscle memory, girl, muscle memory" ("Secrets"). Prior to thought and even feeling is the archaic knowledge of the body—"muscle memory"—which draws on an individual's repetitious actions and a species' millennia of sheer survival. It is knowledge integrally bound up with what Dale despairingly calls "survival of the fittest," and it prompts action, instinctive un-thought action, to ensure one's own survival.

What Shane describes as "muscle memory" may indeed be integral to human behavior, but, at the same time, it blurs the line between human and zombie, as does a shared survival instinct. One recognizably "human" trait that zombies are consistently represented as still possessing is a very rudimentary, corporeal memory—that's why the zombies flock to the mall in Romero's *Dawn of the Dead* and hew to the places and the tasks that formed their habitual lives in the opening of *Land of the Dead*—and it's why Morgan's wife, in "Days Gone Bye," haunts the house where she died and where her husband and son still live. In season three, when Milton tries to test his hypothesis that "there might be a trace of the person they were still trapped inside"—"like an echo," as he puts it ("Walk with Me")—he looks to memory to provide evidence of the persistence of the person. Milton repeatedly enacts certain rituals with a man dying of cancer and then tries to induce him to repeat those actions once he has re-animated; Milton's zombie subject does indeed seem fleetingly to demonstrate memory, but then Andrea shoots him in the head before we can be sure ("When the Dead Come Knocking").

As Richard Shusterman defines it, muscle memory is "a term commonly used in everyday discourse for the sort of embodied implicit memory that unconsciously helps us to perform various motor tasks we have somehow learned through habituation"—either through intentional training or "unconscious learning from repeated prior experience."[29] Actions performed from muscle memory are accomplished without our conscious awareness, thus constituting an integral part of our zombie consciousness. Koch explicitly identifies as "muscle memory" all those "unconscious mechanisms" that "subserve" much of what we do and that he calls "zombie agents." "Collectively," he writes, "this zombie army manages the fluid and rapid interplay of muscles and nerves that is at the heart of all skills and that makes up a lived life." Constant repetition "recruits an army of zombie agents," making the skill effortless, and so "emptying your mind" when you're doing something and "free[ing] up your inner zombie."[30] While all of us inevitably (in order to function at all) have such "zombie agents" at work inside, Shane is exemplar *par excellence* of this way of being—not only in his explicit exhortations to Andrea to let go of emotion and thought when she confronts an antagonist but also in his own repeated resistance to thought at all. While Rick, Dale and Hershel debate their decisions, often second-guessing themselves, Shane is typically mute and unwavering, embodiment of the process by which "emptying your mind ... frees up your inner zombie."[31]

Zombie Consciousness iii: Mimetic Desire

It is important to note that despite his unwillingness to defend his choices, Shane is nonetheless to some degree *aware* of the ways in which he is impelled by the survival mandate and by muscle memory. He articulates these impulses and gives conscious assent to them, although he may not be aware of *how much* they guide him—and some of what he articulates is after-the-fact rationalization of actions he may not have been aware of choosing *at the time*. For Shane, as for all of us, zombie consciousness and conscious choice are imbricated, clarifying the fact that they are not opposed *alternatives* but opposing poles of a *continuum*. A final aspect of the neurological unconscious embodied by Shane, though, mimetic desire, seems much more thoroughly beyond the reach of conscious control.

Mimetic desire fundamentally circumvents conscious choice. As elaborated by René Girard, it is the mechanism by which we desire not an object of our own free choice but, unconsciously, an object of someone else's choice: we desire someone or something *because someone else does*. Girard writes that we "literally do not know what to desire and, in order to find out, we watch the people we admire: we imitate their desire. Both models and imitators of the same desire," he continues, "inevitably desire the same object and become rivals." Girard describes the contagiousness of mimetic desire, arguing that the desire of the imitator infects the desire of the model, and thus both come to desire the object with an increasingly virulent intensity: "Their rival desires literally feed on one another: the imitator becomes the model of his model, and the model the imitator of his imitator." Girard ends by describing how mimetic desire can spread to the entire group: "these imitative or mimetic rivalries can become so intense and contagious that not only do they lead to murder but they spread, mimetically, to entire communities."[32] This "spreading" is due at least in part to the unconsciousness of the mimetic mechanism: the imitator does not know why he or she desires the rival's object; the rival does not know why he or she suddenly desires his or her own object more; and the community as a whole does not understand why conflict spirals out of control.

Several recent studies have posited the possible origins of mimetic desire in the brain, exploring, specifically, the links between mimesis and mirror neurons. The discovery of mirror neurons has confirmed that imitation is foundational to human development: mirror neurons in the brain are activated not only when we do something, but *when we see someone else do something.*[33] Indeed, psychiatrist Jean-Michel Oughourlian argues that mirror neurons are making it possible to re-think desire, which needs no longer to be "hidden away in in a part of the psyche arbitrarily isolated under the name of 'the unconscious,'" but which will, instead, finally be understood "as located in the *other*, on the level of neurons and physiology."[34] Scientists are proposing, in other words, that desire is fundamentally rooted in what neuroscientist Vittorio Gallese aptly calls "intercorporeity," the biological basis of intersubjectivity.[35] In ways that are outside of our conscious control, our bodies thus play a major role in shaping our relationships to others. Scientists working on mirror neurons, including those drawing connections to Girard's work on mimesis, typically emphasize the positive aspects of "incorporeity"—our ability to identify and empathize with others. Girard insists, however, that mimetic desire is also the root of violence.[36] As a post-apocalyptic narrative, *The Walking Dead* inevitably explores the darker side of our biological propensity to imitate each other. That neurons in our brain may well be behind mimetic desire, along with the contagious rivalry and conflict that ensues, is one more variety of automaticity inherent in our bodies. It is also a bodily propensity—an immanent contagion—thoroughly embodied by Shane.

Disclosing the fundamentally imitative nature of his desire at the end of season one, Shane articulates what has been clear since the beginning of the series—his desire for Lori *as Rick's wife.*[37] Telling Lori what happened when he left Rick at the hospital as the epidemic broke out, he says: "I would have traded places with him, I would have. I would trade places with him right now. I love you"—after which he tries unsuccessfully to force Lori to have sex with him ("TS-19"). The temporal sequence of these sentences demonstrates the priority of Shane's love for Rick. Indeed, when Dale accuses him of trying to kill Rick, Shane tells him that Rick is "a man I love. I love him like my brother" ("Secrets"). Shane's love for Rick, which he says would have made him trade places with him in the past—he wishes *he* were the one who had been shot— seems literally to generate his desire for Rick's wife and his desire to trade places with him *now.*

While on the surface mimetic desire seems to be about love and desire, it also breeds conflict. Gallese notes that "appropriative mimicry" (the desire to have another's object of desire for oneself) is "the main source of aggressiveness and violence characterizing our species."[38] And in *The Walking Dead*, the mimetic desire that rivets Rick, Shane, Lori (and Carl) does in fact produce much of the series' violence. Shane shoots Otis and leaves him for bait, for instance, not only for his own survival but also to save Carl's life and to prove to Lori that he can protect her and Carl more effectively than Rick can. This drive to "protect" Lori and Carl—which is really about appropriating them for himself—is also behind Shane's wrenching open Hershel's barn doors, triggering the mass slaughter of the walkers, and it motivates Shane's drive to kill Randall as a threat to the group (i.e., to Lori and Carl). As Lori says to Rick, "Shane thinks I'm his. He thinks the baby is his. And he says you can't protect us. That you're gonna get us killed. He's dangerous, and he won't stop" ("Triggerfinger"). After Lori articulates the threat Shane poses, the violence starts to spread uncontrollably. Everyone (except for Dale and Andrea) decides they want Randall dead, for instance—and Dale tells them that the group is now irretrievably broken, that the people they were are "dead" ("Judge, Jury, Executioner"). Dale is killed, then Randall, then Shane—and then the walkers overrun the farm. Mimetic desire, as Girard writes, breeds an "epidemic of reciprocal violence that never becomes explicit as such."[39] This plague is fully realized when the zombie hordes spread over Hershel's farm in "Beside the Dying Fire," utterly destroying the survivors' sanctuary. Literally brought to the farm by the shot fired (by Carl) during Rick and Shane's confrontation, the walkers materialize "the epidemic of reciprocal violence" bred by a mimetic desire that has Shane at its center.[40]

One sign of the escalation of mimetic desire is the proliferation of what Girard calls "mimetic *doubles*."[41] Like the plague itself, which is "universally presented as a process of undifferentiation, a destruction of specificities,"[42] the generation of doubles destroys individuality. Just as the walkers are for the most part de-individualized in *The Walking Dead*, appearing only as a horde, so mimetic desire, centered on Shane, produces an attenuation of his (human) distinctiveness. Indeed, Shane is represented increasingly as double, not least in his persistent mirroring by walkers. As early as the second episode of the first season, for instance, Lori is alone in the woods looking for food when she hears noises made by what she thinks is a walker: instead, Shane lurches out at her ("Guts"). In another instance, after he kills Otis, Shane attends his funeral staggering like a walker ("Cherokee Rose"). His doubling of the walkers occurs yet again near the opening of "Pretty Much Dead Already." Shane looks in the barn (they've just found out it's full of walkers). There's a shot of his face, centered on his eye, looking through a large gap in the wood, and then there's an immediate reverse shot to a walker looking back, a sequence that joins Shane and the walker. The visual alignment of Shane with the walkers culminates in the episode in which he dies, the penultimate episode of season two. Early in the episode, Shane kills Randall, and both before and after this event, he looks like a zombie—blood on his face, vacant expression, lurching movement. Similar kinds of shots cluster around Shane's attempt to kill Rick: his expression is blank, his breathing guttural. And throughout the episode, he seems inarticulate, as if he's struggling to say anything at all ("Better Angels"). In the last episode, "Beside the Dying Fire," once we learn that the survivors are already infected, it seems in hindsight that Shane evinced the symptoms of infection *before death*. Driven by mimetic desire toward violence, toward a dizzying proximity to the zombies, Shane is increasingly positioned as their mimetic double.

Before Shane becomes his own zombie double, before he dissolves into the endlessly reproducing mimetic doubles of the zombie horde, Rick too is drawn into the mimetic dynamic—drawn, despite himself, into a violence he abhors. When Rick stabs Shane in "Better Angels," convinced that Shane is going to kill him, he disclaims responsibility for the act, asserting that it was Shane who did it: "This was you. Not me. Not me. You made me do this." This moment represents an unusual evasion of agency on Rick's part. He claims a kind of determinism—that he had no choice—that has more often been Shane's domain, and that thus indicates Rick's doubling of Shane. There is, moreover, a confusion of identities in Rick's claim that Shane did it, not him, even though Rick literally held and used the knife. Shane's imitation of Rick, his desire for what is Rick's, has escalated and spread, and Rick has now come to imitate Shane—that is, he kills to survive.

Rick's and Shane's collapse into each other—Rick's becoming infected by what Shaviro has called the "chain of mimetic transference"[43]—is visually suggested by a very odd set of three flash cuts inserted into the narrative after Shane dies. We see three quick shots of zombies feasting on bloody flesh—not actual diegetic walkers-in-the-woods but rather some nightmarish extradiegetic images, perhaps an attempt to capture an *internal* state ("Better Angels"). On the one hand, these shots could be a visual marker of Shane's imminent return as a walker—but Shane is already dead, and the last (and only other time) flash cuts like this interrupted *The Walking Dead's* narrative was in season one when Jim was dying—infected by a zombie bite *but not yet dead* ("Wildfire"). If these shots represent visually the "consciousness" of the living-yet-infected not-quite-zombie, then they could represent Rick's interiority—the only "live" human there. Indeed, while in "Wildfire" the shots were anchored clearly to Jim's consciousness, here they seem to hover somewhere *between* Rick and Shane, joining the two men, and implying Rick's following Shane in his fall into zombie consciousness.

In the end, *The Walking Dead* adumbrates a persistent question, an always-lurking anxiety, about the origins of our choices. Do we have free choice or are we determined by forces of which we're unaware? This question has been (re)animated in the twenty-first century by popular expositions of the neurological unconscious, all of which suggest we are driven by forces immanent in our bodies—automatic consciousness, muscle memory, mirror neurons, mimetic desire. In truth, this question about our capacity for choice, for self-awareness, is one of the most important and persistent with which we grapple. As Marco Iacoboni puts it: "Traditionally, biological determinism of individual behavior is contrasted by a view of humans capable of rising above their biological makeup to define themselves through their ideas and their social codes."[44] The existentialists inhabited one pole of this implied dichotomy, especially Sartre who emphasized the *cogito*, the thinking, freely-choosing human—eschewing any shred of biological determinism. There "is no explaining things away by reference to a fixed and given human nature," wrote Sartre. "In other words, there is no determinism, man is free, man is free-dom."[45] Recent scientific discoveries—of strata of automatic action, of muscle memory, of mirror neurons—tend toward the opposite pole, suggesting that we are more determined by our bodies than we know: "Mirror neuron research," says Iacoboni, who is at the forefront of such research, "suggests that our social codes are largely dictated by our biology."[46] People who may never read the esoteric writings of either existentialist philosophers or neuroscientists recognize the central questions taken up by such work—and they are able to work through such questions by watching popular texts like *The Walking Dead*, which brilliantly dramatizes both existentialist free choice and varieties of biological determinism—condensing "big" questions in concrete conflicts discussed endlessly on blogs and message boards: Was Shane right to shoot Otis? Should the group execute Randall? Was Rick right to shoot Shane? Who is the better leader in a post-apocalyptic world—Shane or Rick? In raising these questions, *The Walking Dead* animates perennial questions about human subjectivity—human nature, biological determinism, and human choice—locating enduring questions within the insights provided (and anxieties provoked) by the philosophy and science of its historical moment.

NOTES

1. Shaviro, *The Cinematic Body*, 85, 103.
2. Warner, *Phantasmagoria*, 357, 367, 368.
3. Lauro and Embry, "A Zombie Manifesto," 89–90.
4. Dendle, "Zombie Movies," 183.
5. Boon, "The Zombie as Other," 54.
6. Ibid., 55.
7. Webb and Byrnand discuss the zombie in a similar way, suggesting that it illuminates "something about the constitution and functioning of the self—and particularly of the

inaccessibility of (much of) the self to the laws of language, culture and society." They suggest that this inaccessibility is in part about the automatic functioning of the body, citing neurologist Richard Cytowic who writes: "'Part(s) of us are *inaccessible to self-awareness*, the latter being only the tip of the iceberg of who and what we really are. The 'I' is a superficial self-awareness constructed by our unfathomable part.'" Webb and Byrnand, "Some Kind of Virus," 88–89.

8. Zombie consciousness is similar to what Anna Gibbs has called the "corporeal unconscious." Gibbs defines the corporeal unconscious slightly differently, more narrowly, than my "zombie consciousness": the "corporeal unconscious is animated by sympathy, a putative affinity between certain things—including bodies and organs—which makes them liable not only to be similarly affected by the same influence, but more especially to affect or influence one another." Gibbs's definition certainly applies to my later discussion of mimetic desire and mirror neurons, and Gibbs references, fleetingly, both Girard's mimetic desire and mirror neurons. Gibbs, "Panic!," 135, 144, 140.

9. Bargh and Chartrand, "The Unbearable Automaticity of Being," 464.

10. Ibid.

11. Koch, *Consciousness*, 78–81.

12. Esposito, *Third Person*, 24.

13. Ibid.

14. Derksen and Hick, "Your Zombie and You," 15.

15. Kempner, "The Optimism of *The Walking Dead*," 146.

16. Sartre, *Existentialism*, 15.

17. Webb and Byrnand, "Some Kind of Virus," 86. The phrase "all dark inside" is from philosopher David Chalmers, *The Conscious Mind*, 96.

18. Rick makes this choice numerous times—notably when he runs into the woods to try to save Sophia ("What Lies Ahead"); when he goes into town to get Hershel ("Nebraska"); when he saves Randall ("Triggerfinger"); and when he saves Shane ("18 Miles Out").

19. Chalmers, *The Conscious Mind*, 96.

20. Jenner's attempt to distinguish the "human part" from the brain stem is misleading, since the brain stem *is* the "human part." Neuroscientist Antonio Damasio has argued that brains begin building conscious minds "not at the level of the cerebral cortex but rather at the level of the brain stem." "Primordial feelings," he writes, which happen in the brain stem, "are not only the first images generated by the brain but also immediate manifestations of sentience." Damasio, *Self Comes to Mind*, 23.

21. Moody, "Conversations with Zombies," 197.

22. Bargh and Chartrand, "The Unbearable Automaticity of Being," 464.

23. Damasio, *Self Comes to Mind*, 29, 30.

24. Kahneman, *Thinking Fast and Slow*, 4.

25. Eagleman, *Incognito*, 4.

26. Koch, *Consciousness*, 77.

27. Esposito, *Third Person*, 24.

28. Derksen and Hick, "Your Zombie and You," 15.

29. Shusterman, "Muscle Memory."

30. Koch, *Consciousness*, 80, 78, 80, 81.

31. Koch, *Consciousness*, 81.

32. Girard, "Violence and Religion," 9–10.

33. For scholarship drawing connections between Girard's theory of mimetic desire and mirror neurons, see Garrels, "Imitation, Mirror Neurons, and Mimetic Desire"; Oughourlian, *The Genesis of Desire*, esp. 92–95; and Gallese, "The Two Sides of Mimesis."

34. Oughourlian, *Genesis of Desire*, 93–94.

35. Gallese, "The Two Sides of Mimesis," 33.

36. Garrels has argued that "there still remains a suspicious absence, among imitation theories, of considerations of the role that reciprocal mimesis has in generating acts of social rivalry, conflict, and ultimately violence." See Garrels, "Imitation, Mirror Neurons, and Mimetic Desire," 50.

37. In an essay on the comic series, Kempner notes how Shane "is attempting to live Rick's former life." "Shane wants to be the perfect husband, father, cop, and protector," he continues, but since "he can't be those things himself, he has to steal them from Rick. As Rick is trying to change into a new sort of person, Shane is literally trying to turn into Rick." He writes later that Shane "can't stand the nothingness and freedom," so "he has to become Rick, to take his place, to be someone by stealing Rick's identity." Kempner, "The Optimism of *The Walking Dead*," 149–150. Since Shane makes only a relatively brief appearance in the comic, being shot by Carl fairly early on, it's not particularly surprising that the TV series, in expanding Shane's role, dramatically extends the theme of Shane's mimetic desire.

38. Gallese, "The Two Sides of Mimesis," 21.

39. Girard, "The Plague in Literature and Myth," 845.

40. Fischer suggests that in the TV series "Darabont opens up the possibility that the plague is, in fact, caused by Shane's illicit love for Lori." Even in the comic series, he notes that "Shane's long-deferred love for Lori may be the unconscious cause of the catastrophe, the male sex drive displaced into the wholesale *Thanatos* of zombie cannibalism." Fischer uses language from Freudian psychoanalysis and doesn't develop his theory about Shane, but the idea is similar to my own reading of Shane's mimetic desire as the unconscious driving force of at least some of the devastation wrought in season two. Fischer, "Meaninglessness," 78, 76,

41. Girard, "The Plague in Literature and Myth," 840.

42. Ibid., 833.

43. Shaviro, *The Cinematic Body*, 97.

44. Iacoboni, *Mirroring People*, 269.

45. Sartre, *Existentialism*, 122–123.

46. Iacoboni, *Mirroring People*, 269.

"Talking Bodies" in a Zombie Apocalypse

From the Discursive to the Shitty Sublime

GARY FARNELL

In an iconic moment from the first episode of AMC's television series *The Walking Dead*, Rick Grimes wakes from his hospital bed to a zombie apocalypse. Wandering through the hospital, he comes across a double door with the words "Dont [sic] Open Dead Inside" ("Days Gone Bye"). "Dead Inside" signifies an alternative title for the whole series, for it defines the condition of the zombies who are themselves the living (walking) dead, the uncanniest of *flâneurs*. This door scene has generated an entire popular imaginary of the uncanny undead. And rightly so ... the director Frank Darabont has clearly taken great pains to ensure the whole shot comes out right. He films the door image in such a way that it interrupts the narrative flow on screen, announcing itself as the (disjointed and "illiterate") *leitmotiv* that it is. What Darabont stages is a talking point, hence the discussion that takes place in this essay. A certain unpacking of the significance of the image is invited from the moment it appears before Rick's and our eyes. A picture speaks a thousand words *at least*.

What, then, is the meaning of "Dead Inside"? The question refracts the key problem of meaning in the new millennium. Meaning itself breaks down by virtue of its very marketability in our age—one of free-market capitalism's hegemony. Here, the ascendancy and grossly matter-of-fact rule of exchange value entails not just a certain usurping of use value but also the subordination of public values, of progressive politics, and of human-scaled social relations, generating a weird new illiteracy in the culture and in the commodity-as-system. In this type of civic illiteracy, not knowing how to read words overlaps with an inability to read the world. The zombie emerges as a figure standing in a symbolic relation to this situation. Hence the appropriateness, to an extent, of the element of illiteracy in that warning about the threat posed to sentient beings by zombies: "Dont [sic] Open Dead Inside." That the zombies are not able to *speak* themselves and their world, revealing a truly psychotic breakdown of their basic linguistic constitutivity—or the pornography of authoritarianism itself—is the important thing. Why? Because it is not that the zombies in Darabont's universe suffer a major loss of consciousness through becoming "dead inside." These zombies are not like the somnambulistic Jessica Holland in *I Walked with a Zombie*, Jacques Tourneur's 1943 *film noir* (how different is the *walking* in Darabont from that in Tourneur!). They sense Rick's presence on the other side of the locked double door and begin clawing at the opening down the middle. Nor, moreover, are these zombies "dead inside" as Sarah Juliet Lauro and Karen Embry describe them in their epoch-making "A Zombie Manifesto" of 2008. For Lauro and Embry, the *living dead* are pre-eminently creatures of the boundary, deconstructing the "third space" of inside-and-outside. As a result, life-death infects death-life and vice versa. Insightful as this argument is, because it links zombies with the question of consciousness rather than that of language, it does not fully explain "Dead Inside" and its refracting of a post-millennial problem of meaning.

Aphasia

The sense in which the properly post-millennial zombies are "dead inside" is in terms of their peculiar form of aphasia. They are both traumatically and obscenely *hyper-aphasic*. They suffer an immediate, total loss of speech upon their being bitten, hence the zombie's familiar rasp, gurgle, cry. This loss of speech, however, does not return the zombie to a pre-verbal infant stage, the Latin etymology of which—*infans* = speech-*less*—Jacques Lacan has investigated so acutely. Rather, the zombies exhibit a condition of total language loss, but one which will have been, in the *futur antérieur*, mediated by the famous "linguistic turn" of twentieth-century thought (from Saussure to Jakobson to Lévi-Strauss to Julia Kristeva as essayist of "abjection"). In other words, they are a negative means of exploring precisely how both the subject and meaning are *not*—are not pre-given outside of language (theorized as production). Zombies, especially those of today's new illiteracy, tend to epitomize a situation inhabited by individuals unable to speak themselves from a position of agency—that is, from symbolic points of enunciation. They thus bring into focus a crisis of democracy, no less, where speech becomes emptied of content and sapped of substance through the very workings of so-called "free" markets, replacing meaningful exchange and public debate with the dead language of a generalized, consumer-driven zombification (a state of affairs first critiqued at the dawn of the present age in George A. Romero's aptly-titled 1978 shopping mall satire *Dawn of the Dead*).

Elaine Scarry's classic study *The Body in Pain*, sub-titled *The Making and Unmaking of the World*, reads as a commentary on what is signified regarding the "illiterate" zombies' deadness to which our attention is drawn via the door *leitmotiv*. For Scarry, "what is quite literally at stake in the body in pain is the making and unmaking of the world."[1] Here, the speaking subject who loses the power of speech by dint of bodily pain loses a great deal: the sheer constitutivity of the signifier. Thus, word-making encapsulates the human capacity to make a world. Scarry writes: "To witness the moment when pain causes a reversion to the pre-language of cries and groans is to witness the destruction of language."[2] She adds, "but conversely, to be present when a person moves up out of that pre-language and projects the facts of sentience into speech is almost to have been permitted to be present at the birth of language itself."[3] For the living dead, however, there is no moving up out of "pre-language"; they remain condemned to a life of pain, to a state of existence (a monstrous bondage no less) of the wordless zombie body *qua* pain. Here we have the antithesis of any kind of dizzying disembodiment idealized in postmodern culture or in New Age religion: a grotesque realism that mimes what is fantastically real *in* capitalist modernity. Whenever a zombie flares up in a rage of wrathful, rasping ineloquence, this is doubtless part of the message that is meant to be conveyed to us: the problem of meaning—crisis of literacy, crisis of democracy—is "articulated" in that very gesture.

"He say somethin'?"

That language itself is the issue is revealed by inversion a couple of scenes later in the first episode of *The Walking Dead*. Rick finds his way home but is hit in the face by a survivor, Duane, who is carrying a shovel: Duane's father Morgan rushes over while Rick is recovering and quickly asks his son, "He say somethin'?" In a sense, this is a very twenty-first-century question to ask. Morgan knows implicitly by now that the test of being able to talk—and *not* any test of consciousness (Rick is half-conscious at this point)—is the true test of not being dead in the zombie sense, that is, *dead inside*. Quite a lot is made of the fact that Rick is a rather taciturn character: he confides to his friend Shane that his wife Lori complains that he never *speaks*. But this taciturnity of course constitutes an altogether different condition to the kind of language destruction experienced by the zombies who nonetheless often resemble human beings like Rick at the level of outward bodily semblance.

The Walking Dead continually plays with the idea that it is often quite difficult to differentiate between the living and the dead, between those who are human and those who are not. The first human Rick encounters in the landscape of the zombie apocalypse—a blonde-haired little girl in dressing gown and slippers—turns out not to be human at all, as Rick discovers once she turns round to face him directly and displays her ghastly visage. Indeed, the tendency to refer to "zombies" as "walkers" in *The Walking Dead* has a specific humanizing effect *vis-à-vis* the zombies. In this respect, Darabont's television series joins with wider debates about the nature of the human condition—at times, the posthuman condition—under late or neo-liberal or global capitalism. So, for example, there is a nice play on words in the title of Carl Cederström and Peter Fleming's *Dead Man Working*, an account of the world of work under late capitalism, *late* capitalism in that their starting point is that "capitalism died sometime in the 1970s." In their account, capitalism itself represents the paradigmatic case of living death and of parasitic predatoriness.[4]

The title *Dead Man Working* is meant to recall the "dead man walking" on death row as well as *The Walking Dead*: Cederström and Fleming are nothing if not "savvy" with their cultural references. What these authors argue is that the "feeling of non-living is no more pervasive than among the multitude of workers trapped in the modern corporation."[5] It is no accident that the world of modern corporate life they describe as a *"dead end"* (their pun) frequently evokes the way of life (the right way of putting it?) of a mere corpse, of a *less-than-bare-life* associated with the figure of the zombie.[6] This witty critique adds stylishly to the increasing number of apocalyptic (hence biopolitical, hence *global*) accounts of "late" capitalism today (all of them pertaining to, in the horror idiom, a fundamentally creepy capital of 24/7 ideology). But, it is a type of Beckettian repetitiveness regarding the *Dead Man Working* that is the subject of study here ("Try again. Fail again. Fail better," from *Worstward Ho*). Analysis of a reversal of the linguistic turn at the level of a problematic of polysemy is not a subject on Cederström and Fleming's agenda. Nevertheless, the absence of this type of discussion in their work, given the emphasis on the work involved in making a world (discursive work as much as physical work), throws this selfsame issue into relief.

Everything that is *negative* about the zombies' penetration of this language question (or, the problem of meaning in the new millennium) fulfills the following function: it throws into relief that which may be seen as positive about humans' inhabitance of the signifier (in Lacanian terms)—a process that makes humans subjects, speaking animals, and so not *dead inside*. To a remarkable extent, *The Walking Dead* is a television series that is *not* about zombies: it is, of course, really about *us*. The subject of the show is the "inner lives" of the main protagonists, delineated through the various moral dilemmas they face. Remarkable, indeed, is the extent to which, as the first season shifts into the second, the script features zombies markedly less. The narrative is less mobile as well: Hershel Greene's farm is firmly established as both the place of the survivors' refuge and the site of their continuing moral dilemmas.

"Talking Bodies"

What, then, becomes of the zombie hyper-aphasics, those who are "Dead Inside," in their state of loss and negativity? By means of a fascinating dialectical reversal (that is, a strange somatic innervation), as they lose the power of speech on the inside, they turn on the outside into "talking bodies." "Talking bodies" is Sigmund Freud's term for hysterics.[7] It seems an apt description for the rasping zombie, for whom the speech function, not to mention the whole language system, has been displaced into (or re-topologized as) a series of somatic symptoms, each of which, as Freud would suggest, operates as a type of signifying system in its own right.

It is without doubt these extraordinary "somatic symptoms" for which zombies are best known: not just the staring eyes, the grinning teeth, the shuffling gait but also more generally the domination by drive and destruction of everything associated with what it means to be a social being. Regarding this nexus of aphasia and corporeality, it is surely misleading for Lauro and Embry to suggest that Victor Frankenstein's creature in Mary Shelley's story is a zombie[8]: the shambling, over-sized, Thing-like creature's acquisition of language *subjectivizes him* and, indeed, ensures that he is not "dead inside." Again, the fact that the "talking" the zombies do is of the body throws into relief the articulate richness of the inner being of Rick and the others. The conclusion to the pilot episode of *The Walking Dead* sees Rick holding a gun, trapped inside a tank, internally debating whether or not to kill himself. Of all things, it is a voice on the radio—a Lacanian object-cause of desire if ever there was one—that calls him back to human interdependence, to the discursive sublime, to society itself ("Days Gone Bye"). Thus, the talking bodies in *The Walking Dead*, the zombies in their condition of the surplus and shitty sublime, exist for the sake of the speaking animals. As hyper-aphasic hysterics, they are a means of determining, within a post-millennial problem of meaning (crises like zombies are everywhere!), that we are not (the) "Dead Inside."

What If Zombies Could Talk as Well as Walk?

Raargh! RAARGH! This is the problem of meaning from the zombie's point of view ... all expressed as the zombie is walking towards us, arms outstretched, offering a fatal embrace.

There is, in fact, an eerie silence surrounding the hospital door that reads "Dead Inside." Then, as the zombies on the other side become aware of Rick's presence, there is a violent shove as they try to break through the door held fast by a makeshift bolt. Through the opening down the middle of the double door emerges not just clawing hands but also a rising chorus of groans and murmurs, a becoming frenzy of an invisible-yet-furious flash mob. So, Rick decides to make a hasty exit. This represents a degree-zero moment in the narrative. Rick must find a new way of living from this point on. And this new way of living will thenceforth be set in counterpoint to the form of living death encountered by him amongst the "Dead Inside." This element of counterpoint will now structure the story of the post-apocalyptic survivors, who will try to build a new life, a new *socius* (a new *human*) for themselves throughout the rest of the series.

The counterpointing as such, setting human beings and the walking dead in a sonata form of their own, is represented in an especially clear way in the finale of the first season, which brings out forcefully what is at stake in the difference between the living and the dead, between those able to project "the facts of sentience into speech" and those who, in this regard, are merely "talking bodies."[9] Our point of reference is the science lesson the pathologist Dr. Edwin Jenner gives to the survivors inside Atlanta's Centers for Disease Control. Inside the CDC, the survivors think they have at last found a place of safety from the zombie plague—at which point Dr. Jenner proffers a scientific explanation for why humans and zombies have become as different as they are.

This scene, the science lesson itself, is a powerful means of making sense of the zombie phenomenon, along certain lines, as we shall see. Jenner plays a short film for the survivors of a functioning brain that becomes infected with the zombie virus; the patient dies at the moment of brain death. Then, after a period of "resurrection time," the brain is re-started but only at the brain stem and with limited functioning: the patient has been turned into a zombie. Or, in other words, this is an account of the making of the walking dead, the same thing as the unmaking of living human beings. What is perhaps especially interesting about this whole account is the scientific nature of Jenner's way of explaining what has just happened in the film. His commentary on the film, which captivates those watching and listening, explicates what it is to be a living human being specifically in terms of the human *qua* organism.

This is indeed no more than we might expect, given that Jenner is a pathologist with a special interest in neurology. So, as the synapses of a properly functioning human brain are shown flashing on the screen, Jenner explains it all in the following way: "Somewhere in all the organic wire, in all those ripples of light is *you*, the things that make *you* unique as humans" ("TS-19"). The speech is met with appreciative, not to say rapt, silence. The laboratory, with its dimmed lighting, its high-tech projection screen, together with the hushed silence surrounding Jenner's vocal self-assurance, has become a grand theater of scientific spectacle, an absolutized enunciative apparatus in its own right. Not only that, everything Jenner says whilst on this "stage" is indeed true in its own terms, namely, the biologistic (if not strictly neuropathological) terms used to describe human uniqueness.

And so everything Jenner says is true at the level of the human *qua* organism rather than that of the human *qua* subject. Moreover, what makes the difference in this respect is the subject's "languaging" of itself (as a certain conflation of "articulation" and "suture") through the power of speech. Human constitution through language, what we might regard as the very process of subjectivity's discursive sublime, is what materializes a (per)formative act of self that has to do with "representing oneself" to oneself and others in order to confirm the fact of *human* existence. This is the theory of language as production, wherein both the subject and meaning are *not*, in the absence of any pre-given—that is, pre-verbal or radically speechless—form of subjectivity.[10] It is ironic that Jenner should exemplify this key idea of profoundly performative speech when he constitutes himself as a figure of scientific authority, speaking on his "stage" in his laboratory. His account of "what makes us human" has nothing to say about language and its ramifications in this regard. He misses what marks *him* as human, what, in a strong sense, *makes* him human—nothing other than discourse itself—even as "the human" is the subject of his own discourse.

The point is made well for us by David McNally in his account of "bodies of meaning" in his book of that name. Crucially, McNally is clear that the experience of the body *of* meaning "is simultaneously organic and psychic."[11] Here, the fact of this simultaneity is hugely consequential for all bodies of meaning (for all strangely sentient flesh). Beyond the organic, it is such things as trauma and fantasy, desire and language, McNally argues, that are thus constitutive of "this erotogenic body [that] is not reducible to the life-history of the physiological body."[12] Beyond the organic, in other words, it is this critical irreducibility of the "erotogenic" to the "physiological" body that lays out the basis of liberation for the human *qua* subject from the human *qua* organism. So, among other things, human desire supersedes biological instinct. The human as such is set free from the entanglements of (Jenner's) "organic wire," leaving all this latter stuff as just so much sublime excrescence—put crudely, as de-formed defecation and as de-subjectivized shit.[13] We shall return to Edwin Jenner's condition of the shitty sublime—that is, of impossible monstrosity—in a moment.

Organic Wire

Language acts. Not only that, it acts as the definition of the human. Such indeed is the thesis of the linguistic turn of twentieth-century thought. Central to this very "turn" is the work of the linguist Émile Benveniste, notably his 1956 (Lacan-inspired) paper "Remarks on the Function of Language in Freudian Theory" published at the front of the then-new journal *La Psychanalyse*, edited by Lacan (and devoted to "speech and language"). Drawing on Freudian insights in the investigation of the human psyche, Benveniste sets forth the at once historical and constitutive character of language, remarking that "[l]anguage is the instrument by which the world and society are adjusted."[14] It had been whilst working as a neuropathologist, in fact, that the early Freud had begun laying the foundations of psychoanalysis; thus, with his first book, *On Aphasia*, published in 1891, he ironically made the *loss* of speech into a veritable *fons et origo* of Freudian theory.[15] Vitally important in this regard is the dialectic of language itself. Language functions as a system, the very nature of which is to enable acts and events that transcend language's limits *as a system*, whence arises the peculiar productivity—the inherent creative labor—of the speaking animal, the linguistic *living* being. In short, language in action is nothing other than discursive work that gives rise to the *production* of meaning out of meaning's very *problem*.

So, it is not surprising to see "the language question" brought forward in the context of the materialist critique of today's present crisis, our era of apocalyptic reckoning. In his *Zombie Politics and Culture in the Age of Casino Capitalism*, Henry A. Giroux holds strongly to the following key idea: "Language ... creates the conditions for dialogue, thoughtfulness, and informed action."[16] In this way, a robust democratic society is set in counterpoint to such things as "zombie language" and the "politics of the living dead." This whole scenario is one that is played out for us in what comes directly after Edwin Jenner's science lesson on the unmaking of human life as the making of a zombie. Let us, therefore, return to the last scenes in the first-season finale of *The Walking Dead*, "TS-19." Here is a narrative of the survivors of the apocalypse seeking to set themselves free from a basic conception of the world—a form of living death—that is bound up with the all-too-fatal notion of "organic wire."

That this organic wire is meant to be seen ultimately as a form of meshing that entraps human life is clear from the narrative dynamic of these last scenes. Jenner gets left behind by the survivors, and the process by which he gets left is significant in terms of its details. As if acting from Giroux's script ("Language creates the conditions for dialogue," etc.[17]), the survivors enter into a debate with Jenner about the choices available to them regarding their situation in the CDC. They discover that the fuel is running out and the Centers are beginning to power down. It is as if the CDC is dying, much like the body in Jenner's fMRI, with the implication that the process of becoming zombie has in fact already started. This is what Rick and the others need to escape. "I don't want this," Rick says to Jenner. What Rick rejects is Jenner's will-to-death: Jenner believes that there is no hope on the outside, and so he resigns himself to death as the CDC's self-destruct mechanism begins its countdown to destroy its store of deadly viruses. As some of the others (Daryl and Shane) use brute force to try to break through the steel doors that have been closed in the lockdown, it is Rick who makes a breakthrough by means of dialogue.

He argues a case against Jenner's position. Jenner, indeed, had admitted a moment ago that, in terms of knowing what is happening in the world beyond the CDC, "I've been in the dark for almost a month." Rick argues that the morality of choice means having a *chance*: Jenner's will-to-death has deprived his group of the possibility of having this chance notwithstanding that the situation outside the CDC may indeed be hopeless. Jenner, whose basic conviction that the situation is hopeless remains unchanged, accepts Rick's argument and opens the laboratory door, thereby allowing the survivors to escape. The survivors then blast their way out of the Centers using a stolen hand grenade. The key point symbolized in the narrative is that those survivors who choose to take a chance in this way "win the argument" with Jenner. It is the process of dialogue underlying this victory, as its enabling condition, that is affirmed. The organizing principle for this dénouement is thus the very notion of linguistic instrumentality (found in Benveniste as well as in Giroux) that bespeaks the capacity of language-users to posit themselves as "subject," and that is ultimately the basis of the counterpointing of the living and the undead staged in *The Walking Dead*.

All this is demonstrated in that moment when Rick and the others leave Edwin Jenner behind. Jenner leans over to Rick and whispers something in his ear. Jenner's whisper is inaudible, and thus he exemplifies, at the diegetic level, a certain loss of speech that differentiates him from all the others who are more properly creatures of dialogue. This moment of parting is then a symbol of Jenner's narrative positioning closer to that fatal form of aphasia that determines zombies as "talking bodies" rather than as linguistic-laboring bodies, as "abject" rather than "subject," and as uncanny nomads rather than canny survivors. No wonder Edwin Jenner, an effectively wordless apostle of the "organic wire," does not survive into an apocalyptic "post-humanism" as the finale to the first season of *The Walking Dead* comes to a close.

It should be added that Jenner is not exactly a creature of silence rather than speech in that moment when he whispers into Rick's ear as the Centers for Disease Control count down to their destruction. Rick reveals what Jenner has said to him in the finale of the second season of *The Walking Dead*. He has been told by Jenner, "We're all infected" ("Beside the Dying Fire"). This disclosure explains why Jenner himself had taken the view that there was no point in leaving the CDC, even as it was shutting down. At the same time, "We're all infected" is a game-changing statement and as such sets in motion (in part retroactively) a new and intriguing set of narrative possibilities regarding the theme of the "fate of the human" in *The Walking Dead*. From a narrative point of view, only time will tell whether or not it is an endgame that is being played out by Rick and the other survivors, especially since the finale of the second season is not the end of the television series.

There is, in fact, a certain heightening of narrative tension in connection with Jenner's revelation—for the latter stages of the second season of *The Walking Dead* are marked by a single symbolic event: the death of Dale. Dale had been the group's most forceful and articulate spokesperson for the value of democratic debate in dealing with the various challenges faced by the group, including the question of killing or releasing a human outsider whom they held prisoner. That Dale loses this vote, is bitten by a walker when alone afterwards, and is subsequently the subject of a mercy killing (to which he appears to consent) at the hands of Daryl is strikingly symbolic. There had been signs earlier that the survivors, including Rick, were starting to lose their moral compass, coming to behave more and more like the walking dead. All this squares with the suggestion "We're all infected." Arguably, the group's decision, against Dale's wishes (and, indeed, against his vehement opposition to their cut-throat mentality), to kill rather than release their prisoner indicates a new brutalism. The loss of Dale as the living embodiment of the group's moral center in these circumstances is clearly a means of heightening the tension about what is going to happen to the other survivors (about what it might mean for them to be "infected"). "The centre cannot hold," as Yeats writes in "The Second Coming." "Mere anarchy is loosed upon the world." Worth noting in this respect is the fact that Dale's death marks a significant departure from *The Walking Dead* comic script, in which Dale lasts much longer as, again, a type of wise elder within the group. So, the very vulnerability of their predicament could hardly be reinforced more strongly when Rick informs them, at this critical juncture when the second season is coming to a close, of what Edwin Jenner had told him at the end of the first season. Above all, the symbolism of the loss of the strongest embodiment of democratic values accentuates all the more sharply how this story, via the rich iconography of the figure of the zombie, deals with the eminently "millennial" issues identified above: the death of democracy itself and the rise of a new brutalism (with fascism as the "symptom" of capitalism), the crisis of literacy (in language as in society), the becoming comatose of moral human beings, and so on.

From the Discursive to the Shitty Sublime

The trajectory from the "discursive" to the "shitty" sublime is what points us towards the problem of meaning in the new millennium. It brings zombies into view within the frame of what we might see as the pornography of authoritarianism, where market-driven hysteria generates a great deal of the unbridled materialism of the ethically somnolent, commodity-fetishizing undead, who, as such, are left without the power of self-determination in their "democratic" lives. There can be no question that, in this light, *The Walking Dead* signifies in an iconic and over-determined fashion as an ideological text in the superstructure of today's neo-liberal conjuncture of hegemonic free-market capitalism and bourgeois society. Like the hysterical symptoms—the signifying systems—we have been examining here (primarily those of "talking bodies"), this aforementioned ideological superstructure is the very locus of signification of otherwise repressed bodily forces (the social as well as the human body). And so the zombie comes to light as an apt metaphor for the monstrous nature of some of the leading tendencies and shaping pressures of our present times. This truly epochal figure displays across its surface—remember that zombies are "talking bodies"—the proverbial signs of the times in which we live. Think only, perhaps, of protestors from the Occupy Movement dressing themselves as zombies so that Wall Street bankers may see them "reflecting the metaphor of their actions."

So terror springs from torpor, creating a situation, in the language of the living dead, of *dead-lock*. Or, putting it differently, now is the time for monsters, as indeed was argued by Antonio Gramsci, reflecting on authoritarianism's threat to democracy in the economic crisis of the 1930s. As he wrote from within a fascist prison, "The crisis consists precisely in the fact that the old is dying and the new cannot be born." He continued that "in this interregnum a great variety of morbid symptoms appear."[18] "Morbid symptoms" seems exactly the right way of putting it—hence the symptomatology of "talking bodies" elaborated in this account of the present grave situation, the contours of which closely resemble those of the 1930s. The transition to the current period of crisis has been charted by James Donald, again employing the devices of a modern horror genre to do so. He notes "what's at stake" in vampire films regarding a 1980s transition, seen in retrospect, connecting vampiric bloodlust with a new round of predatoriness (a frenetically faster dance of death and a purer culture of greed) associated with the emergence in hegemonic mode of the newly freed-up markets of contemporary capital.[19] What is different today in regard to the horror film that is the lived reality of an ongoing crisis situation, however, is that, as many commentators have suggested, "zombies are the new vampires."[20]

Zombies are the monsters of the moment by virtue of their sublime ugliness and their beautiful excrementalism. Vampires have lost the edge to zombies in these horror stakes, not least because the latter connote the end of civilization itself. As is well known, the zombie is the eschaton-made-flesh. The new hordes of *rageful* zombies take us back, in Hegelian terms, to the Night of the World, to "that orgy of un-meaning," in Terry Eagleton's words, "before the dawn of subjectivity itself, in which bloody stumps and mangled bits of bodies" loom at us out of chaotic darkness.[21] Like the anamorphic skull in Hans Holbein's *The Ambassadors*, the zombie, seen in a sideways glance perhaps, is a priori and forever a reminder of the end of worldly vanity. In particular, its gaping mouth evokes both the making and the unmaking of the human subject in language. It is a mouth (a whole gaping abyss) that can never even say "I feel like shit!"[22]

This reading of *The Walking Dead*, then, discloses the allegorical aspect of its meaning vis-à-vis the structure of civilization's present problem of meaning. In capitalist society, exchange value rationalizes, precisely, the privatization of public values, thus undermining the social fabric and producing the specter of apocalypticism—hyper-predatory "zombie" capitalism. A radical discourse with which to articulate an alternative sense of politics is called for—a means of response to toxic developments in the socio-economic realm. *The Walking Dead* exemplifies a contribution to this sort of discursive project. That the root meaning of the word *monster*, from the Latin *monere*, is "to warn" is an important point in this regard.[23] For the new monsters of the moment, the zombies themselves—especially in *The Walking Dead* in respect to their focalizing an argument between social language and dead language (hence all the symbolism of "Dead Inside")—are indeed a warning to us of what is happening in our post-millennial moment. Like all monsters, zombies are a form of warning in the register of the fantastically real. So, when a whole zombie landscape emerges, with the specific connotations of catastrophe that it implies, it indicates a danger that we ignore at our peril. But, at the present time, the zombie metaphor, as well as the whole iconography of the living dead, does indeed serve as a means of "representing the crisis." By the same token, as we have seen, it serves also as a means to find an exit from that selfsame crisis.

NOTES

1. Scarry, *The Body in Pain*, 23.
2. Ibid., 6.
3. Ibid.
4. Cederström and Fleming, *Dead Man Working*, 1.
5. Ibid., 2.
6. Ibid.
7. See Freud, *On Aphasia*, and Kristeva, *Language—the Unknown*, 272. See also Freud's suggestion that hysterical symptoms, for instance, Fräulein Elisabeth von R's legs, may be seen as "'joining in the conversation'" during the analytic session. Breuer and Freud, *Studies on Hysteria*, 383, 217, 91.
8. Lauro and Embry, "A Zombie Manifesto," 102n.
9. Scarry, *The Body in Pain*, 6.
10. On the theory of language as production, see Kristeva, *Language—the Unknown*, 272–275.
11. McNally, *Bodies of Meaning*, 8.
12. Ibid.
13. On Kristevan "abject" "bodies of meaning," see Kristeva, *Powers of Horror*.
14. Benveniste, "Remarks on the Function of Language in Freudian Theory," 71. On "the comparison of language to an instrument," see Benveniste, "Subjectivity in Language," 223.
15. On Benveniste and psychoanalysis (Freud, Lacan, Kristeva), see Coward and Ellis, *Language and Materialism*, 133–138, especially 136, where "the body also communicates in the symptoms of hysteria."
16. Giroux, *Zombie Politics and Culture*, 49.
17. Ibid.
18. Gramsci, *Selections*, 276.
19. Donald, "The Fantastic, the Sublime and the Popular." For an "updated" treatment of the theme of vampiric free-market capitalism, see Policante, "Vampires of Capital."
20. See Grossman, "Zombies are the New Vampires," and Sirota, "The Zombie Zeitgeist." For the works of a new zombie-inspired "monsterology," see, among others, Harman, *Zombie Capitalism*; Williams, *Combined and Uneven Apocalypse*; and McNally, *Monsters of the Market*.
21. Eagleton, *Holy Terror*, 3–4.
22. On the co-extensivity of language use and human mental functioning, see Benveniste, "Categories of Thought and Language."
23. See McNally, *Monsters of the Market*, 9, and Giroux, *Zombie Politics and Culture*, 31.

Zombie Time
Temporality and Living Death

GWYNETH PEATY

When deputy sheriff Rick Grimes awakens from a coma in the first episode of AMC's *The Walking Dead*, one of the earliest signs that something is awry is the stopped clock beside his hospital bed. The camera lingers on its immobile face, zooming in slowly, before cutting to Rick's expression of dawning horror. Signaling more than mechanical failure, the frozen timepiece indicates absence and abandonment. Without living hands to maintain it, the device has ceased to function. No doctors, nurses, visitors, or other patients are there to notice. Minutes, days, weeks, and months are no longer documented, for the zombie hordes that surround the hospital have no respect for such measures. Instead, the ravenous "walkers" instigate their own form of monstrous temporality—a timeless hungering that drives ever onwards without respite or regulation.

In the context of this onslaught, the series underscores the importance of marking time in the maintenance of identity, order, and humanity itself. Depicting a collapsed world seemingly beyond repair, *The Walking Dead* features people who are fighting to survive the long heralded "end of time," a liminal moment that signals the denouement of human history. As one character obsessively winds his watch each day—keeping time alive—others activate deadly counters to hurry their own demise. Clinging to photographs and memories of times lost, they struggle to preserve the past, comprehend the present, and imagine the future.

Philosopher Paul Ricœur has argued that, while all stories are tales *of* time, only select examples are tales *about* time. All narratives involve events that take place over time, but tales *about* time take it as a central preoccupation: "it is the very experience of time that is at stake in these structural transformations."[1] In this essay, I argue that *The Walking Dead* is indeed a tale *about* time. More specifically, it is a tale in which the concept and experience of time is interwoven with monstrosity. Focusing on the first season in particular, I explore how the reign of the zombie is associated with a notion of monstrous timelessness, unpicking the ways in which both past and future are imperilled, threatened with erasure by a carnivorous, devouring present.

Reflecting a profound unease over the apparent tenuousness of the human trajectory, this wildly popular show offers an intriguing insight into contemporary fears over mortality, ontology, and change in the new century. "The end of the millennium," as Elizabeth Grosz pointed out in 1999, is "marked as a ritualized emblem of the meeting of history (the twentieth century and before) with a future full of promise and yet without form or flesh."[2] This is "the postmodern moment, a moment of decolonization, of resurgence of subjected minorities, of difference."[3] A decade into this new era, *The Walking Dead* gives form and flesh to the future in a manner that is less promise, more dire threat. The future is, for all intents and purposes, dead. And yet the present lives on, somehow, for the millennial meeting between history and future has been re-imagined as a brutal feast—the corpse of the future feeding hungrily on the remains of history. Drawing out key moments that highlight the role of time and its importance in the series, this essay begins to unravel its unique vision of apocalyptic temporality or zombie time.

Once Upon a Time

When Rick stirs from his coma, he finds himself in a new world ("Days Gone Bye"). Between being shot and waking up, he has only a vague memory of his best friend and colleague, Shane, visiting to deposit flowers. It is immediately clear that much has passed since then. The flowers are dead and Shane is long gone. Nobody has watered or replaced the tattered blooms, just as nobody has wound the clock on the wall. When Rick rises from his bed, it is as though he has been dropped straight into the "ever after" without any direct experience of how this came to be. This "after" space, the new "now," has an eerie, dreamlike quality well suited to the end of time. The hospital is quiet, painted with the dried traces of violence and death. The suburban streets are windswept and abandoned, strewn with mess. While the architectural outlines of human civilization and domesticity remain—the houses, cars, gates and fences—their substance has fled, replaced by decomposing bodies and shambling corpses. Between violent zombie encounters, long periods of stillness create the sense that the world is in a comatose state. Suspension of life and time go hand in hand in this surreal atmosphere, which causes Rick to question his own sanity. "Is this real?" he wonders aloud, desperately searching his empty home for wife Lori and son Carl: "Am I here? Wake up!" ("Days Gone Bye").

Time has ceased to order the flow of the everyday in *The Walking Dead* because the everyday has ceased to flow. As Richard M. Gale points out, "time is not a substantial entity which is capable of existing separately from other things: it has no reality independently of the changes that substances undergo."[4] Although it is fundamental to our perceptions of places, people, and objects, time is not a *thing* that takes up space. It is invisible and cannot be represented directly. (A clock may depict the passing of time, but it is still a clock, not time itself.) While its effects may be observable and calculable, and its duration might be measured, time has no physical form; it "disappears into events, processes, movements, things, as the mode of their becoming."[5] In biological terms, it is notable that "there is no dedicated sensory organ for time perception, as there are for perceiving the physical and chemical nature of our environment through touch, taste and smell."[6] Time can only be perceived through things other than itself. It depends upon the processes and cycles that structure human lives, just as these structures depend upon it.

It follows that representing time is no easy feat. Indeed, in their efforts to understand and visualize this phenomenon, philosophers have often turned to abstract symbols. For instance, in an attempt to provide a "simple, diagrammatical account" of temporal order (past, present, future), M.K. Rennie creates equations such as "$(x) (y) (xBy \supset (\exists z) (xBz \,\&\, zBy))$."[7] These calculations grow more and more complex, illustrating the difficulty of building a model that incorporates the many associated variables and unknowns. This kind of project is made even more challenging by the fact that time is culture-specific; studies have shown that different societies have diverse ways of conceptualizing and representing temporality.[8] Time does not hold the same meaning for everyone, nor does it operate in the same way for all cultures.

Given the elusive and ephemeral nature of time, the preoccupation with timelessness in *The Walking Dead* is especially interesting. The series is effectively concerned with representing the disappearance of that which is already invisible. As a visual medium, television might not seem the ideal context in which to undertake such a task. Yet the show persists in making explicit and implicit references to time, narrating its loss and exploring the frightening possibility of an infinite timelessness: living death.

Born from a deadly infection that reactivates the brain post-mortem, forcing the dead body to rise once more, the zombies of *The Walking Dead* overwhelm the present and, by extension, consume the future. Hopes and dreams are shattered as the social and physical world disintegrates. Zombies also cannibalize history, taking the form of lost friends and loved ones who are condemned to walk the earth as bloody shells of their former selves. Gerry Canavan comments on this temporal collapse in his analysis of *The Walking*

Dead comics, stating that "as zombies flatten time they obliterate the present alongside the past and the future."[9] In the television series, this "flattening" is a key sign of the apocalypse. It signals the end of the world and the beginning of monstrous temporality, a timeless, ceaseless drive to destroy that threatens to infect the living and strip them of their last residues of humanity—"everything you ever were or will be: gone" ("TS-19").

Rick's quest to find his family is an attempt to restart not only his life and identity, but time itself. Along with his sheriff's uniform and hat, he wears a wristwatch as he heads out into the apocalypse. These items speak more to his intentions than to reality, for they symbolize his burning desire to correct what is broken and return order, both temporal and social, to his environment. Indeed, Rick's timepiece does not feature prominently until he finds his family and experiences a brief reinstatement of peace and order. Having discovered his wife and child safe in a campsite with Shane and other survivors, that night he falls into a deep sleep and stirs later than usual ("Tell It to the Frogs"). Observing sunlight outside the tent, Rick consults his watch. Echoing his previous awakening in the hospital, the camera moves leisurely from the timepiece to his attentive face—only this time the clock is working. As Carl plays and Lori does washing outside, life acquires a sense of precious normalcy, and time appears to have meaning and relevance again. This is a brief respite, however, for this world no longer allows the luxury of surplus time. Moments later, Rick must leave again, called back into the zombie-infested city. "Dislocation," Eva Hoffman remarks, "exacerbates the consciousness of time."[10] In their fundamentally dislocated universe, survivors are made hyper-conscious of time's absence. What little they have is forcibly taken, again and again, leaving them starved, paranoid, and desperate for more.

The End

For characters in *The Walking Dead*, the progression towards living death involves a draining of time, a slide towards monstrous timelessness. "We don't have time" becomes a recurring mantra as survivors seek to evade inexorable surges of zombies. Trapped in a tank on an infested Atlanta street, Rick tries to introduce himself to Glenn over the shortwave radio ("Guts"). "Hey, what's your name?" he asks. Glenn responds with irritation: "Have you been listening? You're running out of time!" Pursued by a perpetually hungering, monstrous mass, there is no time to stop to share pleasantries and polite conversation. There is no time to be concerned with the dictates of society, tradition, or morality, to become preoccupied with empathy and notions of fairness. These are precisely the things, however, that the survivors—Rick in particular—attempt to restore at the end of the world. "Seriously, how long do you think they got?" protests Daryl when Rick shares their guns with another group. "How long do any of us?" he responds grimly ("Vatos"). For the living, maintaining a sense of compassion and civility is an essential part of resisting the pull of monstrosity. Nevertheless, with time in short supply, sharing resources cuts into whatever they have left.

Such scenarios inevitably raise ethical questions. In season one, after a zombie attack that devastates the camp, opinions differ over what should be done with the bodies. Some think they should all be burned, zombies and humans alike, while others demand a proper burial for their deceased friends. Daryl is in favor of burning and becomes frustrated by the discussion: "These people need to know who the hell's in charge here, what the rules are." Rick responds that there are no rules anymore, which prompts a telling outburst from Lori: "Well that's a problem. We haven't had one minute to hold onto anything of our old selves, we need time to mourn and we need to bury our dead. It's what people do" ("Wildfire"). The link between monstrosity and timelessness is explicit here. People, as Lori so succinctly points out, need time. They need time in order to keep doing "what people do," which includes caring for and about others. Otherwise, they lose what makes them people: their humanity. Yet time becomes more and more elusive as zombies stalk the living, mercilessly consuming their life force, their remaining days, hours, and minutes.

Memory becomes a form of resistance in this context. Perceptions of time are enmeshed with nostalgia as many characters focus on preserving history by poring over family photographs and mementos. Morgan strokes a picture of his wife while her undead corpse lurches through the streets and scratches at the door. Lori takes all the photo albums when she escapes town with Carl, keeping the idea of their family alive even as its reality crumbles. Time, Inderjeet Mani explains, "does not appear alone in narrative; it is wound up with events, and involves relationships that hinge on modality and point-of-view."[11] As more survivors are introduced into the narrative, the focus on subjective memory only increases. Direct representations of the past are made possible via flashbacks, allowing viewers to observe past events as they happened. More often, though, survivors recount their tales of better time(s) to others, presenting their experiences as part of an ongoing temporal progression leading up to the present. As Grosz argues, "how we understand the past, and our links to it through reminiscence, melancholy, or nostalgia, prefigures and contains corresponding concepts about the present and future."[12] In *The Walking Dead*, a concern with personal history works to establish a sense of meaningful trajectory—emphasizing the forward motion of time. If the past can be kept alive, if it still exists, surely the/a future *must* exist. Time must be active; the "now" must be going somewhere.

Andrea clings to this view as she carefully marks each day on the calendar, preparing for her sister's birthday. Although the days, months, and years no longer govern the remnants of human society, they continue to have emotional significance. Measuring duration helps Andrea to express her love for Amy, who is much younger. Guilty for having missed Amy's birthdays in the past, Andrea is determined to make up for lost time, but time cannot be regained once squandered—not in a world where it is trickling away. Amy is bitten in a zombie attack, and Andrea must watch her sister die and become a walker on her birthday ("Wildfire"). Before shooting her in the head, Andrea tearfully apologizes to her now uncomprehending sibling: "I'm sorry for not ever being there. I always thought there'd be more time." After Lori dies in season three, Rick makes a similar plea for forgiveness: "I thought there would be time. There's never time" ("Hounded"). The end of time forces characters to reflect on how they have wasted this precious resource, how they have failed to appreciate the value and transience of others' lives.

Of course, for individual humans, time has always been finite. As mortal creatures, our lives are understood to move in a linear progression from birth to death. Time is the inexorable conduit of this advance, dissipating and consuming whether we choose to acknowledge it or not. As the consumer of all things, time already suggests a kind of relentless hungering force that cannot be defeated. One might argue that the survivors are merely experiencing an accelerated version of this passage towards death—the carnivorous power of time embodied by the endless supply of life-taking zombies. And yet, Victor Hugo's expression is perhaps more accurate: *Tempus edax, homo edacior*—Time is a devourer; man, more so.[13] For these zombies are not extensions of the "natural" progression of life towards death. In their own way, they subvert time; but not, I would argue, by restarting it. Instead, the zombies in *The Walking Dead* represent a form of monstrous timelessness that is not infinite time but an infinite lack of time. Theirs is not a glorious immortality, an unfolding journey into the unknown future. They have no future, no destination, aside from the drive to consume flesh. They are what is left once man has devoured time, and, in doing so, devoured himself. It is perhaps fitting that these zombies are not the energetic, hyper-mobile kind, but the more traditional shufflers. They do not run; there is no need to hurry, for they have all the time in the world.

For the survivors, the loss of the future brings with it a loss of hope, anticipation, and excitement. Eugène Minkowski suggests that imagining what is to come is an essential aspect of human life: "We look at the future and we see it in a broad and majestic perspective stretching out to lose itself in the distance. This majesty approaches the mysterious. But this mystery is as indispensible to our spiritual life as pure air is to our respiration."[14] *The Walking Dead* asks: what happens when that future is gone? When bodies that cease to respire continue to walk? When time no longer moves towards the horizon, but folds back upon itself, looped in a moment of perpetual duration? These are not purely philosophical or spiritual concerns but are social, biological, and ontological.

In the series, the agent that causes zombification is not simply an external threat, transferred into the bloodstream via bites alone. Instead, it already exists, lying dormant in the living, waiting to be activated. As carriers, the survivors are all infected, already in the early stages of living death. In other words, as Jeffrey Jerome Cohen puts it, "To be human means to inhabit the zombie's juvenile form."[15] Death is not the end, but the catalyst for this final stage. Destruction of the brain is the only way to escape one's fate. The disease "invades the brain," and it is this tissue that scientist Dr. Edwin Jenner studies in his search for a cure ("TS-19"). Living death is, accordingly, above all a disease of the mind; it affects the neurons and synapses responsible for consciousness, reasoning, emotion, and perception—essential ingredients for the construction of meaningful human experiences.

In *The Walking Dead*, the end of time signals the end of genetic and cultural metamorphosis, of human variation and growth. It is our final stage of evolution. As Jenner puts it, "this is our extinction event." Developments at all levels of society are brought to a standstill. Global movements grind to a halt. The human mind itself is petrified—reset to its simplest, most basic operating level, no longer capable of forging new thoughts, new ideas and connections. In this sense, walkers can be seen as an attempt to neutralize our anxieties regarding the future, effectively short-circuiting any millennial "resurgence of subjected minorities, of difference."[16] After all, the future always brings new monstrosities, with "mutation, metamorphosis—upheaval in directions and arenas with implications and consequences that cannot be known in advance."[17] Trapped in a perpetual present, zombies offer a single, conclusive end state. *Sans* future, the human race as a whole has but one possible destination: "Zombies are our only possible future, our already actual present; zombies inherit the earth."[18] At the point of living death, everyone will be the same.

Such apocalyptic imaginings work to tame the future. They make it knowable, "foreseeable all the way to the end of time."[19] As David Pagano points out, this is, counterintuitively, the fantasy cloaked in the horrors of the apocalypse: safety. "The apocalyptic prophet posits himself as absolutely safe from any risk, contingency, or chance precisely by erasing the futurity of the future, its openness to the unforeseeable."[20] Yet the series does not stop here, for it explicitly associates this erasure with a loss of humanity. Paradoxically, in their battle to survive, the characters are fighting to reinstate mortality as the founding principle of time. Living death annihilates time. To rescue and revive the future, they need real death to reign once more.

Start All the Clocks

Rick is not the only survivor to wear a wristwatch. Dale is known as the timekeeper of the group—an older man with a strong moral code who winds his watch every day without fail. The significance of this act is unpacked when the others challenge his adherence to time during a fireside conversation ("Vatos"):

MORALES: I gotta ask you man, it's been driving me crazy.
DALE: What?
MORALES: That watch.
DALE: What's wrong with my watch?
MORALES: I see you, every day, same time, winding that thing like a village priest saying mass.
JACQUI: I've wondered this myself.
DALE: I'm missing the point!
JACQUI: Unless I've misread the signs, the world seems to have come to an end. At least hit a speed bump for a good long while.
MORALES: Then there's you; every day, winding that stupid watch.
DALE: Time! It's important to keep track, isn't it? The days at least? Don't you think? Andrea, back me up here!
[Andrea laughs wryly and demurs.]
DALE: I like what father said to son when he gave him a watch that had been handed down through generations. He said: "I give you the mausoleum of all hope and desire, which will fit your individual needs no better than it did mine or my father's before me. I give it to you, not that you may remember time, but that you might forget it, for a moment, now and then, and not spend all of your breath trying to conquer it."
AMY: You are so weird.
[Everyone laughs.]
DALE: It's not me, it's Faulkner. William Faulkner.

This scene stands out as a key moment for it explicitly addresses the overarching preoccupation of the series with temporality while highlighting the link between timekeeping and death. Offering an unexpectedly philosophical take on his timekeeping, Dale repeats a famous quote from Faulkner's *The Sound and the Fury* in his attempt to explain the importance of time. Watches attest to the mortality of their wearers, marking the inevitable passing of life, minute by minute. In this sense, they stand as a monument to the inevitability of death. No matter how often you check a watch, there is no real comfort to be gained from consulting it, only in forgetting; yet the very presence of this device offers a kind of reassurance, the ticking arms designed to "keep" time for an individual, recording how much has passed while your attention was elsewhere. As Faulkner himself explains, "you can be oblivious to the sound for a long while, then in a second of ticking it can create in the mind unbroken the long diminished parade of time you didn't hear."[21] The aptly named watch indeed watches time for you, a small sentinel against the overwhelming sensation of time slipping away unheeded.

At the end of the world, this mechanism takes on an even greater significance. The watch does not simply observe time but also produces it, standing testimony to its continued existence and, by extension, attesting to the wearer's progression towards death. The photographs clutched by the characters likewise connote a relationship with mortality and time. As Susan Sontag argues, "all photographs are *memento mori*. To take a photograph is to participate in another person's (or thing's) mortality, vulnerability, mutability. Precisely by slicing out this moment and freezing it, all photographs testify to time's relentless melt."[22] The photograph instantly transforms present into past, memorializing the life of its subjects even before their passing. Roland Barthes has gone so far as to describe photographers as "agents of Death" because they are the creators of "this image which produces Death while trying to preserve life."[23] Similarly, the present becomes history in real time as clocks count down the remaining minutes of an individual's life.

Both watches and photographs foreground the notion that "our bodies are clocks set to expire."[24] They each remind us that time (and life) is finite. This is, perhaps, the important point. While the clock may represent life's passage towards death, the stopped clock presents the living with an even greater horror. If "to be alive is to feel the passage of time, and to have time working through us in every cell, nerve ending and organ,"[25] to be undead is the opposite. If one second is equivalent to one human heartbeat,[26] zombies are the natural inhabitants of the end of time, for their bodies have no heartbeat or internal timer. With the suspension of "time's relentless melt,"[27] humans enter a state of ontological limbo—a condition of timeless monstrosity. In *The Walking Dead*, walkers operate as humans who have transitioned beyond time; their body clocks have stopped, and they are frozen in a present that has no natural end. In this way they have achieved what Faulkner believed impossible—they have conquered time. But at what cost? Zombie bodies exist in a plane of infinite death; they feast and rage without logic or self-awareness. Constantly tearing and being torn, their bodies give bloody testimony to the dire consequences of temporal suspension. Without consideration for the past or the future, they sacrifice all, including their own bodies, in their insatiable hunger for the present.

In this context, mortality seems the lesser of two evils. Death becomes a touchstone as characters fixate on objects that speak to their own demise— yet the survivors of *The Walking Dead* are fighting a battle they have already lost. They are already partially immortal, no longer capable of achieving a natural death. In ontological terms, they no longer experience what Heidegger terms "being-toward-death"[28]: their existence is no longer defined by the unavoidable fact of a future end. Rather, they must live out their remaining lifetime in the knowledge that they will rise again. For Heidegger, being human is synonymous with finite time: existence *is* finitude. In this series, however, "being-toward-death" is subsumed by a kind of "being-toward-undeath." Survivors must face their erasure as individuals as they head towards a transformation that will strip their mind of its humanity. Memory, personality, the ability to form relationships—all will be lost in the synaptic firestorm. An obsession with keeping time and memory "alive," the desire to return to the temporal status quo, reflects the fear that comes with this knowledge.

While the characters of *The Walking Dead* are trying to resurrect a sense of "being-toward-death," this does not mean they greet their end with open arms. The human quest to prolong life continues on a daily basis, even as they battle to reinstate death's natural dominion. After zombies discover their campsite, the survivors make their way to the Centers for Disease Control (CDC), a public health facility in Atlanta rumored to be working on a cure for the zombie outbreak ("TS-19"). The pristine conditions of the building, featuring air conditioning and hot running water, suggest that they have finally found a place that is safe from the monstrous hordes, a place where they can live with some degree of normalcy. In this apparent safety, time awakens again. As Lori and Rick cuddle together on their first night inside, his watch is the main focus, centered in the foreground. Lori grips it tightly as he embraces her, curling her fingers around the timepiece.

Unfortunately, this is yet another false start on Rick's mission to restore the social and temporal order. A more powerful timer is regulating this space. Jenner, the last remaining scientist, works in a large computing room containing what appears to be a big digital clock. As befits his preoccupation with time, it is Dale who ventures a question: "That clock, it's counting down. What happens at zero?" Numbers glowing blood-red in the shadowy room, this timer is not counting the passing of time. Instead, it is counting backwards, ticking off the remaining seconds before the building loses power, going into self-destruct mode. Underscoring the link between time and mortality, this deadly counter offers a drastically foreshortened version of human life. The survivors are not simply moving towards death; they are being pushed at full speed.

While the others panic, the doctor faces his imminent death calmly. "I did the best I could in the time that I had. I hope you'd be proud of that," he tells a photograph of his late wife. "They always think there's going to be more time. But it runs out." As the giant numbers count down in the background, Jenner and Rick debate the value of continuing to live. Fully accepting the end of time, Jenner encourages the survivors to give in and stop fighting, especially for the children: "wouldn't it be kinder, more compassionate to just hold your loved ones and wait for the clock to run down?" Framed this way, their deaths are more euthanasia than suicide—a way (indeed, the only way) of escaping the inevitable horrors of monstrosity. Given the events of the second and third seasons, when many of the group—including the children—face incredible pain, suffering, and living death, this is not an unreasonable point. As Jenner says to Rick, "You *do* want this." Jenner recognizes Rick's quest to restore time for what it is, and he offers what seems like the most obvious answer: death itself. "There is no hope, there never was," insists Jenner, but Rick refuses to admit defeat: "There's always hope. Maybe it won't be you, maybe not here, but somebody, somewhere." This is Rick's role as head timekeeper and law enforcer: to hold his nerve and keep the future alive, as the others work to keep the past alive. Forcing their way out of the compound, they fight for their right to keep winding watches, defying the end of time.

Tomorrow

Reflecting a distinct unease over the perceived tenuousness of both past and future, *The Walking Dead* offers an intriguing insight into contemporary fears about mortality, humanity, and society as we enter the second decade of the twenty-first century. As Hoffman points out, "the problem of time is inseparable from that of meaning. Time *is* the fundamental medium and condition of human meanings.... We think against the horizon of mortality and contemplate first questions against the knowledge of our own ending. What are the uses of a finite life, and what uses do we want to make of it?"[29] In its depiction of the end of the world, the series looks back on the new millennium from an imagined "after" in which all we have is destroyed or slipping away. This is no gleaming horizon, full of promise for the future, but "an endless horrific nightmare" ("What Lies Ahead"). The end, the series shows us, is indeed endless. It carries on into perpetuity, linking and looping the past, present, and future like a snake swallowing its own tail. Human society has lost its forward motion, its ability to change and move in unexpected directions.

Those who remain can only hold on desperately before either being consumed by the inexorable pull of timeless monstrosity or giving up altogether.

As the new millennium begins to build steam, *The Walking Dead* dissects what remains at the end of time—what has been lost and what, if anything, has been gained. It warns of what might be discarded in the rush towards the future: the lessons of history, the value of mortality, the wisdom and empathy that manifest the best of humanity. The series also, however, flags the need for fresh openings and becomings. The future must be allowed to mutate, to take forms as yet unseen, perhaps frightening in their newness. The past may haunt, and the future may threaten, but their erasure is much more problematic. When they are jettisoned, what's left is shown to be monstrous indeed. Without these buttresses, the present transforms into a devouring mass of urgency and unscrupulous hunger as embodied by the zombie hordes. Those trapped within this temporal vortex are left scrabbling for scraps of hope and understanding amidst the timeless overflow.

The series encourages a greater appreciation of time and its role in maintaining empathic human behavior and relationships. When Rick considers killing a potentially dangerous young intruder, Dale suggests that this kind of act warrants more thought and time ("Judge, Jury, Executioner"). "There's got to be a process," he argues, "give me some time to talk to everyone, to figure out another way." Time is a fortification against the "shoot first, ask questions later" philosophy advocated by Shane. It allows for reflection, reason, and sensitivity. "We need time to discuss this," Dale insists. His wristwatch is prominent, flashing gold in the sunlight as he explains his reasoning to Andrea: "The world we know is gone. But keeping our humanity? That's a choice." Dale believes that a human life is "worth more than a five minute conversation." Humans not only need time, they also deserve it. A fast killing may "save" time spent in discussion, but it signifies a much greater loss. The very process of spending time on others, giving people time to think, mourn, and question, is humanizing—even more so when such time is granted to strangers, outsiders, or enemies. But this generosity requires a conscious effort, especially when one feels his or her own meager portion slipping away at an ever increasing rate.

Reflecting tensions over contemporary social change and the evolution of cultural values, the series seeks to connect time with humanity at its most integral level. As the remaining survivors leave the ruins of the CDC, Bob Dylan's "Tomorrow is a Long Time" begins to play ("TS-19"). After the explosion and fast-paced frenzy of their escape, this slow melody marks a return to the bare essentials. It is a song, fittingly, about temporality and about how time seems endlessly to defer perfect union with a loved one.

The experience of time in Dylan's song, is not only that of the clock and the watch, but of the heart—the exertions of which keep the mind and body alive. For Rick and all the characters in *The Walking Dead*, it is the heartbeats of loved ones that bring meaning to their otherwise brutal lives. Tomorrow is indeed a long time if it stands between those who long for each other.

This relationship between love and time is one of the most poignant overarching themes of the series. In season two, Hershel is at first highly suspicious of Glenn who has been romancing his daughter Maggie. After carefully observing the young man in various situations, he decides to accept him into the family. "When you become a father some day you'll understand. No man is good enough for your little girl ... until one is." Hershel marks this development by giving Glenn a family heirloom—an old pocket watch on a chain. The camera lingers on the clock as it passes between them. Meanwhile, the sound of ticking grows louder, overlaying their conversation with a steady rhythm ("Judge, Jury, Executioner"). Living out the passage Dale recounted from Faulkner in the previous season, Hershel gives Glenn a timepiece that has been passed down over generations. It is an item of great symbolic value. A metronome of emotion, it attests not only to the inevitability of death but also to enduring love, responsibility, and trust.

Like Rick and Dale's timekeeping, the pocket watch offers a recurring motif. It appears again when Hershel has his leg amputated and nearly dies ("Sick"). As Glenn waits anxiously, he holds the device, winding its chain around his fingers. The watch is also incorporated into the opening credits of the third season, appearing beside Steven Yeun's (Glenn's) name. It does not operate normally here, however, for its arms are hyperactive—skittering around at an unnatural speed. Love's time is running out, and the accelerated pace of this depletion only makes it more important. At the end of the world, the experience of timelessness is made bearable by family, by those who bring meaning with their very presence. This is the underlying spark that keeps the living going during zombie time, and it is what keeps them human in a world of timeless monstrosity.

NOTES

1. Qtd. in Currie, *About Time*, 2.
2. Grosz, "Becoming ... An Introduction," 6.
3. Ibid.
4. Gale, Introduction, 1.
5. Grosz, "Becoming ... An Introduction," 1–2.
6. Geddes, "The Clock in Your Head," 45.
7. Rennie, "On Postulates for Temporal Order," 133–140.

8. Sinha et al. provide a useful overview of this literature in their article, "When Time is Not Space."

9. Canavan, "'We *Are* the Walking Dead,'" 441.

10. Hoffman, *Time*, 4.

11. Mani, "The Flow of Time in Narrative," 217.

12. Grosz, "Thinking the New," 18.

13. Hugo, *The Hunchback of Notre Dame*, 91.

14. Qtd. in Grosz, "Thinking the New," 21.

15. Cohen, "Grey (A Zombie Ecology)," In The Middle: A Medieval Studies Group Blog, entry posted June 22, 2012, http://www.inthemedievalmiddle.com/2012/06/grey-zombie-ecology.html.

16. Grosz, "Becoming ... An Introduction," 6.

17. Grosz, "Thinking the New," 17.

18. Canavan, "'We *Are* the Walking Dead,'" 441.

19. Pagano, "The Space of Apocalypse in Zombie Cinema," 73.

20. Ibid.

21. Faulkner, *The Sound and The Fury*, 63.

22. Sontag, *On Photography*, 15.

23. Barthes, *Camera Lucida*, 92.

24. Callender, Introduction, 1.

25. Hoffman, *Time*, 62.

26. Geddes, "The Clock in Your Head," 46.

27. Sontag, *On Photography*, 15.

28. Heidegger, *Being and Time*, 290–304.

29. Hoffman, *Time*, 185.

Afterword
Bye-Gone Days: Reflections on Romero, Kirkman and What We Become

Dave Beisecker

Days Gone Bye

Please allow me to begin at the beginning. As we know, that's not where *The Walking Dead* begins, not really. Instead, after a brief pre-apocalyptic prologue that depicts the initial shooting of officer Rick Grimes (which takes but a single page in the comic), the AMC television series opens as Rick finally emerges from his coma in a seemingly abandoned hospital. No doubt this setting witnessed many a struggle for survival, including Rick's own, yet everywhere around Rick bears signs of an epic battle for survival like none before. And behind the barred door to the cafeteria (marked "Dont [sic] Open Dead Inside" in the television series), we finally get to see that battle's evident victors. The medical facility is not as empty as it might at first seem, and Rick is not the first to miraculously arise from a death-like state. The ground indeed was ceded to a new regime: the former patients now run the asylum.

Thus, *The Walking Dead* skips over the real beginning. Perhaps that is because it has become all too familiar to us. We live in an age in which we don't need to be told, as Morgan Jones informs Rick, how to handle the undead; we've already been introduced to their ilk. The true beginning was in 1968 when George Romero released *Night of the Living Dead*, which is sometimes billed as "the first modern-day horror movie."[1] In so doing, he unleashed the contemporary zombie meme into pop-culture consciousness, and what were henceforth known as zombies finally broke free from their vampiric and voodoo origins to become the undead force we now know and love. The public was appalled. The scenes of redneck posses and militia shooting down shambling, cannibalistic cadavers, shot on relatively inexpensive 35mm black-and-white film, reminded viewers of newsreel footage of American soldiers picking off the Viet-Cong (or, worse, immolating Vietnamese villagers). They also called to mind images of the National Guard and law enforcement officers beating down students and civil-rights activists. The latter vision, of course, was only reinforced by the movie's shockingly downbeat ending, in which the calm, collected hero, Ben, who has somehow managed to survive the overnight ordeal in the farmhouse, emerges from the cellar only to be shot in the head by "whitey" and his body unceremoniously consigned to the bonfire. For a populace still unaccustomed to such leads being played by African Americans (and reeling from the assassinations of Malcolm X, Martin Luther King, and Robert Kennedy), such a blatantly pessimistic conclusion was simply too much.[2] The movie had been released nationally as part of a Saturday matinee scarcely a month before the MPAA film-rating system kicked in. Reviewing the film, Roger Ebert spoke of the young girl across the aisle from him, frozen in her seat and weeping at the realization that no one had survived.[3] How dare this George Romero, whose previous experience had been confined to advertising and commercials, flaunt so many cinematic and cultural taboos and compound the crime by exposing such damningly unpatriotic visuals to our impressionable youth? Romero might just as well have been the Bolshevik of Steeltown.

This of course is all ancient history, but I exhume it in part to remind us how revolutionary Romero's living dead were. If *Night of the Living Dead* seems campy or cliché today, then that's only because it was the mold from which later, perhaps more polished, variations on the theme have been cast. Robert Kirkman's *Walking Dead* franchise is perhaps the most wildly successful spawning of Romero's original. Kirkman's vision is to give us "the zombie movie that never ends."[4] One might even call it the first post-apocalyptic zombie soap opera with a story-arc free from artificial timelines imposed by the constraints of cinema. Kirkman freely acknowledges his debt to the creator of the modern zombie, and his walkers and biters are obviously of the slow variety Romero favors.[5] Indeed, Kirkman pays homage to Romero's *Night of the Living Dead* in the very first issue and in the very first episode. It comes in the form of Morgan's young son, Duane, who greets Rick with a shovel to the back of the head. Duane Jones is also the name of the actor (and eventual college instructor) who portrayed the aforementioned Ben in Romero's original.[6]

The widespread, spectacular success of *The Walking Dead* is perhaps the most visible sign that the lowly pathetic zombies have finally arrived. Once reviled and relegated to the B-list, they have now broken through the barricades to our hearts, minds, and souls. Nowadays we consume zombies just as fast as they could ever consume us. We go on zombie walks and to zombie proms, and we let them chase us through the park and the quad as we play Zombies vs. Humans or joyfully romp through a zombie obstacle run. While cynics might suggest that our seemingly insatiable appetite for all things zombie is about to ebb—that the zombie has now gone from eating the shark (think *Zombi 2*, 2004) to jumping it altogether—the remarkable story of how the lowly zombie managed to rise to the top of the horror heap is nevertheless worthy of its own telling. For such a journey might seem improbable for something so patently disgusting and grotesque and yet also fittingly inexorable when viewed in hindsight.

I won't propose to write that story here, though I would suggest that *The Walking Dead* is blessed by coming out in a cultural environment in which we blithely allow zombies simply to be what they are: reanimated mindless corpses, relentlessly consuming the flesh of the living. It wasn't like that in the beginning. In by-gone times, when zombies first appeared on the cultural scene, commentators were quick to read symbolism into the living dead. They couldn't resist likening Romero's "ghouls" or "flesh-eaters" to communists, hippies, the moral majority, the urban underclass, and whatever other untouchable, "un–American" elements of society were currently on their minds. And who could blame them? For J. Edgar Hoover's haunting (and cinematically prophetic) analogy of communism with sickness was surely reverberating inside their skulls:

> Communism in reality is not a political party. It is a way of life—an evil and malignant way of life. It reveals a condition akin to disease that spreads like an epidemic; and like an epidemic, a quarantine is necessary to keep it from infecting the nation.[7]

Such interpretations were only reinforced by Romero's own description of his inspiration. According to Romero, *Night of the Living Dead* was loosely based on Richard Matheson's novella, *I am Legend* (1954). Romero took Matheson's tale to be one of revolution, specifically about the misfortunes that befall those struggling to maintain an old form of life in the face of overwhelming change:

> I ripped off the idea for the first film from a Richard Matheson novel called *I Am Legend*, which is now back with us after a couple of incarnations prior. I thought *I Am Legend* was about revolution. I said if you're going to do something about revolution you should start at the beginning. I mean, Richard starts his book with one man left; everybody in the world has become a vampire. I said we got to start at the beginning and tweak it up a little bit.[8]

In "tweaking it up a bit," Romero didn't wish his confections to be polluted by any association with vampire lore. So, instead of sucking blood, his "ghouls" ate flesh, staggered about freely in the sunlight, and were dispatched by compromising the cranium, not perforating the chest cavity—and they were much more fantastically undead. While Matheson tried to give some sort of pseudo-scientific explanation for his vampires' affliction, Romero (as we shall see in a while) seemed not the least bit concerned about how his living dead got to be the way they were:

> The *T.V. Guide* blurbs on *Night of the Living Dead* begin with, "A returning Venus probe brings this plague ...", and I never meant to imply that.... I don't want there to be a cause, it's just something that's happening, it's just a different deal, it's a different way of life. If you want to look at it as a revolution, a new society coming in and devouring the old, however you want to look at it. That's really my take on it, it doesn't matter.[9]

Romero's living dead didn't exactly pop up out of nowhere, then. Romero was resurrecting earlier, familiar themes and transposing them into a more gory, graphic, and exploitative key. The downbeat apocalyptic and post-apocalyptic messages one can wrench out of *Night of the Living Dead* were, of course, standard fare on the *Twilight Zone*, for which the self-same Richard Matheson was a frequent writer. *Panic in Year Zero!* (1962) and the academy-award nominated *On the Beach* (1959) explored similar apocalyptic and post-apocalyptic themes. The original *Invasion of the Body Snatchers* (1956) was also widely seen as an allegory of how susceptible we were to the communist menace, and, though zombies weren't putting us on the menu in Elia Kazan's *Panic in the Streets* (1950), that film nevertheless exposed us to the idea that we might need to contain a contagion originating from unsavory elements of our own underworld. Even specifically post-apocalyptic racial and sexual tensions had already been explored before Romero in Harry Belafonte's 1959 *The World, the Flesh and the Devil*. It is safe to say, then, that before the release of *Night of the Living Dead*, Americans were already consuming and being consumed by thoughts about the end times, a preoccupation that was not just a product of the atom bomb. As early as 1912, Jack London supplied us with the following description of humanity being wiped out by a global pandemic:

> New York City and Chicago were in chaos. And what happened with them was happening in all the large cities. A third of the New York police were dead. Their chief was also dead, likewise the mayor. All law and order had ceased. The bodies were lying in the streets un-buried. All railroads and vessels carrying food and such things into the great city had ceased running and mobs of the hungry poor were pillaging the stores and warehouses. Murder and robbery and drunkenness were everywhere. Already the people had fled from the city by millions—at first the rich, in their private motor-cars and dirigibles, and then the great mass of the population, on foot, carrying the plague with them, themselves starving and pillaging the farmers and all the towns and villages on the way.[10]

Anyone exposed to the contemporary zombie meme should be struck by how eerily familiar such a passage feels (although the quaint reference to airships lends it a pleasantly steampunk aura!). No doubt, London's description would fit Kirkman's vision of the second evacuation of Atlanta (in case you forgot, *Gone with the Wind* (1939) depicted the looting, destruction, and carnage that accompanied the first). What Romero gave us was the zombie as the face of Armageddon.

What Lies Ahead

Novel or not, the idea of a zombie uprising as an allegory of revolution goes a long way towards explaining much of the original reception of *Night of the Living Dead*. It has become commonplace—even cliché—to construe a zombie outbreak as an allegory for the spread of just about any social threat. Zombies are not just communists anymore. Recently, they've also portrayed Nazis (*Dead Snow*, 2009), exotic dancers and escorts (*Zombie Strippers*, 2008), servants of the aristocracy (*Pride and Prejudice and Zombies*, 2009), technophiles (Stephen King's *Cell*, 2006), and, of course, avatars of mindless consumerism simply returning to the places that were once important to them (*Dawn of the Dead*, 1978). One of my personal favorites, David Cronenberg's *Shivers* (1976), represents a sexual revolution: his infected succumb to carnal abandon and deviance brought on by a parasite spread by open-mouth kissing. Generally, zombies are taken to represent the spread of any despised, "untouchable" segment of the populace that we think needs to be contained: homosexuals, drug addicts, immigrants, the homeless, the proletariat, the religious right, and just about anyone else that might be associated (rightly or wrongly) with either disease or the dismantling of society as we know it. Cleverly playing up the theme of the zombie as disenfranchised, the undead in the short film *Homecoming* (2005) are returning from a war, merely seeking the right to vote out those who sent them off to battle. Indeed, zombies are so regnant with symbolism that it can sometimes be hard to view them literally or just as they are.

However, Romero himself has cautioned us against the temptation to read too much into his living dead. Sure, *Night of the Living Dead* was meant to tap into the deep cultural divisions that were then embroiling us, but Romero always stressed that the zombies were just the situation, not the metaphor. For instance, when asked in an interview for *Vanity Fair* whether "a cigar is just a cigar," he tells us:

> To me, the zombies have *always* just been zombies. They've always been a cigar. When I first made *Night of the Living Dead*, it got analyzed and overanalyzed

way out of proportion. The zombies were written about as if they represented Nixon's Silent Majority or whatever. But I never thought about it that way. My stories are about humans and how they react, or fail to react, or react stupidly. I'm pointing the finger at *us*, not at the zombies. I try to respect and sympathize with the zombies as much as possible.[11]

The real drama, of course, is in our reaction to the disaster as it begins to spread and take over the world. The zombie apocalypse, like apocalyptic narratives generally, exploits anxieties about our seeming inability to contain social threats or to prevent the widespread institutional collapse they might precipitate. And they also serve to remind us how fragile our own humanity and mindfulness might be. As the genre so often makes clear, the real threat is usually not from without but from within. After all, the ones who survive the end times are likely to be the quick and the cunning—as well as the armed and desperate—and so they turn out to be as much, if not more, dangerous than the zombies. Thus we fall prey to the living just as much as we fall prey to any reanimated corpses, and when we do succumb to the latter, usually it can be attributed to actions and betrayals on the part of the former. That is why, when you think about it, the most chilling analogy to the horrors of a zombie holocaust is not the perceived spread of the communist red menace (or the sexual revolution) but rather the killing fields of Cambodia under the Khmer Rouge. The horrors there were all perpetrated by the living as they brought each other down in staggering numbers and in a seemingly random fashion all in the name of bringing about a workers' paradise. Those accused of subversion were, in effect, the walking dead who in their dying confessions brought ever more supporters to their side, while the remaining survivors were themselves the pathogens that acted as the instruments of the dead.

Nietzsche famously warned us, "Whoever fights monsters should see to it that in the process he does not become a monster. And when you look long into an abyss, the abyss also looks into you."[12] Accordingly, as *The Walking Dead* staggers on and on without end in its version of a post-apocalyptic soap opera (replete with major characters variously entering and exiting the show), the drama increasingly revolves around whether Rick himself will turn, not into a zombie *per se* but rather into one of those bona-fide monsters such as the Governor. And Kirkman's question is just the same as Conrad's or Coppola's: when the apocalypse is now, what's to keep your heart from turning to darkness? So we see why it's actually important to both Romero and Kirkman that, at least individually, zombies are as slow and as stupid as they are. That we can eventually fall to such a mindless horde ultimately says much more about our human frailties than it does about theirs. The true tragedy of the zombie apocalypse is not that it's unavoidable;

it's just that the remaining survivors (or holdouts) wind up making things so much worse for themselves.

In *The Walking Dead*, the zombies Romero bequeathed to us have finally managed to become just zombies. *They are just the situation, not the metaphor*, leaving the narrative lens to focus squarely upon the plight of the survivors as they lurch from one disaster to another with no hope for a better life or a way out. In this respect, Kirkman's walkers could be a stand-in for just about any global catastrophe. Romero himself sometimes seems to endorse this view:

> I don't care what they are. I don't care where they came from. They could be any disaster. They could be an earthquake, a hurricane, whatever. They don't represent, in my mind, anything except a global change of some kind. And the stories are about how people respond or fail to respond to this. That's really all they've ever represented to me.... They are a global disaster that people don't know how to deal with. Because we don't know how to deal with any of the shit.[13]

In 1898, H.G. Wells's *War of the Worlds* gave us the canonical chronicle "of the rout of civilisation, of the massacre of mankind," the template of which we still see today in stories like *The Walking Dead's* television rival *Falling Skies*.[14] In Wells's vision, our rapid devolution from civilized individual to hunted prey is not pretty as we scatter like cockroaches out of the paths of malevolent watchers from across the gulf of space. Our resistance is futile, and even our eventual salvation by microbial allies is equally outside our control. As with so much post-apocalyptic fiction, we quickly lose our mindfulness and humanity. In the case of zombie narratives, this loss is both figurative and literal.

Doomsday scenarios come in myriad forms and flavors and can be arrayed according to our degree of involvement in their genesis. *War of the Worlds* lies at one end of this spectrum, in which our demise comes at the hands of natural or even supernatural forces beyond our initial knowledge or control. The darker, more tragic expanses of this spectrum, however, span those Armageddons that we wittingly or unwittingly visit upon ourselves. At least in the comic, Kirkman has remained as little forthcoming as Romero about causality, leaving it entirely open (or up to our own imagination) as to why the dead have arisen. For instance, when asked by one of his readers about the cause of his zombie outbreak, Kirkman writes, "I have ideas ... but it's nothing set in stone because I never plan on writing it."[15] In response to a query about the nature of the plague, he adds: "that starts to get into the origin of all this stuff, and I think that's unimportant to the series itself.[16] There will be smaller answers as things progress ... but never will we see the whole picture." He has even gone so far as to say (in Issue 90) that the topic is not his "prerogative."

Similarly, we've been assured that the television series will also not delve deeply into causality.[17] This is probably a good thing, for it has suffered when it does. For instance, the finale of season one ("TS-19") took Rick and his band on a detour through a CDC bunker that doesn't appear in the comic. Here they are informed by Dr. Edwin Jenner that he has identified a biological pathogen, which reanimates the lower brain stem after death, as the cause of the epidemic. Armed with such information, we are even led to believe that maybe a cure is tantalizingly within reach. Unfortunately, Jenner's revelation paints the series into a corner later when the deaths of Randall and Shane make it apparent that the dead need not first be bitten by zombies in order to reanimate. How, then, are we to account for this fact? By way of explanation, Rick reveals to us and the rest of the survivors that the last thing Jenner whispered to him was that everyone is a carrier of the virus, provoking even more distracting questions. How, for example, did the biological pathogen spread in the first place, and why did it seem to erupt at once all over the globe? And what about zombie bites? Do the walkers now harbor an additional pathogen that leads one to die, thereby activating the original pathogen that Jenner discovered? Such are the troubles when one succumbs to the temptation to offer a naturalistic or quasi-naturalistic explanation of the rising. Rather than reinventing science, we just shouldn't care!

To be fair, I recall hearing that the incineration of the bunker was a sort of pre-programmed self-destruct mechanism for the series in the event that it was not renewed after the first season. That would be fittingly ironic, for, not only did Rick and the other survivors have to find a wholly improbable way out of the sealed bunker (a conveniently-remembered hand grenade), but now the series as a whole must contort itself in order to find its own way out of the episode's attempt to give the contagion a pseudo-naturalistic explanation. Still, this is not the only threat that a series faces when it identifies the cause of a zombie outbreak. When one does so, questions of blame and responsibility inevitably arise, and such questions only threaten to divert attention away from the humans' struggle against the zombies (and against those survivors who might be the true villains). This is especially true if the cause takes the form of some malevolent force, be it human or otherwise. Consider, for instance, *Falling Skies*. At first, this might not strike you as much of a zombie story at all, for the real villains of the piece are the various alien overlords and their minions. Among those minions are human children, however, who have been enslaved by what are essentially alien *bokors*. Thus the zombie element, while largely sublimated, is nevertheless present in its more primitive and humble, voodoo-inspired guise. My point is that these are the more boring kinds of zombies; I seriously doubt the producers of *Falling Skies* would ever run a contest in which the winner lands a role as a harnessed child. Or consider the

Resident Evil franchise, which starts out as your rather run-of-the-mill zombie uprising and first-person shooter game. As the series progresses, however, zombies play an increasingly marginalized role, serving finally as mere distractions, while we await Alice's battle against increasingly powerful Frankensteins emerging from the Umbrella Corporation's laboratories. So, I would argue that Kirkman's steadfast (to date) reluctance to unveil a cause is something we should applaud. The comic and the series both would lose their focus if the writers yielded to the temptation to appease our natural curiosity regarding the outbreak's source.[18] We should be relieved, then, when the hapless Eugene (a character in the comic series who claims to know the cause of the plague) reveals himself to be a fraud.

Pretty Much Dead Already

Though we have seen Romero downplaying the symbolic significance of his zombies, he is no metaphorical nihilist. In *The New York Times*, he disparaged the sub-genre of exploitative films represented by the *Saw* (2004) series and *Hostel* (2005), saying, "I don't get the torture-porn films.... They're lacking metaphor."[19] And he told *The L.A. Times*, "I like to use horror as allegory."[20] Nevertheless, despite the open-endedness of the zombie apocalypse, I can't help but think that Romero's insistence that zombies can stand for any global calamity whatsoever is itself just a bit too metaphorically vapid. Recall that the initial theme or metaphor driving the creation of the contemporary zombie is one of revolution. To lose sight of that is to miss the sub-genre's distinctive poignancy. We can all be chewed apart in the mandibles of alien or mutant super-bugs, but it's especially chilling when our future "selves" are the ones doing the chewing! A zombie apocalypse is thus not your garden-variety apocalypse; it's one in which we are brought down from within, a battle *royale* in which what we have been fights to contain "what we become." Romero and Kirkman might choose to follow Matheson by focusing on the plight of the dwindling ranks of holdouts as they face their imminent destruction, but that doesn't change the fact that they're involved in a struggle for survival between two different and incompatible forms of human existence trying to supplant one another.

To my mind, far too much has been made of the zombie as "Other," not just because the idea isn't literally true, but also because it has become increasingly uninteresting and unproductive. To think of them as some unredeemable alien threat only serves to excavate an unacceptable moral gulf between us that threatens to disconnect us from the potential zombie lurking within each and every one of us. After all, the whole poignancy of a zombie rebellion—the very thing that Romero borrowed from *I Am Legend*—is that the zombies really are us (or at least what remains of us after we've changed). The tragedy is how easily each and every one of us can be claimed by or "cross over" to that other side. This is the reason Romero tells us that he tries "to respect and sympathize with the zombies as much as possible." *Dawn of the Dead* shows them comically slipping on the ice and pressing their faces against storefront windows, as if the rising was a new *Miracle on 34th Street*. *Day of the Dead* (1985) introduced us to the lovable Bub, a heartwarming cadaver akin to a cartoon Frankenstein's monster. Eventually, Bub takes just revenge by shooting (with a gun) Colonel Rhodes after Rhodes killed the good Doctor Logan for showing Bub nothing but kindness. Finally, in addition to zombie landscapers, musicians, and sweeties holding hands, *Land of the Dead* (2005) gives us Big Daddy, a leader of his tribe merely searching for someplace to go.

In all likelihood, the main narrative of *The Walking Dead* will never go so far as to foster such sympathy for those we become. Its gaze will remain transfixed upon the surviving holdouts as they dig in against each other and form circular firing squads with ever-smaller diameters. We can still see, however, enough endearing touches in both the comic and the television series to remind us that the walkers really are us. Here, I don't mean those tragic instances in which former cast members like Sophia reappear in their reanimated guises. Instead, I mean those more entertaining cases in which we notice some "featured" walker reprising its role across multiple episodes or issues, such as the creepy lurker inhabiting the Atlanta bus, leading us, perhaps, to root for its continued animation. Similarly, the promotional webisodes for the second season feature the backstory of "Bicycle Girl," another memorable walker (or crawler) from the first season. In this fashion, we get to follow along with at least a few walkers in their own peculiar journeys, just as we did in *Colin*, the 2008 British film that was the rage of Cannes. Moreover, we might recognize some of the zombies that appear within the pages of the graphic serial and across the covers of the hardbound volumes as having real-world counterparts. Indeed, if fortune smiles, we might recognize a zombified friend, family member, or even our own zombie twin appearing in the series, provided one of us is lucky enough to win one of AMC's contests for a coveted "stagger-on role."[21]

These are the zombies inside each and every one of us, the ones that we like to celebrate when we playfully cover ourselves in fake blood and tattered rags and shamble off to a zombie walk, prom, or flash mob. And these are precisely the zombies we can lose sight of when we yield to the temptation to tie them to some particular social evil or sickness. Interestingly, the emergence of zombie comedies such as *Shaun of the Dead* (2004) and *Zombieland* (2009) has perhaps done more than anything else to cultivate a more enlightened, humanitarian attitude towards the undead. Rather than playing up the idea of zombies as alien or other, the success of many of these zom coms is explained by how well they reverse that theme. For instance, in *Shaun of the Dead* (which Kirkman and Romero both praise), a good portion of the joke is that we've been zombies all along, sleepwalking through our lives to such an extent that not only do we not realize how mindless we've all become, but we also might not even recognize the apocalypse were it to occur under our nose or just outside our favorite pub. Indeed, in the world of these zom coms, it can be hard to tell zombies and humans apart from one another.

As part of the reversal of zombie as other, these zom coms will typically portray geeks, nerds, and other misfits improbably emerging as heroic survivors cut from the same cloth as Bruce Campbell's Ash from the *Evil Dead* series, who must then do battle against hordes of undead "normals." Consider, for instance, the German jewel, *Night of the Living Dorks* (2004)—a veritable *Breakfast Club*-gone-zombie in which the eponymous "*Lebenden Losers*" (if you allow me to refer to the original German) have the misfortune to attend Friedrich Nietzsche High, replete with all the angst-ridden stereotypes to be found in any brat-pack classic. Like the zom coms, the brat-packers thrive by humanizing the geek or outcast in us all as well as by tearing down the mindless pretensions of the in-crowd. *The Walking Dead* is no zom com, but one can see it tapping into the very same cultural currents that have made such zom coms so popular. Specifically, one can find it expressing the same reversal of zombie as other. Consider the ever-dependable Glenn, likely one of the characters with whom fans most identify. By his own admission, Glenn was once the stereotypical geek who now has the opportunity to ride out the ultimate geek-fantasy. He gets to take revenge upon (and denounce as "geeks") all those who once would have strung him up by his underwear in the locker-room but have preceded him to the other side. Plus, in true *Revenge of the Nerds* (1984) style, he gets the girl, too.

A case can be made that the zombies might be the most ordinary human things that remain in the world of *The Walking Dead*, quietly going about their business until disturbed or otherwise molested by a survivor. If there is a message I would like to share, then, it's that we need to stop demonizing the poor, pathetic zombies and begin seeing more of ourselves in them. We might not be cannibals, but in our overwhelming numbers we might possess within us the seeds of destruction of all the social institutions we hold so dear. Even that doesn't make us evil, however. To counter the temptation to think of zombies as alien, evil, or irredeemably other, I'd ask you to engage in one final little thought experiment. One of my favorite recently-released zombie movies is *Fido* (2006), a deliciously dark comedy in which zombies are brought into compliance (and our homes) by shock collars developed by the Zomcom corporation. The title-character is one such endearing figure: a kindly, protective old cadaver who just wants to find love and acceptance in his new family, but, in one of the film's more brilliant tropes, the life of the nuclear family in such a post-apocalyptic world is portrayed with imagery meant to recall the supposedly halcyon times of post–WWII America. In both worlds, close human attachments are virtually impossible: neither friends, family, neighbors, corporations, nor the government are to be trusted. There is another group that poses the greatest threat of all, however: the elderly. For, if they quietly pass along in their sleep amongst you, they just might rise up and carry you along to the other side.

In that vein, let us suppose that zombies are an allegory for an aging "baby-boomer" demographic. After all, in their ceaseless wandering and bewildered expressions, zombies can bear a striking resemblance to those afflicted by Alzheimer's, which has been called the defining affliction (and perhaps greatest fear) of the baby-boom generation.[22] Indeed, the comparison seems apt. Every day, over 10,000 baby-boomers inexorably "crossover" into retirement age, and the overwhelming weight of their numbers, especially by comparison to subsequent "Generations X and Y," threatens to bring down our health care system and social security net (or so we are told).

Generational conflict is hardly new, and it can open up along many fronts as novel ideas and ways of living struggle to supplant the cherished tenets endorsed by the old guard. Though such change can seem threatening or frightening, we should actually embrace it as a sign of social vitality. During the natural course of our lives, we will all have to give way to more youthful thinking, lest the collective yields to the great, grave tragedy of cultural and economic ossification.

This is the kind of zombie narrative that now needs to be told, one that actually demands our taking a more humanitarian attitude toward the zombie, while at the same time recognizing how fragile such humanitarian attitudes are. If zombies are more like the elderly (or even Alzheimer's patients), then our attitudes towards them will need to be complex.[23] There are many around us, who might seem to reside in a foggy world of twilight, for whom we can neither claim that they are dead nor that they are altogether "there." Nevertheless, such folk remain friends and family and are still worthy of our respect, even though they might have lost many of the hallmarks upon which philosophers have pinned the concept of a self. From this point of view, Morgan's attitude toward his wife, Hershel's sequestering of his family and neighbors, and even the Governor's feelings for his zombie daughter are not so easily dismissed or condemned.

Regarded from this angle, zombies aren't inherently bad or even diseased; they're just infirm or perhaps hopelessly set in their ways. But, more importantly, we should be able to see our future selves in such creatures. If aging is the affliction, then, just as Jenner tells Rick, *we are all infected.* So, zombification as an allegory for aging powerfully captures the concern we should have for what we will become. In the natural course of things, there might well come an awkward time of twilight in which we are neither ourselves, nor are we dead. Given world enough and time, we will eventually be hollowed out. Contemplating such an inexorable slide into senescence can be disturbing, and I have no advice about how to descend that slope with any great measure of grace.

Indeed, it can be striking how hard it is to approach the end of our days with any degree of dignity, especially in the kinds of venues that we have set aside for such purposes: hospitals, hospices, or other such end-of-life facilities. And this, of course, brings us around full circle to where *The Walking Dead* begins, a place in which a miraculously revived Rick Grimes arises with the thought that he's alive and hell-bent on finding his family. But, as Romero curiously claims of Matheson's Robert Neville, he might well be wrong. Watch out Carl! Your old man is coming to get you ...[24]

Notes

1. Zinoman, "The Horror Movie."

2. Romero sometimes speaks about hearing of the assassination of Martin Luther King, Jr., while driving from Pittsburgh to New York to sell his film. Ibid.

3. Roger Ebert, "Review of *Night of the Living Dead,*" *Chicago Sun Times,* January 5, 1967, http://rogerebert.suntimes.com/apps/pbcs.dll/article?AID=/19670105/REVIEWS/701050301/1023. For some inexplicable reason, the *Sun Times* website suggests that the original review was written a year before the film actually came out.

4. Kirkman, "The Walking Dead," Issue 37.

5. Frank Darabont, the television series' writer and producer (through the middle of season two), even goes so far as to claim that *Night of the Living Dead* serves as *The Walking Dead's* "Book of Genesis." Ruditis, *The Walking Dead Chronicles,* 46.

6. In another nod to *Night of the Living Dead,* Kirkman also opted to print the comic in black and white. Ruditis, *The Walking Dead Chronicles,* 20.

7. J. Edgar Hoover, "Speech Before the House Committee on Un-American Activities," March 26, 1947, para. 71, http://voicesofdemocracy.umd.edu/hoover-speech-before-the-house-committee-speech-text/

8. McConnell, "Interview: George A. Romero."

9. Curnutte, "There's No Magic." Max Brooks credits Romero with creating the scientific or pseudo-scientific conception of the zombie, but we can see that that's not quite accurate. Indeed, when it matters to Romero to give something like a scientific expla-

nation of an outbreak, it is telling that he *doesn't* give us living dead. Instead, he gives us *The Crazies* (1973). "Max Brooks Discusses George A. Romero's Zombie," Zurvived.it, August 2, 2011, http://zurvived.it/comiccon/max-brooks-discusses-george-a-romeros-zombie.

10. London, *The Scarlet Plague*, chap. 3.

11. Eric Spitznagel, "George A. Romero: 'Who Says Zombies Eat Brains?,'" The Hollywood Blog, VanityFair.com, May 27, 2010, http://www.vanityfair.com/online/oscars/2010/05/george-romero.

12. Nietzsche, *Beyond Good and Evil*, 49; Aphorism 146.

13. McConnell, "Interview: George A. Romero."

14. Wells, *War of the Worlds*, 147.

15. Kirkman, *The Walking Dead*, Issue 54.

16. Kirkman, *The Walking Dead*, Issue 46.

17. Tim Malloy, "'Walking Dead' Writers: We Don't Know What Created Walkers," TheWrap.com, January 14, 2012, http://www.thewrap.com/tv/column-post/walking-dead-writers-we-dont-know-what-created-walker-epidemic-34422.

18. Carroll attributes the pleasure we derive from a horror narrative to our finally coming to solve the mysteries presented to us by the presence of a monster, understood as something we find both disgusting and fascinating in that it violates naturalistic norms. Though zombies certainly fit Carroll's definition of a monster, *The Walking Dead* and other zombie narratives that don't dwell on causation, nevertheless, seem to challenge his idea that our pleasure in horror comes from the satisfaction of our natural desire to know. Carroll, *The Philosophy of Horror*, 178–195.

19. Katrina Onstad, "Horror Auteur is Unfinished with the Undead," *New York Times*, February 10, 2008, http://www.nytimes.com/2008/02/10/movies/10onst.html?_r=0.

20. "The Sunday Conversation: With George A Romero," *Los Angeles Times*, May 30, 2010, http://articles.latimes.com/2010/may/30/entertainment/la-ca-0530conversation-20100530.

21. See Beisecker, "A Stagger-on Role to Die For." So far AMC has sponsored such contests during season one as well as the preview weekend for season three, and now they sponsor contests for roles in *The Walking Dead* video game.

22. Stephen King also explores the idea of humanity achieving Armageddon by way of Alzheimer's in his short story, "The End of the Whole Mess" (2008).

23. For further exploration of this theme, see John Ajvide Lindqvist's *Handling the Undead* (2009).

24. Many folks helped me with this little project, but I especially feel the need to single out Roxana Menes and Scott Schrager for their patience in looking over earlier drafts and exposing potentially embarrassing mistakes and omissions.

Bibliography

Abrams, Ann Uhry. *Explosion at Orly: The Disaster That Transformed Atlanta*. Atlanta: Avion Press, 2002.

Ackermann, Hans-W., and Jeanine Gauthier. "The Ways and Nature of the Zombi." *The Journal of American Folklore* 104, no. 414 (1991): 466–494.

Agamben, Giorgio. *Homo Sacer: Sovereign Power and Bare Life*. Translated by Daniel Heller-Roazen. Stanford, CA: Stanford University Press, 1998.

_____. *State of Exception*. Translated by Kevin Attell. Chicago: University of Chicago Press, 2005.

Ariès, Philippe. "The Hour of Our Death." In Robben, *Death, Mourning, and Burial*, 40–48.

Atkinson, Tiffany. Introduction to *The Body*, 1–11. New York: Palgrave Macmillan, 2005.

Badiou, Alain. *Ethics: An Essay on the Understanding of Evil*. Translated by Peter Hallward. New York: Verso, 2001.

Badley, Linda. "Zombie Splatter Comedy from *Dawn* to *Shaun*: Cannibal Carnivalesque." In McIntosh and Leverette, *Zombie Culture*, 35–54.

Balko, Radley. *Overkill: The Rise of Paramilitary Police Raids in America*. Washington, DC: The Cato Institute, 2006.

Bargh, John A., and Tanya L. Chartrand. "The Unbearable Automaticity of Being." *American Psychologist* 54, no. 7 (1999): 462–479.

Barkman, Ashley. "Women in a Zombie Apocalypse." In Yuen, *"The Walking Dead" and Philosophy*, 97–106.

Barthes, Roland. *Camera Lucida: Reflections on Photography*. Translated by Richard Howard. London: Vintage, 1993.

Bataille, Georges. "Death." In *The Bataille Reader*, edited by Fred Botting and Scott Wilson, 242–247. Oxford: Blackwell, 1997.

Baylor, Ronald H. *Race and the Shaping of Twentieth-Century Atlanta*. Chapel Hill: University of North Carolina Press, 1996.

Beisecker, Dave. "A Stagger-on Role to Die For." In Yuen, *"The Walking Dead" and Philosophy*, 67–79.

Benjamin, Walter. "Critique of Violence." In *Reflections: Essays, Aphorisms, Autobiographical Writing*, edited by Peter Demetz, translated by Edmund Jephcott, 277–300. New York: Schocken, 1986.

_____. *Illuminations*. Edited by Hannah Arendt. Translated by Harry Zohn. New York: Schocken Books, 2007.

_____. "On Some Motifs in Baudelaire." In Benjamin, *Illuminations*, 155–200.

_____. "The Work of Art in the Age of Mechanical Reproduction." In Benjamin, *Illuminations*, 217–251.

Benveniste, Émile. "Categories of Thought and Language." In Benveniste, *Problems in General Linguistics*, 55–64.

_____. *Problems in General Linguistics*. Translated by Mary Elizabeth Meek. Miami Linguistics Series, no. 8. Coral Gables, FL: University of Miami Press, 1971.

_____. "Remarks on the Function of Language in Freudian Theory." In Benveniste, *Problems in General Linguistics*, 65–75.

_____. "Subjectivity in Language." In Benveniste, *Problems in General Linguistics*, 223–230.

Berns, Nancy. *Closure: The Rush to End Grief and What It Costs Us*. Philadelphia: Temple University Press, 2011.

Bickman, Leonard. "The Social Power of a Uniform." *Journal of Applied Social Psychology* 4, no. 1 (1974): 47–61.

Birch-Bayley, Nicole. "Terror in Horror Genres: The Global Media and the Millennial Zombie." *The Journal of Popular Culture* 45, no. 6 (2012): 1137–1151.

Bishop, Kyle William. *American Zombie Gothic: The Rise and Fall (and Rise) of the Walking Dead in Popular Culture*. Jefferson, NC: McFarland, 2010.

_____. "The Idle Proletariat: *Dawn of the Dead*, Consumer Ideology, and the Loss of Productive Labor." *The Journal of Popular Culture* 43, no. 2 (2010): 234–248.

_____. "The Pathos of *The Walking Dead*." In Lowder, *Triumph of "The Walking Dead*," 1–14.

Blandy, Sarah. "Gated Communities in England as a Response to Crime and Disorder: Context, Effectiveness and Implications." *People, Place & Policy Online* 1, no. 2 (2007): 47–54.

Bohm, Robert M., K. Michael Reynolds, and Stephen T. Holmes. "Perceptions of Neighborhood Problems and Their Solutions: Implications for Community Policing." *Policing: An International Journal of Police Strategies and Management* 23, no. 4 (2000): 439–465.

Boluk, Stephanie, and Wylie Lenz. "Infection, Media, and Capitalism: From Early Modern Plagues to Postmodern Zombies." *Journal for Early Modern Cultural Studies* 10, no. 2 (2010): 126–147.

_____. "Introduction: Generation Z, the Age of Apocalypse." In Boluk and Lenz, *Generation Zombie*, 1–17.

Boluk, Stephanie, and Wylie Lenz, eds. *Generation Zombie: Essays on the Living Dead in Modern Culture*. Jefferson, NC: McFarland, 2011.

Boon, Kevin. "The Zombie as Other: Mortality and the Monstrous in the Post-Nuclear Age." In Christie and Lauro, *Better Off Dead*, 50–60.

Borradori, Giovanna, and Jacques Derrida. "Autoimmunity: Real and Symbolic Suicides—A Dialogue with Jacques Derrida." In *Philosophy in a Time of Terror: Dialogues with Jurgen Habermas and Jacques Derrida*, edited by Giovanna Borradori, 85–136. Chicago: University of Chicago Press, 2003.

Boss, Pauline. *Ambiguous Loss: Learning to Live with Unresolved Grief*. Cambridge, MA: Harvard University Press, 1999.

Bostrom, Nick. "A History of Transhuman Thought." *Journal of Evolution and Technology* 14, no. 1 (2005): 1–25.

Botting, Fred. "A-ffect-less: Zombie-Horror-Shock." *English Language Notes* 48, no. 1 (2010): 178–190.

_____. "Zombie Death Drive: Between Gothic and Science Fiction." In Wasson and Alder, *Gothic Science Fiction*, 36–54.

_____. "Zombie London: Unexceptionalities of the New World Order." In *London Gothic: Place, Space and the Gothic Imagination*, edited by Lawrence Phillips and Anne Witchard, 153–171. London: Continuum, 2010.

Bowling, Ben, and Coretta Phillips, "Policing Ethnic Minority Communities." In *Handbook of Policing*, edited by Tim Newburn, 528–555. Devon, UK: Willan Publishing, 2003.

Boycott, A.E. "The Transition from Live to Dead: the Nature of Filterable Viruses." *Nature* 123, no. 3090 (1929): 91–98.

Breuer, Joseph, and Sigmund Freud. *Studies on Hysteria*. Edited by Angela Richards. Translated by James and Alix Strachey. London: Penguin Books, 1974.

Brooks, Max. "Closure, Limited." In *Closure, Limited and Other Zombie Tales*, 17–30. London: Duckworth, 2012.

_____. *World War Z*. New York: Three Rivers, 2006.

Bruce, Barbara S. "Guess Who's Going to Be Dinner: Sidney Poitier, Black Militancy, and the Ambivalence of Race in Romero's *Night of the Living Dead*." In

Moreman and Rushton, *Race, Oppression and the Zombie*, 60–73.

Buckmeier, Bradley. "Setting a Higher Standard for the Evaluation of Problem-Oriented Policing Initiatives." *Policing: An International Journal of Police Strategies and Management* 33, no. 2 (2010): 173–182.

Buscombe, Edward, and Roberta E. Pearson, eds. *Back in the Saddle Again: New Essays on the Western*. London: British Film Institute, 1998.

Callender, Craig. Introduction to *The Oxford Handbook of Philosophy of Time*, 1–10. Oxford: Oxford University Press, 2011.

Canavan, Gerry. "'We *Are* the Walking Dead': Race, Time, and Survival in Zombie Narrative." *Extrapolation* 51, no. 3 (2010): 431–453.

Caputi, Jane. "Films of the Nuclear Age." *Journal of Popular Film and Television* 16, no. 3 (1988): 101–107.

Carroll, Noël. *The Philosophy of Horror: Or, Paradoxes of the Heart*. New York: Routledge, 1990.

Cederroth, Christopher R., Jacques Auger, Céline Zimmermann, Florence Eustache and Serge Nef. "Soy, Phyto-oestrogens and Male Reproductive Function: a Review." *International Journal of Andrology* 33, no. 2 (2010): 304–316.

Cederström, Carl, and Peter Fleming. *Dead Man Working*. Winchester, UK: Zero Books, 2012.

Chalmers, David John. *The Conscious Mind: In Search of a Fundamental Theory*. New York: Oxford University Press, 1996.

Cherokee Nation. "John Burnett's Story of the Trail of Tears." Cherokee Nation: The Official Site of the Cherokee Nation. http://www.cherokee.org/About TheNation/History/TrailofTears/ 24502/Information.aspx.

Christie, Deborah. "A Dead New World: Richard Matheson and the Modern Zombie." In Christie and Lauro, *Better Off Dead*, 67–80.

Christie, Deborah, and Sarah Juliet Lauro. Introduction to *Better Off Dead*, 1–4.

Christie, Deborah, and Sarah Juliet Lauro, eds. *Better Off Dead: The Evolution of the Zombie as Post-Human*. New York: Fordham University Press, 2011.

Clark, W.A.V. "School Desegregation and White Flight: A Reexamination and Case Study." *Social Science Research* 16, no. 3 (1987): 211–228.

Clough, Patricia Ticineto, and Craig Willse. "Human Security/National Security: Gender Branding and Population Racism." In Clough and Willse, *Beyond Biopolitics*, 46–64.

_____, eds. *Beyond Biopolitics: Essays on the Governance of Life and Death*. Durham, NC: Duke University Press, 2011.

Cohen, Ed. *A Body Worth Defending: Immunity, Biopolitics, and the Apotheosis of the Modern Body*. Durham, NC: Duke University Press, 2009.

Collins, Margo, and Elson Bond. "'Off the page and into your brains!': New Millennium Zombies and the Scourge of Hopeful Apocalypses." In Christie and Lauro, *Better Off Dead*, 187–204.

Corkin, Stanley. *Cowboys as Cold Warriors: The Western and U.S. History*. Philadelphia: Temple University Press, 2004.

Coward, Rosalind, and John Ellis. *Language and Materialism: Developments in Semiology and the Theory of the Subject*. London: Routledge and Kegan Paul, 1977.

Crawford, Adam. "'Contractual Governance' of Deviant Behaviour." *Journal of Law and Society* 30, no. 4 (2003): 479–505.

Cullum, Jerry, Catherine Fox, Cinqué Hicks, and Valerie Cassel Oliver, eds. *Noplaceness: Art in a Post-Urban Landscape*. Atlanta: Possible Futures, 2012.

Curnutte, Rick. "There's No Magic: A Conversation With George A. Romero." *The Film Journal*, no. 10 (October 2004). http://www.thefilmjournal.com /issue10/romero.html.

Currie, Mark. *About Time: Narrative, Fiction, and the Philosophy of Time*. Edinburgh: Edinburgh University Press, 2007.

Damasio, Antonio. *Self Comes to Mind: Constructing the Conscious Brain*. New York: Vintage, 2010.

Datta, Ronjon Paul, and Laura MacDonald. "Time for Zombies: Sacrifice and the Structural Phenomenology of Capitalist Futures." In Moreman and Rushton, *Race, Oppression and the Zombie*, 77–92.

Delfino, Robert, and Kyle Taylor. "Walking Contradictions." In Yuen, *"The Walking Dead" and Philosophy*, 39–51.

Dendle, Peter. *The Zombie Movie Encyclopedia*. Jefferson, NC: McFarland, 2001.

_____. "Zombie Movies and the 'Millennial Generation.'" In Christie and Lauro, *Better Off Dead*, 175–186.

Dennett, Daniel C. "The Unimagined Preposterousness of Zombies." *Journal of Consciousness Studies* 2, no. 4 (1995): 322–326.

Derksen, Craig, and Darren Hudson Hick. "Your Zombie and You: Identity, Emotion, and the Undead." In Moreman and Rushton, *Zombies Are Us*, 11–23.

Donald, James. "The Fantastic, the Sublime and the Popular; Or, What's at Stake in Vampire Films." In Donald, *Fantasy and the Cinema*, 233–251. London: British Film Institute, 1989.

Dowler, Kenneth. "Media Consumption and Public Attitudes toward Crime and Justice: The Relationship between Fear of Crime, Punitive Attitudes, and Perceived Police Effectiveness." *Journal of Criminal Justice and Popular Culture* 10, no. 2 (2003): 109–126.

Eagleman, David. *Incognito: The Secret Lives of the Brain*. New York: Vintage, 2011.

Eagleton, Terry. *Holy Terror*. Oxford: Oxford University Press, 2005.

Elsaesser, Thomas. "Between *Erlebnis* and *Erfahrung*: Cinema Experience with Benjamin." *Paragraph* 32, no. 3 (2009): 292–312.

Eng, David L., and David Kazanjian. "Introduction: Mourning Remains." In *Loss: The Politics of Mourning*, 1–26. Berkeley: University of California Press, 2003.

Esposito, Roberto. *Bíos: Biopolitics and Philosophy*. Translated by Timothy Campbell. Minneapolis: University of Minnesota Press, 2008.

_____. *Third Person: Politics of Life and Philosophy of the Impersonal*. Translated by Zakiya Hanafi. Malden, MA: Polity, 2012.

Faludi, Susan. *Terror Dream: Fear and Fantasy in Post–9/11 America*. New York: MacMillan, 2007.

Faulkner, William. *The Sound and the Fury*. London: Random House, 1995.

Fenin, George N., and William K. Everson. *The Western: From Silents to the Seventies*. New York: Grossman, 1973.

Fischer, Craig. "Meaninglessness: Cause and Desire in *The Birds, Shaun of the Dead*, and *The Walking Dead*." In Lowder, *Triumph of "The Walking Dead*," 67–80.

Flanagan, Owen, and Thomas Polger. "Zombies and the Function of Consciousness." *Journal of Consciousness Studies* 2, no. 4 (1995): 313–321.

Frank, Andrew K. "The Rise and Fall of William McIntosh: Authority and Identity on the Early American Frontier." *The Georgia Historical Quarterly* 86, no. 1 (2002): 18–48.

Freud, Sigmund. *On Aphasia: A Critical Study*. Translated by Erwin Stengel. New York: International Universities Press, 1953.

_____. *On Murder, Mourning and Melancholia*. Translated by Shaun Whiteside. London: Penguin, 2005.

Gale, Richard M. Introduction to *The Philosophy of Time: A Collection of Essays*, 1–8. New York: Anchor Books, 1967.

Gallese, Vittorio. "The Two Sides of Mimesis: Girard's Mimetic Theory, Embodied Simulation and Social Identification." *Journal of Consciousness Studies* 16, no. 4 (2009): 21–44.

Garrels, Scott R. "Imitation, Mirror Neurons, and Mimetic Desire: Convergence between the Mimetic Theory of René Girard and Empirical Research on Imitation." *Contagion: Journal of Violence, Mimesis, and Culture* 12–13 (2006): 47–86.

Geddes, Linda. "The Clock in Your Head." *New Scientist* 212, no. 2833 (October 2011): 45–46.

Gibbs, Anna. "Panic! Affect Contagion, Mimesis and Suggestion in the Social Field." *Cultural Studies Review* 14, no. 2 (2008): 130–145.

Gibson, William. *Neuromancer*. London: Harper Collins, 1995.

Gilmour, Michael J. "The Living Word Among the Living Dead: Hunting for Zombies in the Pages of the Bible." In Moreman and Rushton, *Zombies Are Us*, 87–99.

Girard, René. "The Plague in Literature and Myth." *Texas Studies in Literature and Language* 15, no. 5 (1974): 833–850.

_____. "Violence and Religion: Cause or Effect?" *The Hedgehog Review* 6, no. 1 (2004): 8–13.

Giroux, Henry A. *Zombie Politics and Culture in the Age of Casino Capitalism*. New York: Peter Lang, 2011.

Gramsci, Antonio. *Selections from the Prison Notebooks*. Edited and translated by Quintin Hoare and Geoffrey Nowell Smith. London: Lawrence and Wishart, 1971.

Grant, Barry Keith. "Taking Back the *Night of the Living Dead*: George Romero, Feminism, and the Horror Film." In *The Dread of Difference: Gender and the Horror Film*, edited by Grant, 200–212. Austin: University of Texas Press, 1996.

Greene, Richard. "What Your Zombie Knows." In Yuen, *"The Walking Dead" and Philosophy*, 29–37.

Grossman, Lev. "Zombies are the New Vampires." *Time*, April 9, 2009. http://www.time.com/time/magazine/article/0,9171,1890384,00.html.

Grosz, Elizabeth. "Becoming...An Introduction." In Grosz, *Becomings*, 1–11.

_____. *Becoming Undone: Darwinian Reflections on Life, Politics, and Art*. Durham, NC: Duke University Press, 2011.

_____. "Thinking the New: Of Futures Yet Unthought." In Grosz, *Becomings*, 15–28.

_____, ed. *Becomings: Explorations in Time, Memory, and Futures*. Ithaca, NY: Cornell University Press, 1999.

Haraway, Donna. "A Cyborg Manifesto: Science, Technology, and Socialist-Feminism in the Late Twentieth Century." In *Simians, Cyborgs, and Women: The Reinvention of Nature*, 149–182. New York: Routledge, 1991.

Harman, Chris. *Zombie Capitalism: Global Crisis and the Relevance of Marx*. London: Bookmarks Publications, 2009.

Harper, Stephen. "Zombies, Malls, and the Consumerism Debate: George Romero's *Dawn of the Dead*." *Americana: The Journal of American Popular Culture* 1, no. 2 (2002). http://www.americanpopularculture.com/journal/articles/fall_2002/harper.htm.

Hawkes, Gordon. "Are You Just Braaaiiinnnsss or Something More?" In Yuen, *"The Walking Dead" and Philosophy*, 3–15.

Hayles, N. Katherine. *How We Became Posthuman: Virtual Bodies in Cybernetics, Literature, and Informatics*. Chicago: University of Chicago Press, 1999.

Heidegger, Martin. *Being and Time*. Translated by John Macquarrie and Edward Robinson. New York: Harper Collins, 2008.

Hertz, Robert. "A Contribution to the Study of the Collective Representation of Death." In Robben, *Death, Mourning, and Burial*, 197–212.

Hervey, Ben. *Night of the Living Dead*. British Film Institute. New York: Palgrave Macmillan, 2008.

Higashi, Sumiko. "*Night of the Living Dead*: A Horror Film about the Horrors of the Vietnam Era." In *From Hannoi to Hollywood: The Vietnam War in American Film*, edited by Linda Dittmar and Gene Michael, 175–188. New Brunswick, NJ: Rutgers UP, 1990.

Hobbs, Frank, and Nicole Stoops. *Demographic Trends in the 20th Century: Census 2000 Special Reports*. CENSR-4. Washington, DC: U.S. Census Bureau, 2002. http://www.census.gov/prod/2002pubs/censr-4.pdf.

Hoffman, Eva. *Time*. New York: Picador, 2009.

Hopkins, David. "The Hero Wears the Hat: Carl as 1.5-Generation Immigrant and True Protagonist." In Lowder, *Triumph of "The Walking Dead*," 201–215.

Hughes, Gordon, and Michael Rowe. "Neighbourhood Policing and Community Safety: Researching the Instabilities of the Local Governance of Crime, Disorder and Security in Contemporary

UK." *Criminology and Criminal Justice* 7, no. 4 (2007): 317–346.

Hugo, Victor. *The Hunchback of Notre Dame.* New York: The Modern Library, 1941.

Iacoboni, Marco. *Mirroring People: The New Science of How We Connect with Others.* New York: Farrer, Straus and Giroux, 2008.

Inglis, David. "Putting the Undead to Work: Wade Davis, Haitian Vodou, and the Social Uses of the Zombie." In Moreman and Rushton, *Race, Oppression and the Zombie*, 42–59.

Jameson, Frederic. "Reification and Utopia in Mass Culture." *Social Text,* no.1 (1979): 130–148.

Jefferson, Tony. "Pondering Paramilitarism: A Question of Standpoints?" *British Journal of Criminology* 33, no. 3 (1993): 374–381.

Jones, Sharon Foster. *Atlanta's Ponce de Leon Avenue: A History.* Charleston, SC: The History Press, 2012.

Joseph, Nathan, and Nicholas Alex. "The Uniform: A Sociological Perspective." *American Journal of Sociology* 77, no. 4 (1972): 719–730.

Kahneman, Daniel. *Thinking Fast and Slow.* New York: Farrar, Straus and Giroux, 2011.

Keetley, Dawn. "Zombie Evolution: Stephen King's *Cell*, George Romero's *Diary of the Dead*, and the Future of the Human." *Americana: The Journal of American Popular Culture* 11, no. 2 (2012). http://www.americanpopular culture.com/journal/articles/fall_2012/ keetley.htm.

Kempner, Brandon. "The Optimism of *The Walking Dead*." In Yuen, *"The Walking Dead" and Philosophy*, 141–154.

King, Stephen. "The End of the Whole Mess." In *Wastelands: Stories of the Apocalypse*, edited by John Joseph Adams, 3–21. San Francisco: Night Shade Books, 2008.

Kirk, Robert. *Zombies and Consciousness.* Oxford: Oxford University Press, 2005.

Kirkman, Robert, Charlie Adlard, and Cliff Rathburn. *The Heart's Desire.* The Walking Dead: Book 2. Berkeley, CA: Image Comics, 2011.

_____. *Safety Behind Bars.* The Walking Dead: Book 2. Berkeley, CA: Image Comics, 2011.

_____. *Something to Fear.* The Walking Dead: Vol. 17. Berkeley, CA: Image Comics, 2012.

Kirkman, Robert, Charlie Adlard, and Cliff Rathburn. *The Walking Dead* #11. *Miles Behind Us*, Part 5. Orange, CA: Image Comics, 2004.

_____. *The Walking Dead* #14. *Safety Behind Bars*, Part 2. Orange, CA: Image Comics, 2004.

_____. *The Walking Dead* #18. *Safety Behind Bars*, Part 6. Orange, CA: Image Comics, 2005.

_____. *The Walking Dead* #19. *Heart's Desire*, Part 1. Orange, CA: Image Comics, 2005.

_____. *The Walking Dead* #28. *The Best Defense*, Part 4. Orange, CA: Image Comics, 2006.

_____. *The Walking Dead* #29. *The Best Defense*, Part 5. Orange, CA: Image Comics, 2006.

_____. The Walking Dead #37. *The Calm Before*, Part 1. Orange, CA: Image Comics, 2007.

_____. The Walking Dead #46. *Made to Suffer*, Part 4. Orange, CA: Image Comics, 2008.

_____. *The Walking Dead* #49. Orange, CA: Image Comics, 2008.

_____. *The Walking Dead* #54. Orange, CA: Image Comics, 2008.

Kirkman, Robert, and Tony Moore. *Days Gone Bye.* The Walking Dead: Vol. 1. Berkeley, CA: Image Comics, 2004.

Koch, Christof. *Consciousness: Confessions of a Romantic Reductionist.* Cambridge, MA: MIT Press, 2012.

Koolhaas, Rem. "Atlanta: A Reading." In *Atlanta*, edited by Jordi Bernadó and Ramon Prat, 74–85. Barcelona: Actar, 1995.

Kordas, Ann. "New South, New Immigrants, New Women, New Zombies: The Historical Development of the Zombie in American Popular Culture." In Moreman and Rushton, *Race, Oppression and the Zombie*, 15–30.

Kristeva, Julia. *Language—the Unknown: An Initiation into Linguistics.* Translated by Anne M. Menke. London: Harvester Wheatsheaf, 1989.

_____. *Powers of Horror: An Essay on Abjection*. Translated by Leon S. Roudiez. New York: Columbia University Press, 1982.

Kruse, Kevin M. *White Flight: Atlanta and the Making of Modern Conservatism*. Princeton, NJ: Princeton University Press, 2005.

Kurzweil, Ray. *The Age of Spiritual Machines*. New York: Penguin, 1999.

Ladson-Billings, Gloria, and William F. Tate IV. "Toward a Critical Race Theory of Education." *Teachers College Record* 97, no. 1 (1995): 47–68.

Laist, Randy. "Soft Murders: Motion Pictures and Living Death in *Diary of the Dead*." In Boluk and Lenz, *Generation Zombie*, 101–112.

Landis, John. *Monsters in the Movies: 100 Years of Cinematic Nightmares*. New York: DK, 2011.

Larkin, William S. "*Res Corporealis*: Persons, Bodies, and Zombies." In *Zombies, Vampires, and Philosophy: New Life for the Undead*, edited by Richard Greene and K. Silem Mohammad, 15–26. Chicago: Open Court, 2010.

Larsen, Lars Bang. "Zombies of Immaterial Labor: The Modern Monster and the Death of Death." *e-flux Journal* 15 (April 2010). http://www.e-flux.com/journal/zombies-of-immaterial-labor-the-modern-monster-and-the-death-of-death/.

Lauro, Sarah Juliet, and Karen Embry. "A Zombie Manifesto: The Nonhuman Condition in the Era of Advanced Capitalism." *boundary 2* 35, no. 1 (2008): 85–108.

Leverette, Marc. "The Funk of Forty Thousand Years; or, How the (Un)Dead Get Their Groove On." In McIntosh and Leverette, *Zombie Culture*, 185–212.

Leverick, Fiona. *Killing in Self-Defence*. Oxford: Oxford University Press, 2006.

Lewis, Tyson E. "Ztopia: Lessons in Post-Vital Politics in George Romero's Zombie Films." In Boluk and Lenz, *Generation Zombie*, 90–100.

Liaguno, Vince A. "Happy (En)Trails: Violence and Viscera on *The Walking Dead*." In Lowder, *Triumph of "The Walking Dead*," 115–126.

Lightning, Robert K. "Interracial Tensions in *Night of the Living Dead*." *CineAction*, no. 53 (2000): 22–29.

Lincoln, Abraham. "First Inaugural Address." March 4, 1861. http://www.bartleby.com/124/pres31.html.

Lindqvist, John Ajvide. *Handling the Undead*. Translated by Ebba Segerberg. New York: St. Martin's, 2009.

Littmann, Greg. "Can *You* Survive a Walker Bite?" In Yuen, *"The Walking Dead" and Philosophy*, 17–27.

London, Jack. *The Scarlet Plague*. 1915. http://www.gutenberg.org/files/21970/21970-h/21970-h.htm.

Loudermilk, A. "Eating 'Dawn' in the Dark: Zombie Desire and Commodified Identity in George A. Romero's *Dawn of the Dead*." *Journal of Consumer Culture* 3, no. 1 (2003): 83–108.

Lowder, James, ed. *Triumph of "The Walking Dead": Robert Kirkman's Zombie Epic on Page and Screen*. Dallas, TX: Benbella, 2011.

Lowenstein, Adam. "Living Dead: Fearful Attractions of Film." *Representations* 110, no. 1 (2010): 105–28.

Maberry, Jonathan. "Take Me to Your Leader: Guiding the Masses through the Apocalypse with a Cracked Moral Compass." In Lowder, *Triumph of "The Walking Dead*," 15–34.

Mani, Inderjeet. "The Flow of Time in Narrative: An Artificial Intelligence Perspective." In *Time: From Concept to Narrative Construct*, edited by Jan Christoph Meister and Wilhelm Schernus, 217–236. Berlin: Walter de Gruyter, 2011.

Massumi, Brian. "Potential Politics and the Primacy of Preemption." *Theory & Event* 10, no. 2 (2007). http://muse.jhu.edu.

Matheson, Richard. *I Am Legend*. New York: Tom Doherty, 1995.

McAlister, Elizabeth. "Slaves, Cannibals, and Infected Hyper-Whites: The Race and Religion of Zombies." *Anthropological Quarterly* 85, no. 2 (2012): 457–486.

McConnell, Mariana. "Interview: George A. Romero on *Diary of the Dead*." Cinema Blend.com. January 14, 2008. http://www.cinemablend.com/new/Interview-George-A-Romero-On-Diary-Of-The-Dead-7818.html.

McIntosh, Shawn. "The Evolution of the Zombie: The Monster That Keeps Coming Back." In McIntosh and Leverette, *Zombie Culture*, 1–17.

McIntosh, Shawn, and Marc Leverette, eds. *Zombie Culture: Autopsies of the Living Dead*. Lanham, MD: Scarecrow, 2008.

McKendry, Marty, and Michael Da Silva. "I'm Going to Tell Them about Wayne." In Yuen, *"The Walking Dead" and Philosophy*, 53–64.

McNally, David. *Bodies of Meaning: Studies on Language, Labor, and Liberation*. Albany: State University of New York Press, 2001.

_____. *Monsters of the Market: Zombies, Vampires and Global Capitalism*. Leiden, The Netherlands: Brill, 2011.

Miller, Cynthia J., and A. Bowdoin Van Riper. Introduction to *Undead in the West*, xi–xxvi.

Miller, Cynthia J., and A. Bowdoin Van Riper, eds. *Undead in the West: Vampires, Zombies, Mummies, and Ghosts on the Cinematic Frontier*. Lanham, MD: Scarecrow, 2012.

Minsky, Marvin. *The Society of Mind*. London: Simon and Schuster, 1987.

Moody, Todd C. "Conversations with Zombies." *Journal of Consciousness Studies* 1, no. 2 (1994): 196–200.

Moravec, Hans. *Mind Children: The Future of Robot and Human Intelligence*. Cambridge, MA: Harvard University Press, 1988.

_____. *Robot: Mere Machine to Transcendent Mind*. Oxford: Oxford University Press, 1999.

Moreland, Sean. "Shambling Towards Mount Improbable to Be Born: American Evolutionary Anxiety and the Hopeful Monsters of Matheson's *I Am Legend* and Romero's *Dead* Films." In Boluk and Lenz, *Generation Zombie*, 77–89.

Moreman, Christopher M., and Cory

Rushton, eds. *Race, Oppression and the Zombie: Essays on Cross-Cultural Appropriations of the Caribbean Tradition*. Jefferson, NC: McFarland, 2011.

_____, eds. *Zombies Are Us: Essays on the Humanity of the Walking Dead*. Jefferson, NC: McFarland, 2011.

Muntean, Nick, and Matthew Thomas Payne. "Attack of the Livid Dead: Recalibrating Terror in the Post-September 11 Zombie Film." In *The War on Terror and American Popular Culture: September 11 and Beyond*, edited by Andrew Schopp and Matthew B. Hill, 239–258. Madison, NJ: Fairleigh Dickinson University Press, 2009.

Murphy, Kieran. "White Zombie." *Contemporary French and Francophone Studies* 15, no. 1 (2011): 47–55.

Nietzsche, Friedrich. *Beyond Good and Evil*. Translated by Walter Kaufmann. New York: Vintage, 1989.

Norris, Andrew. "Giorgio Agamben and the Politics of the Living Dead." *Diacritics* 30, no. 4 (2000): 38–58.

Osteen, Mark. "Noir's Cars: Automobility and Amoral Space in American Film Noir." *Journal of Popular Film and Television* 35, no. 4 (2008): 183–192.

Ostherr, Kirsten. *Cinematic Prophylaxis: Globalization and Contagion in the Discourse of World Health*. Durham, NC: Duke University Press, 2005.

Oughourlian, Jean-Michel. *The Genesis of Desire*. East Lansing, MI: Michigan State University Press, 2010.

Pagano, David. "The Space of Apocalypse in Zombie Cinema." In McIntosh and Leverette, *Zombie Culture*, 71–86.

Peaty, Gwyneth. "Infected with Life: Neo-supernaturalism and the Gothic Zombie." In Wasson and Alder, *Gothic Science Fiction*, 102–115.

Pierson, George W. *The Moving American*. New York: Knopf, 1973.

Policante, Amedeo. "Vampires of Capital: Gothic Reflections between Horror and Hope." *Cultural Logic: An Electronic Journal of Marxist Theory and Practice*, 2010. 1–20. http://clogic.eserver.org/2010/Policante.pdf

Pollock, Greg. "Undead is the New Green:

Zombies and Political Ecology." In Moreman and Rushton, *Zombies Are Us,* 169–182.

Pye, Danee, and Peter Padraic O'Sullivan. "Dead Man's Party." In Yuen, *"The Walking Dead" and Philosophy,* 107–116.

Pye, Douglas. "The Western (Genre and Movies)." In *Film Genre Reader III,* edited by Barry Keith Grant, 203–218. Austin: University of Texas Press, 2003.

Quigley, Christine. *The Corpse: A History.* Jefferson, NC: McFarland, 2005.

Redding, Arthur. "Frontier Mythographies: Savagery and Civilization in Frederick Jackson Turner and John Ford." *Literature/Film Quarterly* 35, no. 4 (2007): 313–322.

Rees, Shelley S. "Frontier Values Meet Big-City Zombies: The Old West in AMC's *The Walking Dead.*" In Miller and Van Riper, *Undead in the West,* 80–94.

Rennie, M.K. "On Postulates for Temporal Order." In *Basic Issues in the Philosophy of Time,* edited by Eugene Freeman and Wilfred Sellars, 133–144. La Salle, IL: Open Court, 1971.

Richardson, Ingrid, and Carly Harper. "Corporeal Virtuality: The Impossibility of a Fleshless Ontology." *Body, Space and Technology Journal* 2, no. 2 (2001). http://people.brunel.ac.uk/bst/vol02002/index.html.

Rickels, Laurence. "Endopsychic Allegories." *Postmodern Culture* 18, no. 1 (2007). http://muse.jhu.edu.

_____. "Psychoanalysis on TV." *SubStance* 19, no. 1 (1990): 39–52.

_____. "Subliminalation." *Qui Parle* 2, no. 1 (1988): 18–42.

Riley, Brendan. "Zombie People: The Complicated Nature of Personhood in *The Walking Dead.*" In Lowder, *Triumph of "The Walking Dead,"* 81–97.

Robben, Antonius C. G. M., ed. *Death, Mourning, and Burial: A Cross-Cultural Reader.* Oxford: Blackwell, 2004.

Rossell, Christine H. "School Desegregation and White Flight." *Political Science Quarterly* 90, no. 4 (1975): 675–695.

Ruditis, Paul. *The Walking Dead Chronicles: The Official Companion Book.* New York: Abrams, 2011.

Sartre, Jean-Paul. *Existentialism and Human Emotions.* New York: Carol Publishing, 1990.

Scarry, Elaine. *The Body in Pain: The Making and Unmaking of the World.* New York: Oxford University Press, 1985.

Scholthof, Karen-Beth, John G. Shaw, and Milton Zaitlin. *Tobacco Mosaic Virus: One Hundred Years of Contributions to Virology.* St. Paul, MN: American Phytopathological Society, 1999.

Seabrook, W.B. *The Magic Island.* New York: Harcourt, Brace, 1929.

Shaviro, Steven. "Capitalist Monsters." *Historical Materialism* 10, no. 4 (2002): 281–290.

_____. *The Cinematic Body.* Minneapolis: University of Minnesota Press, 1993.

Shaw, L. "The Role of Clothing in the Criminal Justice System." *Journal of Police Science and Administration* 1, no. 4 (1973): 414–420.

Shusterman, Richard. "Muscle Memory and the Somaesthetic Pathologies of Everyday Life." *Human Movement* 12, no. 1 (2011): 4–15. http://bmsi.ru/doc/2fa7c55d-a077-4d68-a67b-2a311f49d9b4.

Sinha, Chris, Vera Da Silva Sinha, Jörg Zinken, and Wany Sampaio. "When Time Is Not Space: The Social and Linguistic Construction of Time Intervals and Temporal Event Relations in an Amazonian Culture." *Language and Cognition* 3, no. 1 (2011): 137–169.

Sirota, David. "The Zombie Zeitgeist." *Open Left,* October 9, 2009. http://www.openleft.com/diary/15458/the-zombie-zeitgeist.

Slotkin, Richard. *Gunfighter Nation: The Myth of the Frontier in Twentieth-Century America.* Norman: University of Oklahoma Press, 1998.

_____. *Regeneration Through Violence: The Mythology of the American Frontier, 1600–1860.* Middletown, CT: Wesleyan University Press, 1973.

Smith, Amy Symens, Bashir Ahmed, and Larry Sink. *An Analysis of State and County Population Changes by Characteristics: 1990–1999.* Washington, DC: U.S. Census Bureau, 2000. http://www.

census.gov/population/www/documentation/twps0045/twps0045.html.

Smith, Geddes. *Plague on Us*. New York: Commonwealth Fund, Oxford University, 1941.

Smith, Henry Nash. "The Western Hero in the Dime Novel." In *The American West on Film: Myth and Reality*, edited by Richard A. Maynard, 31–54. Rochelle Park, NJ: Hayden Book Co., 1974.

Sontag, Susan. *On Photography*. London: Penguin, 1977.

_____. "The Imagination of Disaster." In *Against Interpretation and Other Essays*, 209–225. New York: Octagon, 1978.

Steiger, Kay. "No Clean Slate: Unshakable Race and Gender Politics in The Walking Dead." In Lowder, *Triumph of "The Walking Dead*," 99–114.

Stratton, Jon. "Zombie Trouble: Zombie Texts, Bare Life and Displaced People." *European Journal of Cultural Studies* 14, no. 3 (2011): 265–281.

Strozier, Charles B. "The World Trade Center Disaster and the Apocalyptic." In *Terror and Apocalypse: Psychological Undercurrents of History*, volume 2, edited by Jerry S. Piven, Paul Ziolo, and Henry W. Lawton, 42–65. Lincoln, NE: iUniverse, 2002.

Studlar, Gaylyn. "Wider Horizons: Douglas Fairbanks and Nostalgic Primitivism." In Buscombe and Pearson, *Back in the Saddle Again*, 63–76.

Tait, R. Colin. "(Zombie) Revolution at the Gates: *The Dead*, The 'Multitude' and George A. Romero." *Cinephile* 3, no. 1 (2007): 61–70.

Thacker, Eugene. "Necrologies; or, The Death of the Body Politic." In Clough and Willse, *Beyond Biopolitics*, 139–162.

Tripp, Andrew. "Zombie Marches and the Limits of Apocalyptic Space." *Nomos Journal*, August 7, 2012. http://nomos-journal.org/content/media/2012/08/zombie-marches-apocalyptic-space.pdf.

Valdez, Al. *Gangs: A Guide to Understanding Street Gangs*. 5th ed. San Clemente, CA: LawTech Publishing, 2009.

van der Kolk, Bessel A., and Alexander C. McFarlane. "The Black Hole of Trauma." In *Traumatic Stress: The Effects of Overwhelming Experience on Mind, Body, and Society*, edited by van der Kolk, McFarlane, and Lars Weisaeth, 3–23. New York: Guilford Press, 1996.

Wald, Priscilla. *Contagious: Cultures, Carriers, and the Outbreak Narrative*. Durham, NC: Duke University Press, 2008.

Walker, Jason. "What's Yours Still Isn't Mine." In Yuen, *"The Walking Dead" and Philosophy*, 81–95.

Warner, Marina. *Phantasmagoria: Spirit Visions, Metaphors, and Media into the Twenty-First Century*. Oxford: Oxford University Press, 2006.

Wasson, Sara, and Emily Alder. *Gothic Science Fiction, 1980–2010*. Liverpool: Liverpool University Press, 2011.

Webb, Jen, and Sam Byrnand. "Some Kind of Virus: The Zombie as Body and as Trope." *Body and Society* 14, no. 2 (2008): 83–98.

Wells, H.G. *The War of the Worlds*. New York: New York Review of Books, 1960.

Wetmore, Kevin J. *Post–9/11 Horror in American Cinema*. New York: Continuum, 2012.

Williams, Evan Calder. *Combined and Uneven Apocalypse: Luciferian Marxism*. Winchester, UK: Zero Books, 2010.

Wills, Garry. *Nixon Agonistes: The Crisis of the Self-Made Man*. New York: Mariner, 2002.

Wolfe, Cary. *What Is Posthumanism?* Minneapolis: University of Minnesota Press, 2010.

Wood, Robin. *Hollywood from Vietnam to Reagan*. New York: Columbia University Press, 1986.

Young, Alison. *The Scene of Violence: Cinema, Crime, Affect*. Abingdon, Oxon: Routledge, 2010.

Yuen, Wayne, ed. *"The Walking Dead" and Philosophy: Zombie Apocalypse Now*. Chicago: Open Court, 2012.

Zatz, Marjorie S., and Edwardo L. Portillos. "Voices from the Barrio: Chicano/a Gangs, Families, and Communities." *Criminology* 38, no. 2 (2000): 369–402.

Zinn, Howard. *A People's History of the United States*. New York: Harper & Row, 1980.

Zealand, Christopher. "The National Strategy for Zombie Containment: Myth Meets Activism in Post–9/11 America." In Boluk and Lenz, *Generation Zombie*, 231–247.

Zinoman, Jason. "The Horror Movie: Killer Instincts." *Vanity Fair,* March 2008. http://www.vanityfair.com/culture/features/2008/03/horror_films 200803.

Žižek, Slavoj. *First as Tragedy, Then as Farce.* New York: Verso, 2009.

_____. *For They Know Not What They Do: Enjoyment as a Political Factor.* 2nd ed. New York: Verso, 2002.

_____. "Melancholy and the Act." *Critical Inquiry* 26, no. 4 (2000): 657–681.

_____. *The Plague of Fantasies.* New York: Verso, 1997.

_____. *Violence: Six Sideways Reflections.* New York: Picador, 2008.

List of Episodes

9.	The Suicide King	February 10, 2013
10.	Home	February 17, 2013
11.	I Ain't a Judas	February 24, 2013
12.	Clear	March 3, 2013
13.	Arrow on the Doorpost	March 10, 2013
14.	Prey	March 17, 2013
15.	This Sorrowful Life	March 24, 2013
16.	Welcome to the Tombs	March 31, 2013

About the Contributors

Xavier **Aldana Reyes** is a research fellow in English at Manchester Metropolitan University, where he also teaches in the MA in English program. He is the author of the forthcoming *Body Gothic: Corporeal Transgression in Contemporary Literature and Horror Film* and co-editor, with Linnie Blake, of a collection on digital horror. He has published widely on the Gothic, horror, transgression, corporeality and affect theory.

Dave **Beisecker** is an associate professor and chair of philosophy at the University of Nevada, Las Vegas. He has written extensively on the philosophy of mind and language, including articles on philosophical zombies. Always fascinated by apocalyptic and post-apocalyptic narratives, he has contributed essays to *Race, Oppression and the Zombie* (McFarland, 2011) and *The Walking Dead and Philosophy* (Open Court, 2012).

Chris **Boehm** is an instructor in the College Writing Program at Washington University in St. Louis and has taught courses in film adaptation and critical theory. He is preparing his dissertation for publication as a book; it focuses on the relationship between the psychonalaytical concepts of super ego and fantasy, and their manifestations in the "slasher" horror villain and the meth addict.

Paul **Boshears** is a PhD candidate at Europäische Universität für Interdisziplinäre Studien (the European Graduate School) in Saas-Fee, Switzerland. He is founder and co-editor of the journal *continent* and his first book, *Spectacular Agency*, is forthcoming. His research interests include the role of learning in self-cultivation and the opportunities provided by widespread digital publishing.

Gary **Farnell** teaches English at the University of Winchester in the United Kingdom. A member of the International Gothic Association, he has published widely in the Gothic genre, including work on Walter Benjamin's "Gothic Marxism" in *New Formations* and in *Historical Materialism*. He is the co-author, with Peter Billingham, of the entry for "Melodrama" in *The Encyclopedia of the Gothic* (Wiley-Blackwell, 2013).

Christine **Heckman** is an adjunct instructor of humanities at the College of Lake County in Grayslake, Illinois, where she teaches a course on women and the arts. Her research interests include global virtual literature circles as pedagogy and performance, and the evolution of the 21st-century American superhero. She is in the master's program in English literature at Northeastern Illinois University.

Dawn **Keetley** is an associate professor of English at Lehigh University in Bethlehem, Pennsylvania, where she teaches American literature and popular culture with an emphasis on the Gothic, violence, and horror. She has recently published articles on the TV series *American Horror Story* and on George Romero's *Diary of the Dead* and Stephen King's *Cell*. She is completing a book project on Jesse Pomeroy, "the Boy Fiend" of 1870s Boston, a portion of which was recently published in the *Journal of American Studies*.

Laura **Kremmel** is a PhD student at Lehigh University in Bethlehem, Pennsylvania, where she also teaches. She holds a master's degree in Gothic literature from the University of Stirling, in Scotland. Her work dissects the agency and productivity of unwhole bodies in Gothic literature of the Romantic period, but her research and teaching endeavors extend to all facets of the Gothic. She published an article on Robert Mapplethorpe and the Gothic in the collection *Transgression and Its Limits* (Cambridge Scholars, 2012).

Angus **Nurse** is a senior lecturer in criminology in the School of Law at Middlesex University and a senior researcher in Middlesex's Centre for Crime and Conflict Research. He was previously with Birmingham City University and the Law School at the University of Lincoln. He researches crime and popular culture and has also published widely on the topics of wildlife and environmental crime, and civil justice.

Gwyneth **Peaty** is an honorary research fellow at the University of Western Australia. She completed a PhD exploring the grotesque in popular culture, and her wider research interests include monstrosity, post-humanism, horror and the Gothic. Previous publications include "Infected with Life: Neo-supernaturalism and the Gothic Zombie" in *Gothic Science Fiction: 1980–2010* (Liverpool University Press, 2012). Forthcoming publications include essays on exploitation films and monstrous video gaming.

Steven **Pokornowski** is a doctoral candidate in English at the University of California, Santa Barbara. In his dissertation, he examines the rhetorics of infection and security in literature, film, and comics, tracing the ways that the biomedical and the political have become bound in the popular imagination.

Philip L. **Simpson** is provost of the Titusville Campus of Brevard Community College in Florida. He has served as president of the Popular Culture Association and sits on the editorial board of the *Journal of Popular Culture*. He has published two books, *Psycho Paths: Tracking the Serial Killer through Contemporary American Film and Fiction* (Southern Illinois University Press, 2000) and *Making Murder: The Fiction of Thomas Harris* (Praeger, 2009), and numerous other essays on film, literature, popular culture, and horror.

P. Ivan **Young** is a lecturer of poetry and creative writing at Salisbury University in Maryland. His scholarship focuses primarily on the role of poetry in the Irish Conflict and on pop culture as a mirror for American identity. As a poet, he has presented on the use of the Proustian effect in the creative writing classroom and is the author of *A Shape in the Waves* (Stepping Stones Press, 2009).

Index

Index